Tibetan Treasure Literature

Tibetan Treasure Literature

Revelation, Tradition, and Accomplishment in Visionary Buddhism

Andreas Doctor

Snow Lion Publications
Ithaca, New York
Boulder, Colorado

Snow Lion Publications
P.O. Box 6483
Ithaca, New York 14851 USA
(607) 273-8519
www.snowlionpub.com

Printed in USA on acid-free recycled paper.

ISBN 1-55939-236-3

Cataloging-in-Publication Data is available from the Library of Congress.

Text designed and typeset by Rafael Ortet

Table of Contents

Foreword

Our Teacher, the Buddha and Transcendent Conqueror, possesses infinite wisdom and love and is like a great unknown friend to all limitless sentient beings. In this world he turned innumerable dharma wheels of both sūtra and mantra. In Tibet, through the kindness of the Abbot, the Master, and the Dharma King, as well as the translators and the paṇḍitas, the complete teachings of sūtra and mantra came to spread and flourish throughout the country. As for the profound teachings of mantra, the Ancient School of the Early Translations has maintained its limitless teachings on the Great Secret within the long lineage of Transmitted Precepts, the short lineage of Treasures, and the profound Pure Vision teachings. Among these, in the short lineage of Treasures, we find the profound Treasures of the emanated great Treasure revealer Urgyen Chokgyur Dechen Shigpo Lingpa compiled into a collection of 39 volumes.

Within Chokgyur Lingpa's Treasure of the *Seven Profound Cycles,* the text known as the *Practice Manual of Combined Activity for the Single Kīla of Innermost Mind* belongs to the profound activity of the kīla tantric system. To elucidate this practice, Tsawa Bhande Karma Rinchen Namgyal composed a commentary entitled *Instructions of the Knowledge-holders: Clearly Arranged Deity Guidance for the Single Form of the Most Secret Kīla of Mind.* These two texts, together with the *Gem that Clears the Waters: An Investigation of Treasure Revealers* composed by the Lion of Speech, Mipham Rinpoche, have now been translated into English by my direct disciple Andreas Doctor who has extensively studied and contemplated the profound key points of Buddhism and possesses an open and altruistic intellect. On this fine accomplishment, achieved through much hard work, I hereby scatter flowers of praise.

May this book be an excellent circumstance for its readers to expand the wisdom of study and reflection, and may they give rise to the extraordinary experience and realization of the meaning of the tantras.

This was written in Nepal by Chökyi Nyima, who bears the name of Tulku, on March 3, 2005.

Preface

In contemporary society, Buddhism is often portrayed as a 'science of the mind' rather than a religious tradition based on faith. Considering the importance that Buddhist scholarship traditionally has placed on analyzing the workings of the mind and the transformative influence that such philosophical endeavors have exercised on the minds of many Buddhists, this description does indeed seem to have a relevance and value. It does not, however, do adequate justice to the comprehensive ritual practices and profound devotional approaches that equally abound in Buddhism.

Historically, wherever Buddhism has flourished it has done so by adapting its teachings to the needs of the people it encountered. Accordingly, as a response to those seeking spiritual fulfillment only outside the realm of the reasoned and scientific, a wealth of Buddhist traditions centering on faith, meditation, and the workings of the transcendent arose across Asia. Among these we find the Tibetan Treasure tradition (*gter lugs*). Rich in legend, revelation, esoteric practice, and enlightened vision, this form of Buddhism is a living expression of the confidently devoted spirituality that—rooted in the practice and experience of individual awakening—has been a life pillar of the Buddhist tradition since its very early days.

It is this system of practice that we are concerned with here. As this book can present only a few of the many visionaries, writers, and texts that have influenced and contributed to the Treasure tradition over the last millennium, I have sought to focus on elements within this system that would have a bearing on the tradition as a whole. First, this book seeks to answer the seemingly simple question of what a Treasure is. As it turns out, the positions on this issue vary considerably among writers, traditions, and time periods and so no easy answer is found. Nevertheless, from the perspective of the tradition itself, certain broad identifications and typologies may still be identified and extracted, which is the concern of chapter 1.

The emergence of the Treasures coincided with the second spread of Buddhism in Tibet, a renaissance of the Tibetan efforts to import Buddhist thought and practice from India. As these events unfolded, the question of authenticity arose almost immediately upon the first revelations of Treasure. This topic is examined in chapter 2, which looks at the traditional Tibetan polemics on revelation and examines the influence of this eristical literature on the subsequent perceptions of the Treasures in the West. In conclusion, this chapter offers additional thoughts on Treasure authenticity centered on a brief text by the Tibetan scholar-practitioner Ju Mipham Gyatso (1846-1912), who himself has been considered a significant Treasure revealer. Blunt and biting in his description of the impostor, Mipham here considers critically the question of Treasure authenticity and the relevance of revelation as such in late nineteenth century Tibet. The text, which in this way offers a unique intra-traditional evaluation, is presented in chapter 3 in translation and juxtaposed with Mipham's original Tibetan.

Whereas the first part of this book is concerned with the phenomenon of revelation as such, the middle part focuses on a particular, classical expression of visionary Buddhism—the life and revelations of the Treasure revealer Chokgyur Dechen Lingpa (1829-1870), whose visionary activity has had a defining influence on contemporary views of Buddhist revelation. Chapter 4 introduces the biographical sources for Chokgyur Lingpa's career, followed by a brief look at his past lives as recounted by tradition. Next, chapter 5 offers a detailed survey of Chokgyur Lingpa's revelations and the historical circumstances surrounding them. This section concludes with an account of the numerous masters who have assumed responsibility for upholding his rich spiritual legacy.

Finally, the last chapters of this book present translations of two individual texts from the Treasure tradition, both of which concern the practical application of the Treasure to achieve the liberating accomplishment of Buddhahood—the underlying teleological justification for Treasure revelation *per se*. Both texts, introduced in chapter 6, belong to the tradition of Chokgyur Lingpa and focus on the deity Vajrakīlaya, the personal deity of the Indian master Padmasambhava and one of the most central figures of the Treasure pantheon. Each translation represents a distinct genre of Treasure literature. The *meditation ritual*, translated in chapter 7, is a concise text adapted by Padmasambhava from the original root tantra to support the meditation of the individual practitioner, while the *deity instruction*, presented in chapter 8, is a detailed commentary on the practical application of the meditation ritual. This latter text is composed by Karma Rinchen Namgyal (nineteenth century) who was a close personal disciple of Chokgyur Lingpa.

By presenting the Treasure tradition in this manner I have wished to highlight central aspects of this visionary tradition that, although at first seemingly isolated and removed from each other, upon closer inspection reveal an intricate mutual connection, influence, and dependency.

A Note on Tibetan

A perennial challenge to those working in the field of Tibetan studies is how to best present Tibetan names and technical concepts in a way that is accurate and yet decipherable by the un-initiated reader. Since, as of yet, no satisfying solution has been established to meet this challenge, some compromise is often attempted, which is also the approach taken here. I have translated technical terms into English and listed their spelling according to the Wylie system of transliteration in parenthesis on their first occurrence. Titles of texts and collections of texts have similarly been translated into English and listed alongside their Tibetan original in the glossary. As for personal and place names, I have presented these according to a somewhat intuitive (though hopefully not excessively idiosyncratic) phonetic system that would be pronounceable by readers not familiar with Tibetan. Again, all such names are also listed in their technical format in the glossary. As for deities with Sanskrit names, I have kept their titles in that language. I have generally transcribed the names of deities and spirits lacking a Sanskrit form in the same way that other Tibetan personal names have been listed. In part III, however, I have deviated from this policy and translated the names of the ten female wrathful consorts into English because the concurrence of both Sanskrit and Tibetan appellations in the very same sentence seemed more troubling to my eye than any benefits achieved from adhering to a strict editorial policy. Likewise, when names are applied in epithetical contexts, I have also translated these into English to better evince the meaning underlying their usage.

Acknowledgements

While preparing this book I have been fortunate to receive much help, support, and guidance from a number of learned scholars and accomplished practitioners. First and foremost I am indebted, in so many ways, to Tulku Chökyi Nyima Rinpoche, the abbot of Ka-Nying Shedrub Ling Monastery in

Boudhanath, Nepal. It was Rinpoche who first encouraged me to study the Treasure tradition and advised me to prepare a study of Chokgyur Lingpa's tradition focusing on his Vajrakīlaya Treasure cycles. Rinpoche also directly assisted my research by granting me access to his extensive private library and throughout this project he has been a wonderful inspiration and a true treasure-mine of insight, knowledge, and wisdom.

At Ka-Nying Shedrub Ling Monastery, I am most grateful for the opportunity to receive transmission and teachings on Vajrakīlaya practice from Tsike Chokling Rinpoche, the fourth reincarnation of Chokgyur Lingpa, as well as his son, Phakchok Tulku Rinpoche, who granted me detailed and lucid explanations on Karma Rinchen Namgyal's Vajrakīlaya instructions. I am also thankful to Tenga Rinpoche and Urgyen Tobgyal Rinpoche for their kindness in answering numerous questions that I brought to them.

In addition to these great masters I am also indebted to Khenpo Tashi Palden, Khenpo Sherab Zangpo, Karma Özer, Kunga Sangpo, and Karma Gelek for generously sharing with me their time and expertise in elucidating difficult passages.

In Nepal I have been fortunate to receive much advice, encouragement and inspiration from the lotsāwa Erik Pema Kunsang, the leading western authority on the tradition of Chokgyur Lingpa, who, over the years, generously has shared with me his impressive knowledge of the Treasure tradition and kindly offered many detailed suggestions and corrections to both Vajrakīlaya translations whereby they improved greatly.

A major part of this manuscript was initially written as part of my doctoral work at the Department of Religious Studies, University of Calgary. In Canada I benefited from the knowledge and expertise of Dr. Leslie Kawamura, who guided my studies with kindness and insight. I also received much expert assistance from a number of other eminent scholars who, in conversations and correspondence, have contributed to this book. In particular I wish to thank John Makransky, Tom Tillemans, Eva Neumaier, Dan Martin, David Germano, Per Kvaerne, and Wayne McCready for many helpful discussions, comments, and suggestions that opened up the topic of Treasure revelation to me in a number of new and enriching ways. Much gratitude is also felt towards the Danish Research Agency, which generously supported my doctoral studies.

I am also much obliged to Kathmandu University - Centre for Buddhist Studies at Rangjung Yeshe Institute for generously sponsoring the latter stages of writing. At the Centre for Buddhist Studies I have benefited from the help of many of my colleagues and friends, in particular my brother, Thomas Doctor, who critiqued the manuscript in its various stages, assisted me in translating a number of difficult passages, and offered much support and encouragement throughout the writing process. Likewise, I am thankful to James Gentry, Heidi Köppl, Douglas Duckworth, Thomas Roth, and Cortland Dahl for their insightful and much appreciated critique and comments. At Ka-Nying Shedrub Ling Monastery I greatly enjoyed the excellent library facilities created by George MacDonald and Kathy Morris. Much gratitude is also felt to Namdrol Gyatso for all the hospitality he has shown my family throughout the years that we have lived in Nepal. I also wish to thank Matthew Zalichin for skillfully editing the manuscript, Daniel Kaufer for proofreading the text, and Rafael Ortet for lending his artistic gifts to the layout and design of this book.

I am always thankful to my mother, Kirsten Doctor, and her husband, William Sherwood, for their untiring help at all stages of this project and to my brother, Jonas Doctor, and his wife, Sangye Lhamo, for many enriching discussions. I am also most grateful to the whole Appave family—Jacqueline, Dorrine, Didier, Sonny, Marinel, Nathan, and David—for their warm friendship and generous hospitality during my times in Calgary. Finally, I thank my wife, Jennifer, and our darling son, Lukas, for all their love and support.

Any faults and errors this book may contain are my own, and I sincerely regret and apologize for them. Whatever goodness may arise from its publication I dedicate to the welfare of all beings.

Andreas Doctor
Boudhanath, March, 2005

Part One

Treasure Revelation

I

What is a Treasure?

The Nyingma School of Tibetan Buddhism is home to a transmission of Buddhist teaching known as the "Treasure tradition" (*gter lugs*), a unique religious system that only recently has become the focus of attention in the West.[1] This tradition propagates the reverence of religious material known as "Treasure" (*gter ma*), blessed words and objects said to originate in the enlightened intent of buddhas and bodhisattvas. Broadly, the Treasures belong to a tripartite system of scriptural and oral transmission defined by the Nyingma School as the "three great transmissions" consisting of (a) the long lineage of Transmitted Precepts, (b) the short lineage of Treasure, and (c) the profound Pure Vision Teachings.[2] According to the Nyingma School, the Treasures are most often comprised of spiritual instructions concealed by enlightened beings for the purpose of discovery at a later predestined time when their message will invigorate the Buddhist teaching and deepen spiritual understanding.[3] Central to this process is the figure of the Treasure revealer (*gter ston*)—the person who acts as a medium for the re-emergence of this inspired material into the human world.[4] Accordingly, beginning in the eleventh century and continuing into the present, the Nyingma School identifies a large number of Treasure revealers and grants authoritative status to their discoveries.[5]

The idea that religious truth lies concealed within the world of phenomena awaiting discovery by spiritually gifted people is by no means a concept exclusive to the Nyingma School or Tibetan Buddhism as a whole. Throughout Buddhist literature there are numerous descriptions of teachings being inherently present in the phenomenal world ready to be perceived by individuals possessing inspired levels of consciousness and, accordingly, spiritual revelations have surfaced on numerous occasions throughout the course of Buddhist history.[6] The Nyingma School is therefore unique not so much in its acceptance of revealed truth as in its institutionalization of such spiritual discovery and its ability to maintain a continued revelatory output.[7] Considering the fluidity of the Buddhist canons in India and the central role of scriptural production and revelation in the religious life of medieval Indian Buddhism where the Mahāyāna and Vajrayāna traditions continuously accommodated, accepted, and authenticated inspired revelation as the genuine voice of the buddha(s),[8] it is paradoxical that the Tibetans, in their attempt to adopt and preserve the Indian Buddhist traditions, should abandon this approach to revelation and give rise to an essentially non-Mahāyānic notion of a closed canon.[9] Regardless, the Tibetan acceptance of a closed canon meant that the Treasure tradition, since its early days, has found itself at the center of disputes of authenticity, defending the validity of its scriptures against the criticism of skeptics. This situation will be discussed later, but first we must look more closely at the Treasures and see how they were defined and understood by the tradition itself.

Although the Nyingma School developed numerous systems of Treasure classification according to their content, nature, manner of concealment, etc., all Tibetan Treasures share the claim that they were concealed during the golden age of the Yarlung dynasty (seventh to ninth centuries C.E.) by enlightened Buddhist masters who considered the needs and inclinations of future followers. During this period Buddhism entered Tibet and became the state religion through the sponsorship of so-called "religious kings" (*chos rgyal*) who embraced Buddhism and supported its spread.[10] This was also a time when Tibet enjoyed considerable prosperity and political fortune on the international scene. At the height of its glory the Tibetan empire traced its southern border along the Ganges River in the Indian plains; to the east large parts of China had been conquered, and Tibet had emerged as one of the dominant powers in the region. It is therefore understandable that a number of Tibetan historians later would come to look at this period as the epitome of political as well as religious Tibetan greatness.[11]

As Tibet converted to Buddhism, considerable wealth acquired from victory in warfare was reinvested into the task of propagating Buddhist thought and culture. Later legends, revealed as Treasure from the twelfth century onwards, recount this part of Tibet's history by focusing on the Indian esoteric master Padmasambhava (eighth/ninth century) and his role in the conversion process. In these texts we are told that, having been invited to Tibet in order to pacify demonic obstacles to the construction of Samye, Tibet's first monastery, Padmasambhava stayed on and assumed the leading role in transmitting the tantric tradition to Tibet.[12] Although these later Tibetan accounts accredit

Padmasambhava with this central and all-important role in the conversion of Tibet, little historical data exist to verify these claims.[13]

At any rate, over time the followers of the Nyingma School continued to reveal a vast number of Treasure texts centering on Padmasambhava's religious feats in Tibet whereby his status and importance retroactively became embedded in a legendary narrative that came to play a pivotal role in the self-conception of the Nyingma School. In this literature Padmasambhava is described as the main author and concealer of the Treasures.[14] It is recounted how he taught a small group of students at the court of the Tibetan king Trisong Detsen (ca. 740–798), subsequently concealed a great number of these teachings, and prophetically declared that they would be discovered in the future by reincarnations of those very students. The future Treasure revealers would then propagate Padmasambhava's teachings to audiences whose karmic needs and propensities would call for such instructions. In addition to this soteriological purpose, on a more mundane level the Treasures also appeal to a basic human fondness for novelty, which undoubtedly also contributed to their success and popularity. Still, while the Treasures appeal in their recency, they ironically also possess a concomitant attraction to Tibetans by linking the present "dark age" to the celebrated past when Buddhism was introduced and the empire was at its zenith.[15]

The transmission of the Treasures is traditionally described in terms of six events, or stages, whereby the teaching moves from its original formulator in a dharmakāya realm to the devotee in the present.[16] Among these six stages, the first three are the well-known transmissions of tantric material according to the teachings of the Nyingma School: the realization lineage of the conquerors, the symbolic lineage of the vidyādharas, and the hearing lineage of ordinary people.[17] The remaining three transmissions, specific to Treasure revelation, are: empowerment by aspiration, prediction of the transmission,[18] and entrustment to the ḍākinīs.[19] According to Longchenpa (1308-1363), these three events unfold within the symbolic lineage of the vidyādharas.[20] During these latter stages Padmasambhava first teaches a suitable student and ensures that his or her understanding is authentic and genuine. Once the student has properly received the teaching, Padmasambhava prophesizes the circumstances of the future revelation and finally conceals the teaching and entrusts the ḍākinīs to guard it until the time has come for revelation.

As Treasure revelation in Tibet dates back almost 1000 years, it is not surprising to observe significant changes to the tradition over this period. Recent western studies have focused on the works of late Tibetan exegetics like

Jamgön Kongtrul (1813-1899), Do Drupchen Tenpe Nyima (1865-1926), and Dudjom Yeshe Dorje (1904-1987),[21] who view the tradition through a syncretic lens that occasionally leaves out historical developments in consideration of philosophical clarity and traditional homogeneity.[22] Due to the prominent position held in contemporary Tibetan religious circles by these late exemplars of Treasure ideology, their views have at times been portrayed as normative for the Treasure tradition at large or, when discrepancies are found, as authoritative.[23] Although this may be justified in view of the influence of these works on contemporary Tibetan religion, there remain, however, a number of historical details to be discovered only outside of these later sources.[24] In the following we shall look closer at some of these as they relate to the topic of Treasure identification and classification.

During the history of visionary revelation in Tibet various systems of Treasure taxonomy developed. The many classificatory systems of the Treasures still await a detailed study, and here we shall merely examine a few influential systems of classification, selected for their philosophical variety as well as their historical representation of several centuries of Treasure revelation. To establish a preliminary genealogy of Treasure taxonomy, we shall study the taxonomical classifications of early figures in the Treasure tradition such as Nyangral Nyima Özer (1124-1192), Guru Chökyi Wangchuk (1212-1270), Urgyen Lingpa (1323-?), Longchenpa Drime Özer, and Ratna Lingpa Pal Zangpo (1403-78) and compare these to the later position formulated by members of the famed, but little studied, nineteenth century ecumenical tradition (*ris med*) as represented by Jamgön Kongtrul, Jamyang Khyentse Wangpo (1820-1892) and Chokgyur Dechen Lingpa (1829-1870).[25] This present survey is neither exhaustive in its scope nor final in its conclusions, but aims to offer some initial reflections on which a firmer genealogy of Treasure identification and classification may later be constructed.

Although the Nyingma School traditionally traces the beginnings of Treasure revelation in Tibet to the master Sangye Lama (eleventh century); Nyangral Nyima Özer's writings a century later are the first to show a self-conscious movement with actual descriptions of the tradition including taxonomical features. The primary source is the seminal hagiography of Padmasambhava known as the *Copper Temple Life Story* after its place of discovery at the Samye monastic complex south of Lhasa.[26] As part of Nyangral's account of Padmasambhava's feats in Tibet, two short chapters discuss his concealment of the Treasures.[27] They divide the Treasures into two major rubrics of "religious Treasures" (*chos gter*) and "wealth Treasures" (*nor gter*).[28] In this way, during

Nyangral's time, we can see that the Treasures were classified based on their content and general nature which is much different from the later taxonomies of the ecumenical tradition where, as we shall see below, the Treasures instead were arranged according to their various modes of revelation. As for religious Treasures and wealth Treasures, neither of these two terms was created by Nyangral as both commonly appear throughout translations of Indian Mahāyāna sūtras but in Nyangral's writings they refer specifically to Treasures concealed by Padmasambhava in Tibet and as such both terms become enduring categories in the Treasure tradition.

Besides these two important terms, the *Copper Temple* introduces several Treasure subcategories that were elaborated upon in the works of subsequent commentators. In addition to the categories of religious Treasures and wealth Treasures, Nyangral speaks of "life force Treasures" (*bla gter*), "black magic Treasures" (*mthu gter*), "handicraft Treasures" (*bzo gter*), "medicinal Treasures" (*sman gyi gter*), and "spiritual Treasures" (*thugs gter*).[29] However, the *Copper Temple* does not describe most of these beyond merely mentioning their names so any conclusive interpretation of these terms is rendered problematic.

Nevertheless, the category of spiritual Treasure is particularly important. The *Copper Temple* seems to understand it simply as a precious teaching originally formulated in the spirit (*thugs*) of a buddha or a realized master. Passages stating that Padmasambhava concealed his spiritual Treasures in physical locations such as the hermitage of Chimpu and a cave at Namke clearly refer to a physical substance rather than a mental event.[30] In the fourteenth century, however, this notion of spiritual Treasure appears to function as the etymological inspiration for the concept of "mind Treasure" (*dgongs gter*), which, although at first a semantic synonym for spiritual Treasure, is developed by later writers such as Jamgön Kongtrul and Jamyang Khyentse Wangpo into a prominent Treasure category by denoting a Treasure that is concealed in and revealed from the Treasure revealer's mind. Still, before pursuing this discussion further, we must first consider the revelations of Guru Chöwang who, a century after Nyangral, was the second major contributor to Treasure taxonomy and one of the most influential Treasure hermeneutists in the entire history of the Nyingma School.

The interpretation of spiritual Treasure as referring simply to a precious teaching rather than a specific Treasure is supported by Guru Chöwang's *Great Treasure Chronicle*, which likewise speaks of spiritual Treasures as physical entities.[31] Contextual awareness is therefore required when relating to this term and, in any case, its semantic equivalence to later understandings of mind

Treasure must be doubted. The *Great Treasure Chronicle*, composed in the thirteenth century, is the earliest known detailed treatise on the Treasure tradition. In this text, Chöwang uses four main categories to define the Treasures. The first is "ordinary material Treasures" (*thun mong rdzas kyi gter*). This grouping contains the subdivisions of "supreme material Treasures" (*mchog gi rdzas gter*), which refers to Buddhist ritual substances such as skull cups and the flesh of humans who have had seven consecutive Brahmin births;[32] "special material Treasures" (*khyad par gyi rdzas gter*), referring to jewels; and "ordinary material Treasures" (*thun mong gi rdzas gter*), such as valleys, water, building materials, and magic tricks.[33] The second is "especially purposeful Treasures" (*khyad par yon tan gter*), again subdivided into the categories of "Treasures of truthful speech of emanated Bön" (*bon 'phrul ngag bden pa'i gter*), "astrological Treasures" (*rtsis kyi gter*), "medicinal Treasures" (*sman gyi gter*), "handicraft Treasures" (*gzo'i gter*), and "magic Treasures" (*'phrul gyi gter*).[34] Third is the category of "supreme Treasures of body, speech, and mind" (*mchog gyur sku gsung thugs kyi gter*). "Body" refers to the physical appearance (revelation) of a buddha manifesting in the world, self-manifested representations of enlightened form, and representations made by humans. "Speech" refers essentially to the entire Buddhist teaching, while "mind" includes physical representations of buddha mind such as stūpas and vajras.[35] The last main category is the "definitive Treasure of suchness" (*de kho na nyid nges pa'i gter*), which represents the realization of all the buddhas. This realization is said to be self-secret and is considered a Treasure because it is concealed from the general perception of sentient beings.[36]

In presenting these categories, Chöwang argues that Treasures are not only religious texts and artifacts hidden by Padmasambhava and his students but should be understood in broader terms as the complete Buddhist textual corpus and, on an even larger scale, indeed the entire world. In support of this Chöwang quotes the *Sūtra of Mañjuśrī's Play*:

> Mañjuśrī! Just as the four elements appear from the Treasure of the sky so all teachings appear from the spiritual Treasure of the Victorious one. Therefore, you must know to appreciate the significance of Treasures.[37]

Thus, Chöwang attempts to root the Treasure tradition within the normative Mahāyāna philosophical tradition where the "articulated dharma" (*lung gi chos*) is said to manifest precisely through the creative potential of the "dharma of realization" (*rtogs kyi chos*). As a description of the kind of Treasures that Chöwang and his Tibetan Treasure tradition commonly would come to reveal it is, of course, very broad indeed. Chöwang can therefore not be said to engage in an actual phenomenological study of Tibetan Treasure revelation, but rather a philosophical exercise to connect the Treasure tradition to the nondescript dharmakāya reality from which, according to Mahāyāna Buddhists, purposeful activity ceaselessly manifests in any conceivable form. This is no insignificant point, however, and one that Tibetan Treasure analysts repeatedly returned to as Chöwang's classifications were adopted by some of the most influential commentators of the Nyingma School.[38]

The earliest occurrences of the term "mind Treasure" appear to stem from the fourteenth century works of Longchenpa (in particular his *Innermost Essence of the Ḍākinī*)[39] and Urgyen Lingpa (in his famous *Chronicle of Padmasambhava*),[40] although in the latter the term occurs only twice among a plethora of other general Treasure categories.[41] The *Chronicle of Padmasambhava* presents four main Treasure categories: "ancestral Treasures" (*mes gter*), "filial Treasures" (*sras gter*), "magistral Treasures" (*dpon gter*), and "essential Treasures" (*yang gter*), each containing 18 different kinds of Treasure (each one again subdivided 18 times!).[42] Unfortunately, these terms are not further defined in the *Chronicle of Padmasambhava* and their meaning is elusive. The term translated here as "essential Treasure" is the same designation later used by Kongtrul, where it is probably best rendered "rediscovered Treasure." However, in the early sources the meaning of "rediscovered" appears absent and the term seems instead to refer to an "essential" or "particular" Treasure.[43] Mind Treasure, however, is not a prominent category in Urgyen Lingpa's writings.

Longchenpa, on the other hand, uses that term much more frequently in the *Innermost Essence of the Ḍākinī* where it appears to have a similar meaning to the earlier notion of spiritual Treasure. Here Longchenpa speaks of mind Treasure in reference to both the *Innermost Essence of the Ḍākinī* (his own writing) as well as the *Heart Essence of the Ḍākinī* (a Treasure already in circulation),[44] which indicates a much different understanding of the term from that of later scholars, such as Kongtrul and Do Drubchen, for whom mind Treasures are immaterial revelations that are utterly isolated from any potential interpolation by the Treasure revealer.[45] An explanation for Longchenpa's attribution of his own works to the category of Treasure is found in the writings of Dudjom who explains that the *Innermost Essence of the Ḍākinī* was dictated directly to Longchenpa by Padmasambhava, Yeshe Tsogyal, and the protector Yudrönma,[46] thus implicating Padmasambhava as the source of Longchenpa's writings (although, arguably, one would expect this to situate the *Innermost Essence of the Ḍākinī* within the lineage of pure vision rather than the lineage of the Treasures). Still, this would not exclude the possibility that during the fourteenth century the meaning of this concept was identical, or closely related to, the similar term spiritual Treasure (i.e., a precious teaching) and that only later did a real distinction develop between these two. In that case, the attribution of both the *Heart Essence of the Ḍākinī* and the *Innermost Essence of the Ḍākinī* as precious teachings would seem accurate.

Still, this period of Treasure history warrants more thorough research, and drawing firm conclusions is at present a doubtful enterprise. We should note, however, that Kongtrul also displays some ambiguity in classifying Longchenpa's Treasures by listing him as a revealer of both "earth Treasures" (*sa gter*) and mind Treasures.[47] The classification as revealer of earth Treasures is based on Longchenpa reportedly receiving the *Heart Essence of the Ḍākinī* "in actuality" from the ḍākinī Shenpa Sokdrubma even though these texts had already been previously revealed by Rinchen Tsultrim Dorje (thirteenth century).[48] His mind Treasure revelation is the *Innermost Essence of the Ḍākinī* just described. Interestingly, although Kongtrul mentions that Longchenpa's mind Treasures were "established in the form of treatises"[49] (i.e., their identity as Treasures might not be readily apparent to the ordinary person), he simultaneously hails Longchenpa as the king of all revealers of mind Treasure.[50] Still, such seeming paradoxes seem to have posed no difficulty for the followers of the Nyingma School, who appear to have been comfortably settled in the belief that the manifestations of enlightened wisdom ultimately defy mundane conceptual structures. Thus, schemas and classifications become imbued with an elasticity that allowed for the harmonious union of otherwise seemingly contrasting classificatory notions. Finally, we may note that Longchenpa appears to have been the first Treasure commentator to identify the Treasures with the classical five-fold division of body (*sku*), speech (*gsung*), mind (*thugs*), qualities (*yon tan*), and activity (*phrin las*), thus further contributing to the taxonomic richness of Treasure hermeneutics.[51]

In the century following Longchenpa we find an influential Treasure treatise, lauded by Jamgön Kongtrul as one of the most significant authorities on the polemical defense of the Treasures, the *Great Treasure Chronicle: The Illuminating Lamp* by Ratna Lingpa Pal Zangpo.[52] Like Guru Chöwang before him, Ratna Lingpa claims to have a two-fold purpose for composing his treatise: to elucidate the philosophy of Treasure interpretation as construed by the Nyingma School and to counter continuing criticism raised against the

Treasures by outside skeptics. Having discoursed at length on the nature of the Treasures, he remarks:

> In this way... although these instructions have elucidated individually the general, specific, and particular categories of Treasure, in reality the Transmitted Precepts and the Treasures are said to be an indivisible unity. Nevertheless, I have presented them here so that those who possess the eye of wisdom and have valid, honest minds may feel confidence and become uplifted. For those who are linked through past aspirations and positive karmic residue and today feel interest in the Treasures, follow them, practice them genuinely, and are able to gain accomplishment, this treatise will increase their experience of joy and inspiration, give rise to limitless devotion and conviction through certainty, and engender renunciation, diligence and so forth. Even so, I have also explained extensively in order to defeat those sectarian intellectuals who lack vast learning, understanding, and reasoning; who are destitute with respect to renunciation, pure perception, and wisdom; who are devoid of any real understanding although they know the names of a few categories; who pretend to be learned while deluded by ignorance; and who do not benefit themselves by training and meditation nor help others through teaching and exposition.[53]

We shall return to discuss the gentlemen for whom this latter part was intended. First, however, let us consider the divisional elements in Ratna Lingpa's Treasure taxonomy. The text is divided into five main chapters that explain: 1) that all the teachings of the Buddha are Treasures; 2) how the classical Buddhist teachings of India were all revealed as Treasure; 3) the way the Treasures were revealed in Tibet; 4) the way Ratna Lingpa's individual Treasures were revealed; and 5) apologetic arguments in favor of Treasure revelation.[54] The primary discussion of Treasure definitions is found in chapters one to three. Although the inspiration of Guru Chöwang's *Great Treasure Chronicle* is felt throughout these first chapters, there are nevertheless notable differences in terms of topical structure and emphasis.

While Chöwang devotes the majority of his treatise to defining the Treasures, Ratna Lingpa focuses primarily on the process of concealment and revelation, leaving the explanation of Treasure identity as a secondary theme that only occasionally surfaces throughout his larger account. Ratna Lingpa adheres predominantly to the categories defined by Chöwang centuries earlier, such as those of body, speech, and mind (statues, teachings, and stūpas), as well as Treasures of astrology, medicine, and handicraft (notably, no mention of Bön). However, he also renames Chöwang's four primary Treasure divisions with terminology of his own. Thus, Ratna Lingpa presents a Treasure category termed "outer variegated Treasures" (*phyi sna tshogs pa'i gter*) referring to the elements, valleys, wealth, etc. Next are the "inner Treasures bestowing eminence" (*nang mchog stsol ba'i gter*) comprising the specifically Buddhist Treasures of body, speech, and mind. Third are the "secret, naturally appearing, naturally concealed, and naturally realized Treasures" (*gsang ba rang byung rang gab rang rtogs pa'i gter*). This category is not further defined by Ratna Lingpa but we may reasonably assume that it refers to the realization of the buddhas classified by Chöwang as "the definitive Treasure of suchness." Last in the group of four is the category of "indefinite variegated Treasures" (*ma nges sna tshogs pa'i gter*), which refers to the arts of medicine, astrology, magic, and handicrafts.[55] In this way Ratna Lingpa provides yet another demonstration of the innovative spirit that continuously shaped and developed the Nyingma School during the first centuries of revelatory activity where, even as commentators increasingly saw themselves as belonging to a textually institutionalized tradition (and so must have felt inclined to adopt already established taxonomies), the creative urge of these writers gained the upper hand, and the taxonomy of the Treasures was reinvented with almost every new commentarial scripture.

The Treasure ideology of the ecumenical tradition, several centuries later, is most thoroughly presented in Jamgön Kongtrul's monumental hagiographical survey of the Treasure revealers entitled *Precious Lapis Lazuli Rosary that Briefly Presents the Emergence of the Profound Treasures and the Accomplished Treasure Revealers*, which introduces his famous anthology of Treasure revelations, the *Store of Precious Treasures*.[56] According to this text there are two main categories of Treasure: earth Treasure and mind Treasure.[57] As we have seen, these concepts are already found in Longchenpa's writings, although without the prominence attributed to them by Kongtrul. The presentation of earth Treasure and mind Treasure as the two major Treasure classifications in fact has roots prior to the ecumenical tradition that Kongtrul represents (at least to the revelations of Jigme Lingpa in the eighteenth century),[58] but precisely how far back is not certain.

In any case, although this bipartite Treasure system had been an element of Treasure taxonomy for at least a century, Kongtrul and his colleagues are unique in developing it into a four-fold sub-classification constructed around the visionary activity of Jamyang Khyentse Wangpo and Chokgyur Dechen Lingpa. The system is based on the following prophecy revealed by Chokgyur Lingpa:

> The river of seven descents—
> The unbroken spoken lineage,
> Profound actual earth Treasures as well as mind Treasures,
> Rediscovered Treasures and recollected Treasures,
> Pure vision and the hearing lineage—
> Will flow into the fortune of the father and son.
> It will enrich the teachings of the degenerate age
> And spread the sunshine of the profound and vast.[59]

Accordingly, in this classification, the earth Treasures are divided into "actual earth Treasures" (*sa gter ngos*) and "rediscovered Treasures" (*yang gter*), while mind Treasures consist of "actual mind Treasures" (*dgongs gter ngos*) and "recollected Treasures" (*rjes dran gter*). The basic division of earth and mind Treasures forms the primary structure for Kongtrul's work while the remaining sub-categories are encountered throughout the text as he discusses the revelations of individual figures, in particular those of Khyentse and Chokling.[60] Following Kongtrul, this system was adopted by subsequent scholars in their treatment of the Treasure literature.[61]

According to this presentation, earth Treasures are revealed in dependency on a physical locality and constitute the only kind of Treasure that is not exclusively transmitted in and revealed from the mental realm. As the name indicates, this kind of Treasure is hidden in the ground, a rock, or another physical location. It may be actual texts but can also consist of religious objects such as vajras, kīlas, or buddha statues, sub-classified as material Treasure, as well as jewels and precious metals, designated wealth Treasures.[62] Rediscovered Treasures are teachings that previously were revealed but, as the conditions for successful revelation were not met, were re-concealed and now discovered anew. Mind Treasures are revealed purely from the mind of the Treasure revealer where Padmasambhava is claimed to have originally concealed them. Recollected Treasures are remembrances from a former life. The Treasure revealers recollect their past existences as spiritual teachers and propagate their earlier teachings once again. The purpose of this form of revelation is to revive past teachings that have been lost or whose spiritual lineage has been interrupted. This particular form of Treasure is predominantly associated with the revelations of Khyentse Wangpo who, as Kongtrul mentions time and again, revived the spiritual transmission of many Treasure lineages in this way.

Lastly, we may note that the great diversity of Treasure classifications is partly mirrored in the multiplicity of masters responsible for their revelation, the Treasure revealers themselves. Commentaries often speak of more than one thousand Treasure revealers to appear in Tibet but focus on a much smaller number of important figures of which the most comprehensive list is found in Kongtrul's treatise on the Treasure revealers mentioned above.[63] From the early days of the tradition, to be considered a major Treasure revealer an individual was required to discover sufficient material to constitute an entire path to enlightenment, which in this case meant teachings related to Padmasambhava, the Great Perfection, and the bodhisattva Avalokiteśvara.[64] Within the larger group of major Treasure revealers there are numerous sub-divisions such as the recent "five royal Treasure revealers",[65] the "three supreme nirmāṇakāyas",[66] the "eleven Lingpas",[67] and the most general and common grouping of the "108 great Treasure revealers".[68]

We have witnessed here some of the complexity involved in classifying and identifying revealed Treasures and seen how the tradition over time went through significant taxonomical and philosophical developments. On that basis it may come as a surprise that the Nyingma School was even able to maintain a unified stance in propagating the Treasures as a continuously increasing number of visionaries all claimed to have discovered the profoundest Treasure of all. While there certainly were voices within the Nyingma School that adopted a skeptical attitude towards the rapidly growing number of revelations, it is remarkable that they were not more plentiful and that the tradition was able to absorb and accommodate this plethora of teachings and masters to the extent that it did.[69] This philosophical ecumenicalism was no doubt in large part facilitated by the Nyingma School's historical composition of multiple lineages that for long avoided institutional amalgamation as this school (unlike the Sakya, Kagyu, and Gelug schools) never encountered the galvanizing effect of major state-scale sponsorship.

Thus, even though the approach to Treasure identification and classification developed over time, the fundamental philosophical position of the Nyingma School remained surprisingly homogenous, consistently placing the *sine qua non* of Treasure discovery within the inexhaustible potentiality of the dharmakāya realm. Notably, the skeptical voices within the Nyingma School were never critical of the *principle* of continued revelation, but instead warned against the potential danger of admitting frauds into the ranks of genuine visionary masters. Ironically, it is therefore precisely within the multiplicity and variety of the tradition that we encounter its unifying force as a dominant eclecticism capable of incorporating a host of idiosyncratic Treasure systems into a relatively homogenous and well-functioning unity. This integrality in turn received its cohesive strength from a continual referral to the Treasures' genesis in the a-historical realm personified by the dharmakāya buddha Samantabhadra and his peers. At least since the time of Guru Chöwang there has been a broad understanding within the Nyingma School that the Treasures, in essence, embody the entirety of the Buddha's teachings and even existence itself. Thus, in the most fundamental equation, anything and everything belongs within the unifying dharmakāya realm from which all Treasures emerge.

In spite of this position being repeatedly advanced by past thinkers of the Nyingma School it has often been ignored or downplayed in contemporary studies of the Treasures. For example, a recent study of Guru Chöwang's *Great Treasure Chronicle* portrays his inclusive outlook on Treasure definition as a unique and eccentric view developed as an apologetical tool for defending his revelations against the critique of outsiders.[70] While there is no question that Chöwang's *Great Treasure Chronicle* in part was meant to rebuke the skeptics of his day,[71] the inclusive interpretations of the Treasure phenomenon that are developed in this text came to influence later commentators profoundly as they adopted the main elements of Chöwang's philosophical vision into the predominant hermeneutical position of the Nyingma School.[72] Guru Chöwang's inclusive attitude therefore represents, not an odd piece of Treasure apology, but a seminal source for the formation of the philosophical position of the Nyingma School in matters of Treasures. Consequently, by focusing predominantly on perceived apologetic "agendas" and "strategies" in the *Great Treasure Chronicle* one risks losing sight of the importance and value of this text as a formative philosophical vision that came to influence the Nyingma School for the better half of a millennium.

Although new Treasure taxonomies developed in partial dependency on previous classificatory formulations, the evolutions within Treasure taxonomy gradually came to involve philosophical change on such a scale that central positions of recent Treasure commentators can be hard to identify in the earliest Treasure treatises of the Nyingma School. A prominent illustration for such developments is the concept of mind Treasure, which, emerging in the fourteenth century from the notion of a spiritual Treasure, at first appears to denote simply a precious teaching in general, while in later Treasure commentaries it evolves into one of the most prominent Treasure categories.[73] As a way to accommodate these many variegated Treasure systems within its ranks, the Nyingma School adopted a broad interpretation of the Treasures, first formulated by Guru Chöwang, which, running parallel to the multiplicity of textual and taxonomic idiosyncrasies, came to conceive of all the buddhas' teachings, and even existence itself, as Treasure. It was this collateral approach to Treasure hermeneutics that allowed the tradition to continue as a homogenous entity in spite of the numerous historical neologies that continuously changed its outward appearance. Still, in spite of the warm reception given to the numerous Treasures by the followers of the Nyingma School they were often met in other quarters with a skeptical reaction that discarded their legitimacy and denounced their propagators as frauds, tricksters, or worse. In the following chapter, we shall look at these opposing positions of the devotee and the skeptic and trace their relationship in Tibet and the West.

2

Are the Treasures Authentic?

It did not take long from the first major Treasure revelations in the twelfth and thirteenth centuries before skeptics from rivaling Buddhist schools began questioning their authenticity.[74] The appearance of the Treasures coincided with the second wave of Indian Buddhist import to Tibet from the tenth to fourteenth centuries. At this time, as the texts and practices of the New Schools (*gsar ma*) and the older Nyingma tradition became increasingly measured against one another, tensions often ran high as the life-giving favors of the political and financial establishment were perceived to be intimately linked to publicly demonstrating the supremacy of one's own religious tradition at the expense of others. The New Schools primarily sought to establish themselves by emphasizing the Indian origin of their texts—an origin the Nyingma School had difficulty proving, in part due to the long time span since its textual import from India in the eighth and ninth centuries. As a verifiable Indian origin became the central measure for authenticating Buddhist scripture in Tibet, the texts and practices of the Nyingma School were quickly disclaimed as Tibetan forgeries and interpolations. Even so, the approach to validation propagated by the New Schools was never rigorously applied internally and would occasionally be suspended with if seen to conflict with the inherited textual corpus of the New Schools themselves.[75] Nevertheless, as this new-found standard of evaluation became increasingly normative in the Tibetan discourse on authenticity, the stage was quickly set for a polemical confrontation over the validity of the Treasures.

Traditional Polemics

The lack of mention of the Treasures in outside sources until the thirteenth century tells us that in terms of adherents and political influence the Treasure tradition must have been a relatively minor movement at least until the time of Nyangral Nyima Özer in the second half of the twelfth century. During the first half of the thirteenth century, however, with the appearance of polemical works denouncing Treasure revelation we may assume that the tradition had gained momentum through the revelations of Nyangral Nyima Özer and Guru Chöwang—the two most prominent figures among the early Treasure revealers. The earliest known critique of Treasure revelation is by the scholar and polemicist Chak Lotsāwa Chöje Pal (1197-1265), who advanced his criticism of the Treasures as part of a general complaint against practices and scriptures circulating in Tibet that he perceived to be spurious in nature.[76] Having argued at length against the general teachings of the Nyingma School he concludes this section of the text with a critique of the Treasures and Guru Chöwang, concerning whom he remarks:

> At the time when Samye Monastery was being constructed Guru Padmasambhava arrived from India and vanquished false teachings. Then, having made a few auspicious connections by accepting students, he returned to India. Later, Pekar, a Gyalpo spirit, entered the body of a Nepalese known as Kakarudzin. He put on a meditation hat, placed feathers in it and put on a brocade cloak. He then went to Samye where he declared himself to be Padmasambhava and taught innumerable perverted teachings and thereafter these numerous wrong teachings spread. The many false teachings were then manipulated by the one known as Guru Chöwang who became possessed when a Radza spirit entered him after telling him that they were Treasure texts. Subsequently, nāgas, demons, and Gyalgong spirits gathered around his false teachings which resulted in outbreaks of leprosy and psychotic fits. These were then taken as his signs of accomplishment. Such texts that appear from Treasures are not authentic.[77]

There were other thinkers of this period, such as Jigten Gönpo (1143-1217),[78] Sakya Paṇḍita (1182-1251), and possibly even Butön (1290-1364),[79] who, like Chak Lotsāwa, saw it fit to issue warnings against the Treasures. In a text attributed to the famed scholar Butön Rinchen Drub the author seems to agree with Chak Lotsāwa's assessment of Guru Chöwang and comments:

Such false teachings, pretending to be the words of
[Padmasambhava],
Were presented as Treasure revelations by Chöwang who was
under the influence of demons.
Thereby numerous incorrect teachings were put into writing
Leading many beings down the wrong path.[80]

He also says:

Likewise, each and everywhere,
Any region has a false Treasure.
Once revealed, they now spread in all directions.
Still, although they are obviously false teachings,
The inhabitants of the Snowy Land perceive them to be true.[81]

Even so, the main objection of the early polemics seems to have been a concern that the Treasures were false Tibetan compositions devoid of spiritual continuity with Buddhist India. Sakya Paṇḍita, in his *Differentiation of the Three Precepts*, offers the following remarks:

There are scriptures that emerge from Treasures,
Traditions that have been copied from elsewhere,
Teachings that are written, teachings that are dreamt,
And traditions that were memorized.

If you pursue the lineage of these back to Vajradhara
Or even receive their transmission from others
It will of course go against the dharma—
But it will also negate our own tradition.[82]

Although the condemnation of the Treasures was often categorical and determined, the early skeptical writings generally offer little historical, philosophical, or philological deduction to support the critique. This did not, however, prevent these writings from becoming standard models for subsequent condemnations of the Treasures by the New Schools. Thus, two centuries following the critiques of Sapaṇ and the other early polemicists, the Treasure apologist Ratna Lingpa sums up the skeptical arguments in the following manner:

> There are some ghostly and sectarian people...who criticize the Treasures. They say that the Treasures are false and never were concealed. Even if the Treasures should happen to be genuine, they will say that they are earth teachings, stone teachings, and wooden teachings as they were concealed in earth, rocks, water, and so forth. Yet other people claim that if the Treasures had been concealed at the time of Urgyen Padma during the early spread of the teaching they would have turned to dust by now. Therefore, since they are still intact, it is claimed that we deceptively hide and discover them ourselves. Still others say that the Treasures are controversial, have little success, and only benefit others slightly while yet other people say that the oral transmission of the Treasures is broken as they do not have an oral lineage. They call them "teachings that burst forth" because it is claimed they have no spoken transmission or empowerment.[83]

Being a Treasure revealer himself, one should of course not uncritically accept Ratna Lingpa's characterization of the skeptical positions as he would have no interest in making this critique appear any more sensible than necessary. Nevertheless, his description of the criticism does indicate that, until the fifteenth century, the critique of the Treasures had developed only slightly from its early formulations quoted above. Furthermore, this hermeneutical *status quo* appears to have continued into the following centuries as well, as the polemical literature increasingly ossified around previous positions. Thus, the arguments set forth by the Gelugpa scholar Sumpa Khenpo (1704-1788) in the eighteenth century remain by and large identical to the critique advanced during the early days. Although the Treasure revealers are no longer portrayed as possessed by demons, Sumpa Khenpo still suggests that the Treasures are best avoided as they are composed by charlatans wishing to deceive the public. Characteristic of the polemical literature, both skeptical and apologetic, Sumpa Khenpo states his position in no uncertain terms but offers no actual arguments in support of his view.[84] This has been noted by Kapstein who quite rightly remarks:

> We should not lose sight of the fact that scholarship consists not of merely arriving at conclusions, but also of justifying them. Sumpa Khenpo doubts the authenticity of the *Testimonial Record of Padmasambhava* and of the *Maṇi Kambum,* but never does he

> give us a detailed and critical account of his reasons for harboring those doubts. This being so, the correctness of his position is anything but self-evident.[85]

Despite the assumptive nature of the skeptical critiques, the Nyingma School clearly felt a need to defend its revelations and, rather than stoically ignoring the criticism, it soon composed a series of vigorous and spirited rebuttals of the charges brought forth against the Treasures. Among the various apologetical writings of the Nyingma School, the most detailed works related to Treasure revelation are the two Treasure chronicles by Guru Chöwang and Ratna Lingpa.[86] Since the main principles of Guru Chöwang's arguments have already been mentioned above, and as they have also been discussed in some detail elsewhere,[87] we shall here focus primarily on Ratna Lingpa's Treasure defense. At first glance, the two chronicles resemble each other as both authors are concerned with demonstrating commonalities between the Treasures and the generally accepted Indian Mahāyāna canons, though Ratna Lingpa's Treasure chronicle is both longer and more detailed. The primary theme throughout this treatise is an attempt to situate the revelatory activity of the Treasures firmly within mainstream Mahāyāna Buddhism. Like Chöwang, Ratna Lingpa claims that Treasures are not only religious texts and objects revealed in Tibet but include anything meaningful that previously has been concealed, in actuality as well as figuratively, from the perception of sentient beings. This may include, but is not restricted to, the Buddha's teaching. Ratna Lingpa defines a Treasure in the following words:

> It is a Treasure because it is concealed. It is a Treasure because it is hidden. It is a Treasure because it is inexhaustible. It is a Treasure because it fulfills needs and wishes.[88]

A significant aspect of this wide definition is, however, inevitably defined as the Buddha's teaching, which, according to both Treasure chronicles, was repeatedly concealed and revealed in India as the archetypal example of a Buddhist Treasure. Having included the generally accepted Buddhist canons within the Treasure phenomenon, Ratna Lingpa concludes that Tibetan Treasure revelation represents no new form of spiritual transmission; in fact it merely continues an already well-established tradition of scriptural revelation in Buddhism. Having argued at length for the equation of accepted Indian scripture with the Treasures of the Nyingma School, Ratna Lingpa devotes his fifth and last chapter to a point-by-point rebuttal of particular objections to the Treasures, defending them against the claims that they are fake, originate in the outer elements, could not have survived into the present, are mistrusted, unpopular and of little benefit, devoid of spiritual lineages, and emerge at random.[89]

Regarding the first claim that the Treasures are essentially fraudulent and therefore inherently unworthy of respect, Ratna Lingpa asks a rhetorical question. If the Treasures were not authentic, he says, how could one account for the prevalence of self-appearing Treasure statues, hidden Treasure valleys, the numerous accomplished masters in the Treasure lineages, and the abundant riches that appear from the Treasures of wealth?[90] This argument is of course dubious as a skeptic would question the authenticity of such phenomena no less than that of the Treasures themselves and, as such, Ratna Lingpa's refutation appears rather analogous to the skeptical approach to polemics witnessed above.[91]

Considering the question of the general authenticity of the Treasures settled, Ratna Lingpa continues his rejoinder by attacking the critique that the Treasures emerge from the five elements. The textual matrix for this rather odd objection seems to be the *Manual of the Single Intent* by Jigten Gönpo, which says:

> There are some who would have it that teachings (chos) without lineages and earth teachings (sa chos), sky teachings (gnam chos), gter-ma [i.e. Treasures] and so on are profound and miraculous. But we hold that the teaching transmitted through a lineage is [truly] profound and miraculous.[92]

However, as we can see, Jigten Gönpo's concern is not that the Treasures issue from the five elements but rather that they emerge without an established lineage. Thus, if taken as a direct reply to Jigten Gönpo's critique, Ratna Lingpa's response would partially misconstrue the original argument. We cannot, however, exclude the possibility that Ratna Lingpa addresses a derogatory oral tradition, which dismisses the Treasures as "earth teachings" and so forth without the underlying hermeneutics of Jigten Gönpo. In any case, whether addressing an actual or a fictive critique, Ratna Lingpa argues that the Buddha himself was composed of physical elements and so was his speech. Furthermore, he notes, since the various precious substances involved in writing, such as gold, silver, copper, lapis lazuli, etc., all are extracted from the earth, that would make any written text an earth teaching; using ink would make it a water teaching; while moving the hand freely through space when writing would make it a space teaching.[93]

Proceeding, Ratna Lingpa argues in a similar fashion against several other seemingly minor objections before he turns to the more serious accusation that the Treasures lack an unbroken spiritual continuity and thus have lost their transformative power and relevance.[94] Ratna Lingpa addresses this charge by arguing that the Treasure revealers already have received full spiritual transmission at the feet of Padmasambhava himself in their past existence. In this view, Padmasambhava came to Tibet as an already fully enlightened Buddha and conferred all relevant empowerments and oral transmissions on his Tibetan disciples, the discoverers to be. Only then were the Treasures concealed along with instructions to reveal them in the future. At the appropriate times the revealers then locate the Treasures based on preliminary Treasure guides (*kha byang*), also concealed by Padmasambhava, that mark the exact location of each Treasure. Still, even though the revealer will thus already have received the complete transmission to the relevant Treasure, to awaken this past karmic imprint, he must enter a period of private appropriation of the Treasure in which he meets Padmasambhava in actuality, vision, or dream. This meeting will then restore the recollection of the past empowerments, prophecies, and oral transmissions. In Ratna Lingpa's view, the allegation that the Treasures possess no spiritual continuity is therefore without any merit and, citing a Treasure prophecy by Padmasambhava, he admonishes his readers to pay no more attention to the skeptical charges than a deer is concerned with the sound of a running stream.[95]

Finally, Ratna Lingpa rebuts the concern that Treasures suddenly appear out of the blue—a phenomenon derogatorily described as "teachings bursting forth" (*rdol chos*). This rebuttal is reminiscent of the one just witnessed in that both are concerned with demonstrating an unbroken spiritual continuity for the Treasures. Here Ratna Lingpa argues that the Buddhist teaching likewise originally "burst forth" from the realization of the Buddha and was transmitted in a line of masters in whose minds realization similarly appeared instantaneously. Therefore, the entire Buddhist teaching, according to Ratna Lingpa, has been transmitted in a process identical to the sudden appearance of the Treasures.[96] In this way, Ratna Lingpa considers the challenge to the Treasures' authenticity effectively reversed and concludes his Treasure chronicle.

There is, however, little reason to believe that Ratna Lingpa's arguments actually ever succeeded in persuading any number of skeptics of the spiritual validity of the Treasures. On the contrary, it seems that the attempts by Treasure apologetics to argue that Treasure revelation is an integral part of mainstream Buddhism—or rather, that mainstream Buddhism *is* Treasure revelation—fell on deaf ears as critics continued to advance their objections in much the same manner of the early centuries.[97] Thus, the exchange of views came to a hermeneutical halt, and as late as the nineteenth century, we find Jamgön Kongtrul defending the Treasures with essentially the arguments of Guru Chöwang against criticisms not unlike those advanced by Chak Lotsāwa.[98]

We have witnessed here some traditional attempts to argue the deceitful nature of the Treasures and followed the subsequent replies to this critique by the followers of the Nyingma School. We have also noticed how a number of basically unconvincing arguments, advanced by skeptics and apologists alike, remained surprisingly stagnant over the centuries and, on the whole, failed to effect any significant change of opinion on either side of the religious divide. Surely, the perceived need by Tibetan scholars to follow established party lines and adhere to positions already formulated by the founders of their respective traditions must have inhibited the vitality of the Treasure debate considerably. Nevertheless, the inherent difficulty of determining the validity of claims of revelation *per se* no doubt also contributed to this situation. Let us now look closer at this issue and try to gauge its effect on the way that the Treasures have been perceived in the West.

The Occidental Adoption

Although Tibetan attempts to bridge the divide between the skeptic and the devotee generally are few and far between, their influence cannot be dismissed offhand. The famed master of the Nyingma School, Ju Mipham (1846-1912), whose views on Treasure revelation we shall consider below, was not the first author to seek broader perspectives outside the traditional dichotomy of right and wrong. One such previous writer was Tsele Natsog Rangdrol (b. 1608), a yogin-scholar of the Kagyu and Nyingma Schools, who in discussing the Treasures of Urgyen Lingpa, acknowledges the value of certain skeptical arguments.[99] Although Tsele fundamentally agrees with the traditional position that Treasure revelation should be appreciated in reference to an a-temporal transcendent realm in which enlightened manifestations can appear in any shape or form, he also concedes that spiritual fraud disguised as genuine revelation is a real and likely possibility. He remarks:

> Although the main part of [the two versions of the *Chronicle of Padmasambhava*] surely is the words of the Great Master, obviously some uneducated and foolish people have interpolated them with colloquial terms and phrases of their invention. Similarly, the famous *Five Chronicles* are unmistakenly a [Treasure] by Orgyen Lingpa. However, no matter how you examine the verbiage and meaning, it is unlike authentic [Treasure] teachings. For example, the assertion that Guru Rinpoche had a son and the predictions of people who later appeared I personally find implausible. The various versions of [the *Chronicle of Padmasambhava*] are for the most part comprised of the teachings of Master Padmasambhava. Of course they possess great blessings, but it is simply hard for me to regard them as reliable historical sources.[100]

Although Tsele offers no further philological elaboration on his assertions, he clearly sympathizes with the concerns that the veracity of certain revealed accounts was questionable.

Critique of religious revelation claiming authoritative origins is not tied exclusively to Treasure revelation but represents a religious and philosophical tension in Buddhism as old as the tradition itself. In India, a number of early Buddhist communities seem to have shown little interest in limiting authentication to mere historical analysis, and instead validated scripture based on soteriological value—an approach that gave rise to a most fertile climate for the emergence and institutionalization of religious scripture.[101] Still, even in this rather liberal intellectual climate, the authenticity of new scriptural traditions never went fully uncontested and frequently met with skeptics advocating a more conservative approach based on historical realist verification.[102]

The Nyingma School defended its Treasures within a framework of soteriologically validated authenticity but in the origin accounts of the Treasures simultaneously narrated a complex account of transmission and revelation, seemingly unfolding within historical time. The apparent conflict between advancing soteriological defenses of the Treasures, while still including historical elements in origin narratives, has been interpreted by some as demonstrating the Nyingma School's concern to maintain historical credentials for its Treasures in a Tibetan religious society demanding so.[103] While this explanation no doubt contains an element of truth, it is, however, not fully satisfying when considering how the historical claims in the origin accounts often became the particular targets of criticism, and instead of raising the validity and respect given to Treasures, these claims became some of the most discredited features in the entire literature of the Nyingma School.[104]

Demonstrating a firm historical identity for one's scriptural tradition surely concerned all the religious schools of Tibet; that the Tibetan canon was compiled on such criteria is evidence to this effect. However, the origin accounts of the Treasures are perhaps better seen as religious elements internal to the tradition rather than as tools to convince a skeptical antagonist in the outside community as, although no one could have been surprised that the historical claims advanced in the Treasures would meet with a skeptical reaction, Treasure revealers continued unabatedly to root their revelations in the legends of the Yarlung dynasty. It seems therefore fair to assume that the historical claims of the Treasure literature were advanced, not in the hope that outside skeptics would abandon their disbelief and become Treasure adherents, but rather as a means for internal communication that traced the origin of the Treasures to a matrix of internally accepted religious authorities.[105] In this way the Nyingma School included these historical narratives as a way to demonstrate, internally, the legendary origin of the tradition to its followers—knowing that these very claims would be viewed by its rival Tibetan schools as *res odiosa*.[106]

As we noted above, the historical claims advanced in the Treasure literature probably never persuaded many skeptical Tibetans to embrace this tradition while, on the other hand, the followers of the Nyingma School already would have been inclined to accept, *a priori*, the general principles of Treasure revelation even in the absence of such legends. This in turn indicates that the authority granting authenticity to Treasure revelation, even internally, must be identified only outside of these historical narratives. Treasure literature frequently states that the historical claims are told to "engender confidence" (*nges shes skye pa*) in the Treasure. However, this confidence is generated, not in a skeptic intrinsically inclined to question the value of the Treasure but in a devotee who has already fundamentally accepted the basic principles involved in Treasure revelation. In this way the historical accounts in the Treasure literature retain only marginal influence for establishing the authenticity of the Treasure compared to other more basic, less philosophical factors, such as the political, financial, and religious support extended to the Treasure revealer by the local elite, combined with the revealer's own ability to magnetize an audience through a charismatic personality. Based on such basal factors a final authentication of the Treasures can then be granted by a broader community of followers. Only then, once a teaching has been accepted within this fundamental validating framework, can the historical narratives come to the fore and fulfill their purpose of imbuing the insider with respect and veneration for the Treasure's exalted origin.

A related issue is the difficulty of evaluating historical claims when little actual material exists from which to derive conclusions. For the overwhelming majority of earth Treasure revelations, the only extant physical evidence linking the Treasure to antiquity is the so-called yellow scroll (*shog ser*) from which the Treasure manifests in the psychic vision of its revealer.[107] In the case of the later mind Treasures, however, no physical evidence whatsoever exists, as the entire revelatory process occurs exclusively within the mind of the revealer.[108] In either case, the actual revelation of the Treasure is predominantly a mnemonic process that leaves little or no historical material from which to judge a potential relation to eighth century dynastic Tibet. Furthermore, it is important to keep in mind that the Nyingma School did not embrace the association of the Treasures with the dynastic period according to the principles of realist historical interpretations, but consistently emphasized the lack of intrinsic existence of time and matter, which allowed for an abstract philosophical approach to such legends.[109]

Although the Treasure transmission eventually sees itself elaborately attached to an "historical reality," it emerges so thoroughly saturated by the events of the realization lineage of the conquerors that any subsequent historical claims simply cannot be separated from this noumenal reality and taken at face value. Therefore, to assert that the Treasure legends were composed primarily as counterevidence to charges of forgery, and that a primary defense strategy was to link Treasures to a Buddha of the Indian Buddhist world, partially misrepresents the intent behind the historical narratives.[110] Although the Treasures do emphasize the role of the Indian master Padmasambhava and his Tibetan disciples in the transmission accounts, the primary function of these historical descriptions is to provide an origin account for the Treasure teachings rather than attempting to convert outside skeptics. The Treasure teachings repeatedly emphasize their roots in the transcendent, and the buddha of the origin account is not always a buddha figure connected geographically to India but rather to the principle of enlightenment itself. In fact, the Nyingma School has often deemphasized the historical link of its canonical scriptures to India. Consider Dudjom Rinpoche's remarks:

> None the less, some jealous persons created discord by, for example, declaring that certain of the ancient tantra had been composed in Tibet because they did not exist in India. However the non-

> existence of those tantras in India did not prove them to be inauthentic. Even the tantras which did exist in India did not originate there: they were brought forth by great accomplished masters from the domains of the gods, nāgas, yakṣas, ḍākinīs and so on...and later they were introduced to India.[111]

Acknowledging the a-historical framework in which they appear allows us to fully appreciate the historical claims found in the Treasures, and to consider the religious purposes that such narratives fulfill as spiritual links, neither fully mundane nor completely beyond, between the practitioner of the Treasures and the transcendent ultimate from which these revelations flow.

As we have seen, even though the body of polemical literature continued to grow, the basic arguments presented by the two opposing parties remained disproportionately static, and the Treasures were repeatedly presented either as true and genuine revelations or conning schemes of trickery. If we consider the link that existed in Tibet between acknowledged possession of scriptural authority and concrete political survival, it is of course understandable that most commentators showed little interest in searching for a middle ground in validating the Treasures. What is surprising, however, is the tendency in a number of Western studies to adopt the very same dialectical parameters metered out by the Tibetan tradition.[112] For example, Michael Aris, in his well-known study of the Treasure revealer Pema Lingpa, repeatedly debunks this figure as a spiritual charlatan but offers little evidence for his assertion.[113] Finally, perhaps sensing that his reader might not yet be fully convinced, Aris advances the following exhortation:

> Most important of all, many of Pemalingpa's contemporaries were of the opinion that he was basically a fraud. If they, with the radical and brilliant skeptic Drukpa Kunley among them, not to mention the "reformed" Gelukpa school, were capable of holding that view, then surely the rational and critical scholars of the twentieth century can do so too.[114]

Aris never explains why a rational and critical scholar should accept the evaluations of Drukpa Kunley (1455-1529), "the madman" (*smyon pa*) as he was also known, whose eccentric views and behavior challenged virtually all established figures and institutions, and those of his fifteenth century Gelugpa contemporaries, well-known for their skepticism toward the Nyingma School, as evidence to Pema Lingpa's spiritual authenticity. It seems clearer, however, that he has appropriated a politicized Tibetan agenda to argue a personal conviction that has not otherwise been convincingly established.[115]

Not everyone has been skeptical of the Treasure revelations of the Nyingma School and Aris in fact makes a point of criticizing several scholars for presenting charitable views of the Treasures.[116] However, generally the passages in question consist of minor remarks and tend to be less definitive in their evaluations of the Treasures. Still, like the skeptical positions, they generally offer little rationale for the way that views are assumed and judgment passed.[117]

Now, considering that to the Nyingma School the very being of the Treasures *per se* defies historical pin-pointing, it becomes clear that the question of authenticity beckons a much broader methodological approach than that which traditional polemicists previously have employed. I have argued above that, in spite of the numerous historical claims associated with Treasure discovery, their ultimate authentication rests on their acceptance, first by established religious authorities, and next by a broader community of devotees. However, fully appreciating this approach to Treasure validation requires us to suspend our notions of veracity as measured in purely historical terms and instead to engage with the Treasures as revelatory products. This implies appreciating them as scripture rather than text.[118]

Within the field of Buddhist studies this approach has been rare but a similar methodological hesitation can be identified in other branches of religious studies. In an insightful study Cantwell Smith has argued that scripture (and the authentication that makes it so) is created from a process of human interactions rather than historical verification.[119] Smith suggests that the academic emphasis on historical methodologies is a strategy created by scholars trying to avoid the hermeneutical challenges posed by the diversity of religions and the variety of interpretations of their beliefs. He categorizes this scholarly reluctance to engage with the notion of scripture as "academic fundamentalism" that refuses to acknowledge value in other traditions or interpretations. Then, as an encouragement to appreciate religious writings in broader ways, he sets forth the following proposition:

> Fundamental, we suggest, to a new understanding of scripture is the recognition that no text is a scripture in itself and as such. People—a given community—make a text into scripture, or keep it a scripture: by treating it in a certain way. I suggest: *scripture is a human activity.*[120]

In this way, Smith points out the simple truth that texts are transformed into scripture only through the validation process of a devotional community. As for Treasure validation, this suggests the fruitlessness of measuring scriptural authenticity merely with the yardstick of historicity, as scripture functions and exists in a realm beyond the measurable. Thus, Smith's statement is an invitation to expand the methodological horizon and look for alternative avenues for exploring the Treasures when perceived as scripture rather than as scrolls. Although both traditional and modern studies of Treasures often omit such alternatives, it would be premature to pronounce the entirety of Tibetan Treasure hermeneutics as caught up in polarized debates of right and wrong. In fact, we have the existence of a fascinating late nineteenth century composition to indicate otherwise.

Mipham's View: A New Hermeneutics?

The text in question belongs to the Treasure tradition and discusses the identity, not of the Treasures, but of the visionaries who claim to have uncovered them. Previous scholarship in this area is sparse and little information on the Treasure revealers is available. This text, entitled *Gem that Clears the Waters: An Investigation of Treasure Revealers*, is composed by the renowned nineteenth-century master of the Nyingma School Ju Mipham.[121] It is more concise than many other works by Mipham, yet it is an excellent source of information on Treasure revealers and questions of their validity. Right from the outset, Mipham acknowledges that the Treasure tradition, to which he himself belonged, contains certain fraudulent elements who exploit the good faith of devotees by posing as genuine Treasure revealers.[122] In this way Mipham does position himself within the traditional polemical framework of right and wrong, and he certainly writes hoping to expose those who unjustly pose as genuine visionary masters. However, in the course of writing, Mipham also touches on a number of issues of intrinsic interest for the study of the Treasure tradition that differentiate his text from the standard presentations of the saint–fraud dichotomy so often found in Tibetan polemical writings on this topic.

Mipham diverts from his usual scholastic writing style and presents a lively critique, full of both humor and sternness, of spiritual fraud in the name of Treasure revelation. His thoughts on this subject are noteworthy for several reasons. Most important, they are a rare acknowledgement that the issue of authenticity is more complex and warrants deeper methodological consideration than the standard polemical evaluations would have us believe. Second, as a critique of the Treasure revealing community from within the tradition itself, it provides important insights into the challenges the Nyingma School faced in curbing what appears to have been a widespread presence of deceit in the name of Treasure revelation. This insider's challenge to the authenticity of proclaimed revealers indicates the difficulty the Nyingma School experienced in maintaining a clean name and reputation in the public perception. Perhaps Mipham felt that this type of challenge would be difficult to address effectively in an environment of traditional philosophical discourse and that by adopting a more colloquial and direct style of writing he could better address the issue in a straightforward manner that would prove comprehensible to both commoners and scholars alike.

Acknowledging the polemical nature of the text, the editors of Mipham's collected works placed it adjacent to his famous replies to Gelugpa criticism of his controversial *Bodhisattvacāryāvatāra* commentary.[123] According to the brief colophon, it was composed "suddenly as it came to mind,"[124] and its style and language convey a sense of freshness and directness rarely encountered in classical Tibetan literature. The text contains no opening verses of praise or prayer and immediately tackles the issue at hand in a straightforward manner free from distracting philosophical sophistications. The fact that this is not an "ordinary" scholastic composition makes it all the more intriguing and fascinating as a window into the Treasure tradition, as Mipham speaks from his heart and addresses the culprits directly in a way that hits home much more effectively than would the elegant prose style for which he is otherwise so well known.

Mipham's homeland of eastern Tibet was generally inclined towards a charitable view of the Treasure tradition, so Mipham is not obliged to defend the tradition's basic premises. Instead he can concentrate on weeding out negative elements within the Treasure culture. In this process, he commences by characterizing the false revealers and then proceeds to evaluate the damage they inflict. Toward the end of his analysis, he offers devotees suggestions on how to identify such imposters. Mipham's admission that charlatans exist within the ranks of Treasure revealers indicates that even the Nyingma School's east Tibetan heartland must have harbored significant public concern that not all revelations could be trusted. Previous studies have for the most part described criticism of the Treasure tradition as stemming from scholars outside the Nyingma School, but Mipham makes it clear that the issue of authenticity was a concern for the Nyingma School as much as for anyone else. In fact, he urges its followers to take the outsiders' critique to heart and calls it "nectar-like advice."[125]

Although Mipham admits to the falsity of certain Treasure revelations, we should not therefore conclude that he generally finds Treasure revelations suspect or spurious. Rather, his goal is to expose the false revealers and expel them from the community so that the inspired lives of genuine Treasure revealing masters can shine unblemished by public mistrust brought on by frauds and imposters. Clearly a level of public criticism of the Treasure revealers existed at the time. The internal controversies over the compilation of the *Store of Precious Treasures*[126] would no doubt have contributed to the tattered image of the tradition, but the misgivings Mipham addresses here seem to have been rooted in a more fundamental and widespread suspicion among the general populace. Mipham acknowledges this mistrust, and speaks to the frauds as follows:

> Hey Treasure revealers! Although all inhabitants of the Snowy Land claim to have heartfelt interest and trust in Guru Padmasambhava, they do feel weary seeing the deceit of liars claiming to be Treasure revealers...so stop lessening the fortune of those who have trust in Padmasambhava.[127]

Later, Mipham supports this statement by quoting from Urgyen Lingpa's *Chronicle of Padmasambhava*, which says "except for dead dogs, anything is revealed as Treasure,"[128] referring, in Mipham's interpretation, to weariness with random objects being presented by imposters as religious artifacts blessed by saints in a bygone dynastic era. The scholarly establishment of the Nyingma School seems to have viewed so-called "new Treasures" (*gter gsar*) with a certain measure of skepticism while referring to the "older Treasures" (*gter rnying*) as genuinely authentic and worthy of practice. The idea that past things are better, of course, reflects a universal concern in matters of religion that spans all cultures and regions.[129] Nevertheless, given that Treasures in their very being represent an endorsement of spiritual and religious innovation, it is fascinating to find Mipham extolling this principle. He makes it clear on several occasions that he prefers the older Treasures and hails such early figures as Nyangral Nyima Özer, Guru Chöwang, Rigdzin Gödem (1337-1408), Ratna Lingpa (1403-78), and Karma Lingpa (1326-?) as authentic masters whose Treasures can be followed with confidence.[130]

Likely, many masters within the Nyingma School were concerned that emerging revelations would include some works of charlatans. As for Mipham, how does he characterize such frauds? He makes no attempt to conceal his disdain for those who deceivingly claim to possess the spiritual qualities required for Treasure revelation. He describes these people as power hungry individuals who will do anything to achieve the fame and economic benefits afforded genuine spiritual masters. In a lively blend of prose and poetry he exposes the many tricks that such individuals employ to gain their desired goals. According to Mipham, these goals are dominated by the wish for fame and wealth and their coveted byproducts. Lamenting the prevalence of such desires, he exclaims:

> When examining closely those who announce Treasure teachings,
> they wish for fame, look for wealth, and search for women and so
> place hope in their Treasures with expectations burning like fire.
> How rare are those free from lies and deceit![131]

These of course are not novel themes in the life of a fraud, but their mention in this text is intriguing as it offers a glimpse into the culture and politics surrounding the Treasure tradition and its revelatory output. As Mipham introduces the schemes of the false revealers we hear of practices such as inserting the names of wealthy people into the preceding prophetic inventory (*byang bu*) of the Treasure, lobbying spiritual authorities for recognition, declaring beautiful women as religious emanations especially suited for partnership, and the common Tibetan (and perhaps universal?) practice of denouncing all adversaries as deceitful demons.[132] The predictable result is that the community's faith is shaken and decreases. Mipham deplores this state of affairs and speaks directly to the imposters in an attempt to change their crooked ways. In addressing the false revealers he adopts a common Tibetan strategy in communicating with obstacle makers by first issuing a polite request followed by a wrathful threat of the unpleasant consequences of non-compliance. He first appeals to the moral conscience of the false revealers by reminding them of the destabilizing effect they have by causing the faithful to question the entire Treasure tradition, thereby severing the connection to the liberating instructions of Padmasambhava. For those who ignore such requests, Mipham then issues a warning of the dire karmic consequences awaiting such liars when, in future existences, they will find their tongues transformed into plows employed for farming. Thus, Mipham reminds the false revealers that there are severe consequences to all parties when someone falsely assumes the mantle of a spiritual adept.

Despite Mipham's lively account of the imposters and their unfortunate effect on the Treasure tradition, the issue of definitively determining the authenticity of such figures has not yet been resolved, and one is still left wondering what to do about the Treasure revealers and their claims. Since Tibetan religious history is amply filled with accounts of respected saints behaving in highly unconventional ways, the roguish actions described above cannot in themselves constitute any final measure for conclusively identifying a fraud. Although the ways of the charlatans appear deplorable by any standard, evaluations based on mere behavioral observation therefore seem insufficient. At the very end of his essay, however, Mipham proposes a measure by which one can, in his view, finally settle the question of authenticity. The text's concluding verse suggests that:

> If you should ever feel doubt in this regard, it is best to resolve this hesitance in the presence of a powerful person.[133]

This simple advice points directly to the fact that although the Treasure community is plagued by a group of deceitful charlatans behaving in outlandish ways, ultimately there is no verifiable evidence to aid the devotee in distinguishing deplorable frauds from those beings lauded by Mipham as authentic compassionate masters. Naturally, the lifestyle of a fraud would be predictably short-lived if it did not outwardly resemble its object of imitation, but the real reason that makes the two groups so difficult to distinguish is that both parties identify the source for their discovery in the mental visions of the revealer, thus suspending the availability of the kind of verifiable evidence on which people ordinarily rely when assessing claims of origin.

Mipham's suggestion that only a spiritually powerful person can determine the validity of the Treasure revealers is an acknowledgment that evaluations based exclusively on historical premises or observations of behavioral conduct will fail to provide any final and definitive answers. According to Mipham, ultimately it is only the spiritual intuition (i.e. the mastery of supramundane knowledge that perceives the minds of others) of authoritative leaders that can validate the claims of the Treasure revealers. On what grounds can he say this? To answer this we must first look at some of the ways in which Treasure revealers traditionally emerged as successful visionaries in Tibet.

The religio-political realities of nineteenth century east Tibet where Mipham lived were to a large extent governed by the mechanics of a feudal-like society in which major decisions were taken by a relatively small and exclusive financial, political, and religious elite. In such a society any suggestion of delegation of authority to the masses would certainly not have been encouraged, if even conceived of. Thus, an aspiring Treasure revealer would often ascend to fame only through active endorsements by the established regional powers.[134] In theory (and certainly rhetorically), this support would be extended based on a recognition of certain spiritual qualities in the Treasure revealer whereby his revelations, by extension, would be considered endowed with the liberating potency of a genuine Treasure. In reality this process was of course open to the negotiations of spiritual or political intrigue, and the outcome not always a given. Nevertheless, although such social and economic realities had a real and lasting influence on the way the Treasure tradition developed and flourished, one must also consider other more diffuse elements to the validation of the Treasure revealer such as the influence of his personal charisma and magnetism, and his ability to fulfill both the practical and spiritual needs of the general populace. Although political and religious connections often could go a long way in advancing a given Treasure revealer's career, Tibetan history is also rich in examples of charismatic visionaries rising to prominence primarily through the strength of their personal magnetism, only subsequently to be aided by established authorities. This latter factor, while more vague and hard to pinpoint than political backing, seems to have been one of the key ingredients in the success of the Treasure tradition, and would occasionally provide a validating capacity rivaling even that of the religious and political establishment.

Regardless of whether Treasure revealers ascended to fame primarily through the support of a religio-political power base or via their personal magnetizing qualities ultimately they would have to persuade a broader public—monastic and lay—of the value of their Treasures so that they could be adopted into a general social religious framework. Considering the hierarchical structure of traditional Tibetan religious society, much of this communal adaptation would certainly have occurred almost by default simply through the type of authoritative adherence that Mipham prescribes. Although it is doubtful whether any ordinary follower of the tradition ever felt blessed with a real mandate to validate the spiritual leaders of the Nyingma School, one should not disregard the influence of the collective devotional following in authenticating religious figures such as the Treasure revealers. Regardless of their charisma or political support, the Treasure revealers would eventually have to sustain and fulfill the needs of a faithful audience through their revelations. Not only in the short term by providing an attractive novelty, but also by establishing over time the value of their revelations to Buddhist practitioners by demonstrating such Treasures to be a reliable medium for spiritual growth and fulfillment for those who embrace them.

The process through which a devotee of the Treasure tradition can arrive at a final conclusion regarding the validity of a given Treasure revealer does, as Mipham points out, not include any foolproof checklist of outwardly observed characteristics. Mipham's solution to this problem is an appeal to authority; a move that in the traditional Buddhist context has long precedence in the practice of relying on the matured wisdom of spiritual elders. In the context of finding authenticity as an insider within a tradition dominated by revelatory activity, Mipham's advice therefore constitutes a traditional but also quite pragmatic approach to validation. Implicit in his advice, however, is the deeper consequence that to invest a spiritual teacher with full authority each devotee is ultimately forced to perform a validation based on a leap of faith. In the absence of any empirically verifiable modes of evaluation, Mipham suggests that the doubtful should rely on "a powerful person" in matters of authenticity, but, of course, identifying such an authority must eventually be performed on similarly faithful grounds as the initial evaluation of the Treasure revealer takes place.[135] Significantly, the validating onus thus returns to the individual devotee who is required, in the final analysis, to form a personal judgment of the Treasure revealer based on the strength of faith rather than any tangible and verifiable evidence of his credentials or the simple endorsement of a religious or political elite.

Recognizing that the final authenticating measures for Treasure revelation lie beyond what can be objectively verified, it appears a less rewarding exercise to perpetuate a debate of the Treasures along a simplified framework of true or false. Instead, looking beyond the traditional saint–charlatan paradigm may allow for other more rewarding perspectives for studying this fascinating literature that would enrich our understanding of the philosophical and hermeneutical value of this unique Buddhist tradition. To acknowledge the influence of the community—a community that is, of course, composed of faithful individuals—in authenticating scripture does not necessarily entail a failure to critically examine the religious claims of the Treasure tradition. Rather, this understanding allows us to engage with the Treasure revealers and their texts in a manner free from the confines of methodologies tainted by the influence of religious politics. In this way we may explore with fresh eyes the intricate drama that unfolds when religious claims, inspired saints, deceitful frauds, and Tibetan politics all come together in the complex phenomenon of Treasure revelation. Although Mipham is firm in his denunciation of fake revealers, we may today, while not abandoning careful philological and historical evaluations of individual Treasure scriptures, modify and soften the rhetoric that so often accompanies Treasure evaluations in Tibet and the West by acknowledging that what makes a visionary a saint or transforms a revelation into scripture is indeed a complex interplay of many factors, among which the faith and intuition of the devoted community plays no small or insignificant part.

༄༅། །གཏེར་སྟོན་བརྟག་པ་ཀུ་དྲངས་ནོར་བུ་ཞེས་བྱ་བ་བཞུགས་སོ། །

ཡང་དང་པོར་ཆོས་འདི་ཐོན་དང་། སྒྲུབས་དང་། ལེགས་པོ་འོང་རྒྱུ་ཡོད་ཅེས་ལུང་བསྟན་ཏེ། དེ་ལྟར་ཡིན་སྙམ་ནས་ནན་ཏན་གྱིས་ཞུགས་པ་དག་ལ་ལུང་བསྟན་པ་ལྟར་འབྱུང་བ་ལྟ་ཅི། བར་ཆད་འཚུབ་ཆ་ཆེན་པོས་མནར་བ་བྱུང་བའི་ཚེ། རྟེན་འབྲེལ་མ་འགྲིགས་པ་ལ་ཁག་འགེལ་བའམ་བར་ཆད་ཀྱིས་ཟིན་ཏོ་ཟེར་ཀྱང་། དད་པས་ཞུགས་པ་དག་བར་ཆད་ཀྱིས་མི་ཟིན་པ་ཆོས་དེས་འགྲུབ་རིགས་པ་དང་། ལེགས་པར་ཞུས་ནས་བསྒྲུབས་པས་རྟེན་འབྲེལ་འགྲིགས་གོ་ཆོད་དགོས་པ་འདྲ་སྟེ། གཞན་ལ་ལན་ཁག་བཀལ་བས་བདེན་གཏམ་དུ་མི་འགྱུར་བ་བློ་ལྡན་དག་གིས་ཤེས་སོ། །གལ་ཏེ་གཏེར་ཆོས་དེ་དངོས་གྲུབ་འགྲུབ་སྲུད་ཞིག་ཡིན་ན། གཏེར་སྟོན་རང་གིས་དེ་ནན་ཏན་བསྒྲུབ་རིགས་ལ། དེས་དེ་ལ་དངོས་གྲུབ་ཀྱང་འབྱུང་བར་རིགས་ཏེ། གུ་རུ་པདྨས་ཆོས་དེ་གདམས་པའི་སྣོད་དུ་གཟིགས་ནས་རང་ཆོས་ལ་རང་ཡིད་ཆེས་པ་དེ་ལ་དངོས་གྲུབ་འདི་ཐོབ་ཅི་ཡང་མ་བྱུང་ན། དེ་ལས་གཞན་ལ་འབྱུང་བ་ཤིན་ཏུ་དཀའ་འོ། །ཕུག་ལ་བྱིན་རླབས་ཐེ་ཡིན་མ་ཤེས་ཀྱང་། འཕྲུལ་དེ་སྒྲུབ་པ་པོ་རྣམས་ལ་བར་ཆད་མེད་ཅིང་ཁ་དགེ་བཀྲ་ཤིས་བྱུང་ན་ཆོས་དེའི་མཐུ་ཡིན་རུང་མིན་རུང་མི་རྣམས་ཀྱིས་ཡིན་པར་སེམས་ནས་དགེ་ཤིས་སུ་རྩི་བ་ལ། དེ་ཡང་ཤིན་ཏུ་དཀོན་ན་གཞན་ཕྱོགས་དག་ཁ་ཟེར་བ་ལ་ལན་ཁག་མི་འདུག་སྙམ་མོ། །དེ་སོགས་ཚིག་འཛམ་རེས་ཕན་ཚིག་བདུད་རྩི་འདྲ་བས་དོན་གནད་གོ་ངེས་སྤྲར་བར་བྱའོ། །ཀྱེ་གཏེར་སྟོན་པ་དག །གངས་ཅན་པ་དག་གུ་རུ་པདྨ་ལ་སྙིང་ནས་མི་མོས་མི་བདེན་ཟེར་ཡོད་མཁན་སུ་མི་འདུག་ཀྱང་།

3

Gem that Clears the Waters

An Investigation of Treasure Revealers by Ju Mipham

First someone gives a prediction that says, "This text should be chanted and practiced and will have a good result." Thinking that it must be true, people then practice with diligence but how could it ever turn out as prophesied? Then, as suffering emerges due to fierce obstacles he blames it on a lack of auspicious circumstances. Even should he acknowledge that obstacles occurred, he will still claim that it is a suitable teaching to practice as faithful followers do not experience such obstacles and that, once it has been correctly received and implemented, things will go well. However, as he puts the blame elsewhere, intelligent people know that his words are false.

If the Treasure were a practice that brought about accomplishment then one would expect the Treasure revealer to practice it sincerely himself. And it would also be reasonable that the practice would bring him some accomplishment since Guru Padmasambhava would have perceived him to be worthy for the instructions of that teaching. Therefore, if he himself has confidence in his own teaching but fails to gain any accomplishment from it, one should think that, compared to him, others would meet with even greater difficulty.

Since those who practice are unaware what blessings ultimately are like, they think it must be the power of the teaching when they temporarily become free from obstacles and experience joy and good fortune. Then, whether or not this is in fact the case, they believe it to be so and venerate it as virtuous and auspicious. Now, since it is actually very rarely so, I don't think that we can blame those other groups who criticize this. Such comments are actually sweet nectar-like advice so one must apply oneself to understanding their real meaning.

Hey Treasure revealers! Although all inhabitants of the Snowy Land claim to have heartfelt interest and trust in Guru Padmasambhava, they do feel

གཏེར་སྟོན་ཡིན་ཟེར་བ་ཆོས་རྫུན་སོགས་ཀྱིས་ཟོལ་མཐོང་ནས་ཡིད་སུན་ཏེ། བྱིས་པ་འོ་མས་ཇ་སོགས་ཞེས་པ་ལྟར་གཏེར་སྟོན་ཚད་ལྡན་ལའང་ཡིད་མི་ཆེས་པ་དེའི་ཁོངས་ནས་བྱུང་འདུག་པ་རྒྱལ་དབང་པདྨ་ལ་སེམས་ཅན་མོས་པའི་སྐལ་པ་ཆུང་ངུ་རམ་བྱེད་ཅིག ཆོས་དེ་དགེ་ཤིས་བྱིན་ཆེ་བྱུང་ན་དད་པ་རྣམས་ལྟ་ཅི། མི་དད་པ་རྣམས་ཀྱིས་ཀྱང་། རྨ་ཁར་ཁྲི་ཆིལ་དཔེ་ལྟར་མ་བླང་ཐབས་མེད་འོང་འདུག་པ་དེ་ཅི་ཡིན་ན། དང་པོར་རྟེན་འབྲེལ་རང་གིས་བརྟགས་ལ་བསྒྲིགས་ཏེ་ཆོས་རྣམ་དག་ཡིན་ན་བསྙེན་སྒྲུབ་ཕྲིན་ལས་རབ་འབྲིང་ཐ་མའི་ཚད་ཅི་ནུས་ཞིག་བསྐྱངས་ན་གཞན་ལ་ཕན་ཐོགས་ཏེ། གཏེར་སྙིང་རྣམས་ནས། གསང་རྒྱ་དང་གཏེར་སྒྲུབ་དགོས་པར་གསུངས། གཏེར་ཆོས་གསར་པར་མ་ཟད། བློ་སྦྱོང་ཕྱག་རྫོགས་སོགས་ཀྱང་རང་གིས་ཉམས་སུ་བླངས་ཏེ་སྨྱོང་བ་ཐོན་པ་དང་། ལྷ་གང་ཡིན་དེ་རང་གིས་རབ་འབྲིང་ཐ་མའི་བསྙེན་སྒྲུབ་རྟགས་ཐོན་པ་ཞིག་གིས་དབང་དང་མན་ངག་གཞན་ལ་བྱིན་པ་དེས་གཞན་ལ་ཕན་ཐོགས་ཆེ་བ་མངོན་སུམ་ཡིན་ཏེ། རང་མ་སྨིན་པས་སོགས་ཞེས་ལེགས་པར་བཤད་པ་བཞིན་ནོ། །འོན་ཀྱང་དབང་ཁྲིད་སོགས་ལ་རང་གིས་སྨྱོང་བ་དང་བསྙེན་སྒྲུབ་ཆེན་པོ་མ་ཐོན་ཀྱང་། སེལ་མེད་ཀྱི་བརྒྱུད་པ་ཁུངས་ཚད་ལྡན་ཡོད་ན་གཞན་ལ་དབང་སོགས་བྱས་པས་དངོས་གྲུབ་ཀྱི་སྣོད་དུ་རུང་བར་འགྱུར། གསར་ཆོས་གཏེར་གྱི་ཁུངས་ནི་པད་འབྱུང་རེད། དེའི་བརྒྱུད་པ་ནི་གཏེར་སྟོན་ཁོ་ན་ལ་ཐུག་པས་དེ་ལ་ཚད་ལྡན་གྱི་དག་སྣང་དང་ཉམས་སྨྱོང་གི་བརྡ་རྟགས་མེད་ན་དེས་གཞན་ཇི་ལྟར་སྨིན་གྲོལ་དུ་འགྱུར་ཏེ། ངེས་པར་བརྡ་རྟགས་ཡོད་དགོས་སོ། །གལ་ཏེ་ཉེ་བརྒྱུད་བྱིན་རླབས་ཆེ་སྙམ་ན། ཉེ་བརྒྱུད་བྱིན་རླབས་ཆེ་བ་ཡིན་སྲིད་ཀྱི། གཏེར་ཆོས་རྙིང་པ་ཚོ་ལ་རིང་བརྒྱུད་དང་། དེའི་སྟེང་ཉེ་བརྒྱུད་ཐོབ་ནས་གཞན་དང་མི་འདྲ་བའི་བྱིན་རླབས་ཚན་ཁ་ཆེ་བར་བྱས་ན་དེ་ལེགས་ཀྱི། གསར་པ་ནི། རིང་བརྒྱུད་མེད་པས་རྟོག་ལྡན་དག་ཡིད་མི་ཆེས་ལ། ཉེ་བརྒྱུད་ལ་ཐེ་ཚོམ་ཟ་བའང་སྲིད་པས་འདོན་ཆ་གསར་པ་ཡིན་ཅི་ལ་དགོས། པད་འབྱུང་ལའང་ཆོ་ག་སྟུ་མ་དང་ཚིག་བདུན་དང་བཛྲ་གུ་རུ་སོགས་ཀྱིས་གསོལ་བ་བཏབ་ན་བར་ཆད་སེལ་བ་དང་དངོས་གྲུབ་ཆོས་ཀྱི་བྱིན་རླབས་འབྱུང་ངེས་ལ། དེ་ལྟར་བྱིན་རླབས་བྱུང་བ་ངེས་དོན་འགྲུབ་ཀྱི། བྱིན་རླབས་འཇུག་པ་ལ།

weary seeing the deceit of liars claiming to be Treasure revealers. As it is said of the child and milk,[136] this causes some people to lose faith even in authentic Treasure revealers as well, so stop lessening the fortune of those who have trust in Padmasambhava, King of the Conquerors.

If a teaching is virtuous, auspicious, and has great blessings then, forget about faithful people, even those without faith will have no way around practicing it, just like the proverb about sores and dog fat.[137] The way it happens is that, first, the Treasure revealer examines circumstances and makes sure they are auspicious. Then, provided the teaching is genuine, he should practice it to the best of his ability to a higher, medium, or lesser measure of the approach and accomplishment activities. Then it will benefit others. In the old Treasures the need for keeping the seal of secrecy and practicing the Treasure were taught. Not only is this also the case regarding new Treasures but also in Mind Training, the Great Seal, and the Great Perfection where one practices by oneself and gains experience, while in deity practices one may grant empowerment and oral instructions to others based on first having manifested a higher, medium, or lesser sign through approach and accomplishment. The greater benefit for others thereby is clearly visible and is also expressed well in statements such as "Not having ripened oneself..."

Furthermore, even though one may not have great realization and extensive experience in the approach and accomplishment practices, it is still possible for others to gain accomplishments when given empowerment and meditation guidance, provided that the ritual is authentically rooted in an unpolluted lineage. However, in new Treasure teachings the source is Padmasambhava and the lineage therefore only consists of the Treasure revealer, so how could he mature and liberate others unless he himself has the fresh signs of authentic pure visions and experience? Surely he needs such signs. One may think that a closer lineage would possess greater blessings and it *is* possible that a close lineage will have greater blessings, but receiving the longer lineage of the old Treasure teachings in combination with a closer lineage creates a unique blessing of great power that is even better.

Still, since the new Treasures do not have a long lineage they do not satisfy the minds of skeptics who may even feel doubt regarding the close lineage, so why do we need these new recitation texts at all? If one supplicates Padmasambhava through the early rituals, the *Seven-Line Prayer*, and the *Vajra Guru Mantra*, then obstacles will surely be removed and accomplishments, the blessings of the dharma, will certainly appear. Since such blessings will accomplish all aims it is certainly not the case that, for blessings to appear, one

དུས་ཀྱི་འགྱུར་བ་དང་གང་ཟག་རེ་རེའི་ངོས་སྐལ་གྱི་ཆོ་ག་འདོན་རྒྱུ་གསར་པ་རེ་རེ་མེད་ན་བྱིན་རླབས་མི་འཇུག་པ་ག་ལ་ཡིན་ཏེ། མདོ་དང་རྒྱུད་སྡེ་ཆེན་པོ་རྣམས་ལ་བསྐལ་པའམ་བསྐལ་པ་ཚད་མེད་པའི་ཕྱི་མའི་མུ་མཐར་ཐུག་གི་བར་དུ་སུས་བསྒྲུབས་ཀྱང་བྱིན་རླབས་དང་དངོས་གྲུབ་མི་འབྱུང་བ་མི་སྲིད་དེ། སངས་རྒྱས་བཅོམ་ལྡན་འདས་བཞིན་ནོ། །དེས་ན་རང་གི་རྩོམ་ཆོས་ལ་གཏེར་བརྫུ་བྱས་ན་ཆེན་པོ་ལ་ལྟོངས་བཏབ་པ་དང་། ཆོས་ལ་དབང་ཟོས་ནས་ལྕེ་ལ་ཞིང་རྨོ་བའི་རྣམ་སྨིན་སྨྱོང་ངོ་། །དག་སྣང་གི་གདིང་ཚོད་དང་དཔེ་ཕྱག་ལུང་གསུམ་འདི་ཡིན་གྱི་གདིང་ཚད་མེད་པའི་ཉམས་རྨི་དངོས་ཀྱི་སྣང་བ་ཟ་ཟིར་ཤར་བ་ནི་ལེགས་ན་ཆོས་ཀྱི་ཚིགས་བཅད་འཆད་རྩོམ་སོགས་རྨི་ལམ་རྨིས་ན་སྔ་གོན་སོགས་ལ་དུས་དགེ་ལྟས་སུ་གསུངས་པ་རང་གི་ཉམས་སྣང་དགེ་བའི་མཚན་མ་ཙམ་ཡིན་སྲིད་ཀྱི། གཞན་སྨིན་ངེས་ཡིན་མིན་མ་ངེས། ལྷ་འདྲེའི་བརྫུ་བག་གིས་རྩོལ་ཆོས་དང་ས་གཏེར་ལྟ་བུ་ནི་ཤིན་ཏུ་གཞན་ལ་གནོད་པའི་ལོག་སྨོན་ཅན་གྱི་སྐལ་བ་ཡིན་པས། ཆོ་ག་ཆལ་ཆོལ་བྲི་ཤེས་པ་ཙམ་གྱིས་གཏེར་སྟོན་ཡིན་རློམ་གྱིས་སྤེལ་མི་རུང་སྟེ། སྔ་འགྱུར་གྱི་ལུང་དང་མན་ངག་ཀུན་ལས། མཁའ་འགྲོ་མ་རང་གི་དབང་དུ་གྱུར་པ་ལ་སོགས་པ་གསུངས་པ་བཞིན་འཇིག་རྟེན་ལྷ་འདྲེ་ཤ་ཟའི་མཁའ་འགྲོ་སོགས་ཀྱིས་རྣལ་འབྱོར་སྒྲུབ་པ་པོ་ལ་རྫོད་ཚུལ་བའི་ཉམས་ཆོས་དང་གྲུབ་རྟགས་སྣ་ཚོགས་ཀྱི་མཐུ་བསྐྱེད་པས། རང་གིས་མངོན་རློམ་དུ་བཟུང་ནས། དེའི་དབང་དུ་གྱུར་ན་མཐར་ཆོས་རྣམ་དག་འགྲུབ་པའི་བར་ཆད་དུ་འགྱུར་གསུངས་པ་ལྟར་ཤེས་དགོས། དེས་ན་ཉམས་སྣང་རྨི་ལམ་ལུང་བསྟན་ཟ་ཟི་བདེན་མིན་བརྫུན་མིན་འདི་འདྲ་ཙུར་མི་བརྒྱབ་པར་གསང་སྟེ་རང་གྲོལ་དུ་བྱས་ན་ཆོས་པ་ལེགས་པོ་འོང་བ་མངོན་སུམ་གྲུབ། རློམ་པ་དང་རྣམ་གཡེང་གྲགས་འདོད་བྱས་ན་བར་ཆད་དུ་འགྱུར་བ་མངོན་སུམ་མཐོང་བས། ད་ཤེས་མི་ཤེས་གྲུབ་མ་གྲུབ་ཀུན་གྱིའང་གཏེར་ཆོས་ཟེར་བའི་ཡི་གེ་མང་པོ་བྲི་རྒྱུ་འདི་བཞག་ན་ལེགས། ཕལ་པ་དག་གིས་ཀྱང་གསར་ངེས་ཧ་ཅང་མ་ཆེ་ན་བསྟན་པའི་བབ་དང་རང་གཞན་ཀུན་ལ་ཕན་ངེས་སོ། །ཁ་ཅིག་གཏེར་ཆོས་བྲིས་ཟིན་ཉབ་ཉོབ་རྣམས་རིགས་བརྒྱུད་དང་སློབ་བརྒྱུད་ནས་འདི་ཉམས་མི་རུང་ཅི་དར་དགོས་ཟེར་ཀྱང་།

needs a new ritual and liturgy for each and every time-period and personal inclination. Throughout all the aeons or limitless aeons until the end of time it will be impossible that blessings and accomplishments should not manifest for anyone who practices the sūtras and the great tantra sections. Just like the Buddha, the Transcendent Conqueror, did.

To make a false Treasure out of one's own religious writings is therefore a pretense to greatness and a disregard for the dharma that results in the karmic ripening of one's tongue becoming a plow. Sometimes uncertain appearances may arise, both in dreams and the waking state that cannot be determined either via the confidence of a pure vision or with the certainty that identifies based on signs, inner experience, and prophesies. In good cases, they will be dreams of writing religious poetry, teaching, or composing. One may then begin to make preparations and proclaim them to be signs of auspicious times. These may be simple indications of your own wholesome meditation experiences, but it is doubtful whether they really will ripen others. Through the deceit of gods and demons there are instructions that are similar to teachings bursting forth and earth Treasures, but as they are the legacy of beings with aspirations to severely harm others, it is wrong to spread them while proudly proclaiming oneself a Treasure revealer just because one knows how to write down some dubious ritual. All the scriptures and oral instructions of the early translations teach that one must bring the ḍākinīs under one's influence because worldly gods and demons, such as the flesh eating ḍākinīs, will conjure up various misleading meditation experiences and signs of accomplishments to a practicing yogin, who will come under their power if he clings to them with conceit. One should know that this has been taught to be an obstacle for ultimately accomplishing the authentic dharma.

One should therefore keep these uncertain and dubious psychic visions, dreams, and predictions secret without making a big fuss about them. It is obvious that a practitioner will turn out well if he is able to naturally liberate them. Since we can see with our own eyes how conceit, distraction, and longing for fame turn into obstacles it would be better if people stopped writing numerous volumes of so-called Treasure teachings explaining all about their knowledge and accomplishment and, certainly, when common Treasure revealers are not absolutely confident then it would benefit the transmission of the doctrine as well as themselves and everyone else if they refrained from writing.

Having composed Treasure teachings, there are some indolent people who speak of the need to spread them as much as possible to make sure that the

བཀའ་རྒྱུད་ལུང་མན་ངག་གི་ཆོས་དང་གཏེར་རྙིང་ཚད་ལྡན་རྣམས་མ་ནུབ་པར་སྤེལ་ཐུབ་ན། དེར་
མ་འདུས་པའི་དོན་ཟབ་མོ་དང་ལས་སྒྲུབ་ཐབས་ཁྱད་འཕགས་པན་དེས་ཅང་མ་མཐོང་བས། མི་
རེའི་ཆོས་ལུགས་འཛིན་པ་འདི་ཆག་བཞག་མེད་པའི་ལུགས་སུ་འགྱུར་བས་བསྟན་རྙིང་གི་གྲུབ་མཐའ་
བསྐྱང་བ་གཙོ་བོར་བྱས་ནས། དག་སྣང་དང་གཏེར་ཆོས་རྣམ་དག་རེ་ཡིན་ན་ཟུར་རྒྱན་ལྟ་བུར་བྱས་
ན་ལེགས་ཀྱི་ནུབ་མི་བྲ་བའི་ཆོས་གང་ཡིན་བློ་གྲོས་ཀྱིས་ཞིབ་དགོས་ཀྱི། ཡི་གེར་བྲིས་ཚད་ནུབ་མི་
རུང་བ་ཅི་ཡོད་དེ། དེ་ནུབ་པས་ཐབས་ཆག་ཅི་ཡང་མི་འབྱུང་། རྒྱུད་ལུང་མན་ངག་གིས་ཟབ་ཆོས་
ཚན་རེ་རེ་ཡིན་ནའང་དོན་ཆེ་བས་མི་ནུབ་པར་འཛིན་དགོས་སོ། །ཡང་བསྒོམ་ན་རྫོགས་ཆེན་རྒྱུད་
ལུང་མན་ངག་གི་དོན་འདུས་ཀྱི་གནད་ཀློང་ཆེན་རབ་འབྱམས་ཀྱིས་གསུང་འདི་ཀོ་བས་གོ་རྒྱུ་ཟབ་
ཅིང་བཟང་བ་དང་། ཉམས་ལེན་གནད་དུ་འགྲོ་ལུགས་གཞན་ཡོད་མི་སྲིད་པས། འདི་བས་ལྷག་
པར་རྫོགས་ཆེན་གོ་རྒྱུ་གསར་དུ་ཅི་འདུག་སྙོམ་ལ། འདི་བཞིན་ཉམས་སུ་ལོངས། འདི་ལ་བྱིན་
རླབས་ཀྱི་ཆ་ཡོད། ཉམས་ལེན་གྱི་བརྒྱུད་པ་ཡོད་པས། དེ་སྔ་མང་པོ་རྟོགས་པ་མཐར་ཕྱིན་པ་ཡིན།
ད་ཡང་རང་མ་ལན་ན་ཆོས་འདི་མི་ལན། བརྟེན་ན་བཀའ་མའི་ཆོ་ག་རྣམས་དང་གཏེར་མ་བཀའ་
དགོངས་སོགས། མདོར་ན་ཉང་ཆོས་དབང་ཕྱུག་གཏེར་རཏྣ་གླིང་པ་ཀར་གླིང་སོགས་དེ་སྔ་མང་པོ་
རྟགས་ཚད་ལྡན་བྱུང་བ་འདི་ཆོའི་གཞུང་ན་ལྷ་རབ་འབྱམས་ཀྱི་སྒྲུབ་ཐབས་ཡོད། དེ་རྣམས་ཀྱང་རྒྱས་
བསྡུས་སྒྲུབ་ཐབས་རང་ཉམས་བསྟུན་པ་ཅི་འདོད་ཡོད། ལས་ཚོགས་སྣ་ཚོགས་གཏོར་སྣ་ཚོགས་ཡོད་
པས་དེ་བཞིན་ཉམས་ལེན་བྱས་ན་བྱིན་རླབས་ཀྱི་བརྒྱུད་པ་ཡོད། དེ་སྔ་ཆོས་འདི་དག་གི་གྲུབ་པའི་
ལག་རྗེས་ཐོན་པ་ཡིན། རང་གིས་འབྱུང་ན་ཆོས་འདིས་མ་འབྱུང་བ་མེད། ད་སྒྲུབ་ཐབས་རེ་ཟུང་
མངོན་རྟོགས་དང་འདོན་ཆ་ཉབ་ཉོབ་ཅིག་དོན་སྔར་བས་ཟབ་པ་པར་ཞིག ཕྱོགས་སུའང་མི་ཕྱིན་པ་
ཞིག་བརྟེན་པས་དགོས་པ་ལྷག་པོ་མི་ཆེ། ཆེ་བསམ་ན་ཅི་འདོད་མཛོད། སྔ་མ་ཚོ་སྒྲུབ་པས་འབྲས་
བུ་མ་གྲུབ་ན་ཆོས་ཀྱིས་མིན་བསམ་ཐུབ།

family lineage and the lineage of students does not disappear. However, if instead they were able to preserve and spread the teachings of the tantras, scriptures, and pith instructions of the Transmitted Precepts together with the authentic old Treasures then I surely cannot see any deep purpose, or any excellent or beneficial activity sādhana, that would not be included in that. Since attachment to the tradition of individuals creates an unstable tradition, it would be better to focus on maintaining the philosophical systems of the older teachings and then adopt as auxiliary ornaments whatever few genuine pure vision and Treasure teachings may exist. Intelligent people need to understand what teachings to preserve instead of just conserving everything simply because it has been written. If much of what has been written should disappear it wouldn't be sad at all. On the other hand, since even a fraction of the tantras, scriptures, and oral instructions has a great purpose they must be preserved.

Furthermore, regarding meditation, Longchen Rabjam taught the key points of the meaning contained in the tantras, scriptures, and oral instructions of the Great Perfection, and you are not going to find some other profound and excellent truth or any other system of key points for practice besides that. Please take a look around to see if there is anything new to understand about the Great Perfection that might be superior to this and then practice accordingly. As it contains a factor of blessings and a lineage of practice, there are many people who previously perfected their realization through that. So now, do not look for fault in this teaching without looking for faults in yourself. As for recitation, there are the rituals of the Transmitted Precepts lineage as well as the Pronouncements and Realizations of the Treasures[138]—in short, scriptures on the sādhanas of infinite deities by many revealers who appeared in the past with authentic signs, such as Nyangral Nyima Özer, Guru Chöwang, The Northern Treasure Revealer,[139] Ratna Lingpa, and Karma Lingpa. In those texts you will find any kind of long or short sādhana you may desire according to your inclination. There are also various activity and protection rituals that, if practiced properly, contain a lineage of blessing that is actualized as the result of practice of these early teachings. If you are able, so are the teachings! Now, forget the idea that the words and meaning of some sādhanas, practice texts, and pointless liturgical scriptures should be more profound than the earlier texts—since they do not even come close I cannot see any particular purpose to chanting them. But if you think it's important, do as you like.

If someone practices the early Treasures but no result occurs, they will not think that it is the fault of the teaching. However, if one does not know whether

གསར་པས་མ་ཕན་མི་ཤེས་པ་འབྱུང་ན་ཐེ་ཚོམ་ཟ་ཞིང་ལོག་ལྟ་སྐྱེ་དེ་ལ་དགོས་པ་ཅི་ཡོད། གལ་ཏེ་ཡིད་ཆེས་ནས་ཚོག་གསར་པ་རེ་བརྟེན་པ་ཙམ་ལ་འགལ་བ་ཆེར་མ་མཐོང་སྟེ། བླ་མ་དག་གིས་ཚོག་སྒྲིག་སྣ་ཚོགས་དང་འདྲ་ཡང་། གསར་པ་ཤ་སྟག་འདོན་དགའ་འདི་མི་ཤེས་པའི་གསར་ངེས་ཆེ་བར་ཟད་དོ། །བསྒོམས་ན་རྟོག་གེ་ང་འདྲས་ཀྱང་ཚིག་ལེགས་པ་དང་། དོན་རྒྱུད་ལུང་མཐུན་པ། མན་ངག་སྣ་ཚོགས་སྤྲོ་མར་བཏབ་སྟེ་བྲི་ཤེས་ཀྱང་། དེ་གཏེར་ཆོས་སུ་བྱས་ན་ཐོག་པོའི་ལས་ག་ལྷ་དང་བླ་མར་རྫུན་ཁེགས་བཀལ་བའི་ལས་མི་བཟད་པར་འགྱུར། བསྟན་བཅོས་སུ་བྱས་ནས་རྫུན་མེད་ཅིང་དད་པ་ཕན་པས་བྱས་ན་མཁས་གྲུབ་རྣམས་ཀྱི་གཞུང་དང་རྗེས་སུ་མི་མཐུན་པ་ཅི་ཡོད། དེས་གཏེར་ལ་ཁུངས་འཕྱི་ན་རྒྱུ་འདི་ངེས་པ་ཡིན་ན་དེར་ཟད། མིན་ན་ཤིན་ཏུ་མི་བཟད་པའི་ལས་ཏེ། གལ་ཏེ་རང་མིན་ཡང་བྱེད་པོ་གཞན་གྱིས་བསླུ་ནས་མ་བྱས་དབང་མེད་ཡིན་ན་ལེགས་ཉེས་ཅི་ཡིན་རང་ཐག་ཆོད་ན་ལེགས། མིན་པར་གཞན་ལ་བྲི་དགོས་བསྐུར་ན་ལེགས་འདྲ།

དེང་སང་གཏེར་སྟོན་ཟེར་བའི་མི་འདི་ཚོ། འཛམ་གླིང་བོད་ལ་ཕན་བྱེད་ཡིན་ནོ་སྐད། །
རང་མགོ་ལེགས་ཐོན་ཆེ་རིང་བདེ་ལྡན་ཞིག །བྱུང་ན་ལེགས་ཏེ་དེ་ཡང་དཀའ་བར་སྣང་། །

གངས་ཅན་འདི་ན་གཏེར་སྟོན་གཏེར་ཆོས་ལ། །ཕལ་ཆེར་མི་དད་ལོག་པར་ལྟ་བ་མང་། །
དེ་དག་མ་སྐྱོབ་ཅི་བྱ་དད་པ་རྣམས། །ལྷག་པར་སྐྱོབ་ན་ཐུགས་རྗེའི་མངོན་རྟགས་ཡིན། །

དེ་ལྟ་ནའང་མ་དད་རྒྱུད་པ་དང་། །དད་རྣམས་ལྷག་པར་དར་བ་ལྟ་ཅི་ཞིག །
ཕལ་ཆེར་གོ་ལྡོག་ཚུལ་དུ་མཐོང་བས་ན། །འདི་འདྲ་ཅི་ཞེས་སེམས་ཀྱི་ཅིས་མི་སྐྱེ། །

or not the new Treasures bring benefit, one may get doubt, give rise to wrong views, and wonder what the need for it is. If someone feels trust, I cannot see anything really wrong with reciting a new text, but although they are similar to the liturgical arrangements of past masters, to only delight in the recitation of new texts is a clear sign of ignorance. When composing texts, even a dry intellectual like myself will know how to write eloquent phrases in a meaning that agrees with the tantras and scriptures and is supported by many esoteric instructions, but presenting this as a Treasure teaching would be the work of a charlatan and incur the terrible karma of arrogantly lying to the deities and the spiritual masters. If, however, it were presented as a treatise it would be free from deceit and would benefit people's confidence. What then, could be in discord with the scriptures of the learned and accomplished masters? If a Treasure really has an authentic source then there is nothing to object to, but if it does not, it is a terrible karma to claim otherwise. Even if the teaching is not initiated by yourself but is requested by someone else so that you feel powerless but to write, you should still examine for yourself whether it will be wholesome or harmful. Unless it will be wholesome it might be better to refer the writing to someone else.

The people who nowadays are called Treasure revealers
Claim to benefit Tibet and the world,
But are driven by their own concerns.
If they achieve long life and happiness, fine; but even that will hardly happen.

In this Snowy Land there are many who mostly look
At the Treasure revealers and their Treasures with distrust and wrong view.
Why should we not protect those?
And yet to especially protect the faithful ones is a true sign of compassion.

However, when things decline for those without trust,
And for the faithful things do not improve,
And we can see how most people end up worse,
How can one not feel doubt and wonder?

ཨོ་རྒྱན་ཆེན་པོས་རྗེས་སུ་བཟུང་ཡིན་ན། །ཉམས་དང་རྟོགས་པའམ་ཆོ་རིང་ཆོས་འཕེལ་ཞིང་། |
བསྟན་པ་རྒྱས་པར་བྱིན་རླབས་མཛད་ན་ལེགས། །འདོན་རྒྱུ་ཙམ་ཞིག་བསྟན་པས་ཅི་ཞིག་བྱ། |

འདོན་རྒྱུ་བྱིན་ཆེན་ཡིད་ཆེས་དེ་སྟ་ཡོད། །གསར་བྱུང་དེ་བས་ཟབ་པ་གཅིག་མ་མཐོང་། |
གསར་ཆོས་ཟབ་པོ་སླམ་ནས་དེ་བསྙེན་ནས། །རང་གི་དངོས་གྲུབ་ཐོབ་ན་ལེགས་ཏེ་དགོན། |

ལེགས་པར་བརྟགས་ན་གཏེར་ཆོས་ཟེར་པ་རྣམས། |
གྲགས་འདོད་ནོར་འདོན་བུད་མེད་འདོད་པའི་ཕྱིར། |
གཏེར་ལ་རེ་ཞིང་སྐྲམ་ཆགས་མི་ལྷར་འབར། །རྫུན་དང་ཟོག་པོ་མེད་པ་དགོན་འདི་ཅི། |

ངེས་པར་པདྨའི་བྱིན་རླབས་ལས་ཙམ་ནི། །སངས་རྒྱས་མཐོང་ཞིང་དེ་ཡིས་དངོས་སློབ་དང་། |
འདྲ་ཕྱིར་གཞན་ལས་ཁྱད་འཕགས་ཡིན་ངེས་ཀྱང་། |
མཁྱེན་བརྩེ་ནུས་པ་བརྟགས་ན་གཞན་དང་མཚུངས། |

དེ་འདྲས་གངས་ཅན་བདེ་སྐྱིད་སྤེལ་བ་ལ། །ཐེ་ཚོམ་ཟ་ཡང་རང་བསྟོད་གཏེར་ལུང་གིས། |
རང་ཆེ་འབྲིན་ཞིང་གཞན་སྨོད་བྱུང་སེམས་ཀྱི། །རྩ་ལྷུང་ཁྲུར་ལེན་འཚོལ་རྟོག་སྤྱོད་པ་མང་། |

ཀྱི་མ་དུས་ངན་འདི་ལ་རྩུལ་ལྡན་གྱི། །དགེ་སྦྱོང་དགོན་ཕྱིར་སེམས་ཅན་རྒྱུད་པ་བདོ། |
དགེ་སྦྱོང་གཞན་ལས་འཕགས་རློམ་སྤྲུལ་པའི་སྐུ། |
གཏེར་སྟོན་འདི་ཙམ་མང་འདི་དུས་དང་འགལ། |

གལ་ཏེ་བཟང་པོ་མང་ཕྱིར་བསྟན་འགྲོའི་དཔལ། །འཕེལ་ན་བསྟན་པ་སྤྱི་དང་རྙིང་མ་པ། |

It is good if one is accepted by the great Master from Oḍḍiyāna,
And creates blessings for experience and realization,
Or longevity, growth of the dharma, and spread of the teaching.
But what is the use of merely presenting something to chant?

As for chanting, the earlier Treasures possess great blessings and can be trusted,
And I have not seen a single newly revealed Treasure that was more profound.
If, relying on new teachings believing them to be more profound,
You should reach accomplishment, fine; but it is rare.

When examining closely those who announce Treasure teachings,
They wish for fame, look for wealth, and search for women,
And so place hope in their Treasures with expectations burning like fire.
How rare are those free from lies and deceit!

If they truly are the destined ones of Padma's blessing,
They should surely be superior to others.
It would be like beholding the Buddha and his close disciples.
But when examined, their wisdom, love, and capacity are just like anyone else's.

Whether they spread happiness and joy in the Snowy Land is doubtful,
But with their Treasure prophecies praising themselves,
They commit the root bodhisattva downfall of aggrandizing themselves and belittling others,
And carry out many perverted actions.

Alas! Since genuine practitioners are rare in these sad times,
The decay of sentient beings is rampant.
So it seems untimely that so many nirmāṇakāya Treasure revealers
Conceitedly consider themselves superior to other practitioners.

If the splendor of the teaching and sentient beings were to expand
Because of so many excellent masters,

ལྷག་པར་བདེ་འབྱོར་རྒྱས་པར་རིགས་ན་ཡང་། །དེ་རྣམས་ལྟོས་བཅས་ལྷག་པར་རྒྱུད་འདི་ཅི། །

ཏ་ཏ། ཡང་གཏེར་ཆོས་དེ་གཏེར་སྟོན་དེ་ལ་གུ་རུས་གདམས་པ་དངོས་སུ་མཐོང་བའམ། མངོན་ཤེས་ཀྱིས་ཤེས་པ་མེད་ན། གང་ཟག་དེས་ཚིག་ལ་ཡིད་སྟོན་ན་གུ་རུའི་གསུང་དུ་འཛིན་དགོས་པས། གང་ཟག་དེ་ཚད་ལྡན་དགེ་བའི་བཤེས་གཉེན་ཆེན་པོ་ཞིག་མིན་ན། འདི་ངའི་གཏེར་ཆོས་ཡིན་ཅེས་པ་ཙམ་གྱིས་དང་། ཚིག་སྒྲོས་ལེགས་པའམ་བྲག་ནས་བཀོས་པ་ཙམ་གྱིས་ཡིད་ཆེས་དཀའ་འོ། །གལ་ཏེ་དུས་འཁོར་རྩ་རྒྱུད། ཀྱི་རྡོར་རྒྱུད་འབུམ་ལྔ་སོགས་རྒྱུད་ཚད་ལྡན་བོད་ན་མེད་པ་དང་། ཤིན་ཏུ་གོ་རྒྱ་ཡོད་ངེས་ཀྱི་བརྟག་པ་བརྒྱད་སོགས་དང་། གཟའ་སྐར་གྲུབ་རྩིས་ཀྱི་རྩིས་འགྲོ་སོགས་རིགས་གནས་ཀྱི་གནད་ལ་ཕན་ངེས་སྤར་མེད་ཡིག་ཆ་ངོ་མཚར་ཅན་དང་། རྒྱུད་དང་མདོ་སྡེའི་དཀའ་གནད་མི་ཤེས་པ་ཐམས་ཅད་འགྲོལ་བས་གཞུང་དང་། ལུང་བསྟན་གསལ་བ་དུས་ཀྱི་འབྱུང་འགྱུར་བསླུ་མེད་སོགས་མདོར་ན་གོ་རྒྱ་ཆེ་བ་མདོ་རྒྱུད་དང་མཐུན་པ། དེ་མཐོང་ན་དགོངས་གནད་ལྷག་པར་གསལ་བ་སོགས་བློ་ལྡན་མགུ་བ་བསྐྱེད་པའི་གཞུང་གལ་ཏེ་གཏེར་ནས་ཐོན་ན་ནུབ་མི་ཐུབ་བར་བདེན་ནོ། །གཞན་ཡང་བྱེ་བྲག་བཤད་མཛོད་ཆེན་མོ་སོགས་ནང་པ་དང་། ཕྱི་པའི་གཞུང་གི་སྒྲ་རྩལ་གྱི་བསྟན་བཅོས་སོགས་སྐབས་སུ་མཁོ་བ་དག་ཀྱང་གཏེར་ནས་བཏོན་ན་ངོ་མཚར་ཆེ་ཞིང་ནུབ་མི་ཐུབ་བར་གདའ། གཞན་ཡང་དཀོན་བརྩེགས་ཀྱི་ལེའུ་ལྷག་མ་ཡོངས་རྫོགས་སམ་ཅི་རིགས། མདོ་དྲན་པ་ཉེར་བཞག་གི་ལྷག་མ་ཅི་ཡོད་སོགས་གཏེར་ནས་འབྱུང་ན་ངོ་མཚར་ཆེ། གཞན་ཡང་བོད་ཀྱིས་བསྟན་བཅོས་གཉུབས་ཆེན་གྱི་མདོ་འགྲེལ་སོགས་སྤར་ཡོད་དུ་མ་ཞིག་ད་ལྟ་མི་སྣང་བ་སོགས་མཁའ་འགྲོས་ལུང་བསྟན་ལ་བརྟེན་ཏེ་གཏེར་ནས་བྱུང་ན་ལེགས་ཏེ། གཏེར་ནས་ཕྱི་རོ་མིན་པ་གང་ཡང་འབྱུང་། །ཞེས་གསུངས་པས་མཁོ་བའི་ཆོས་གང་ཡང་གཏེར་ནས་མི་འབྱུང་དོན་མེད་ལ། ནད་ཞི་བའི་སྨན་དྲི་ཆོར་བ་ཙམ་གྱིས་ཕན་པ་དང་གསོ་དཔྱད་ངོ་མཚར་གྱི་གཞུང་སོགས་གཏེར་ནས་རྙེད་པའམ། གཞན་ཡང་དཔེ་ཆ་ལག་ཏུ་བྱུང་ནའང་སྐལ་ལྡན་གྱི་གང་ཟག་གཞན་ལ་ཕན་བྱེད་ཡིན་འདུག་པས། གཏེར་སྟོན་ཆོས་དེ་ལྟར་པད་འབྱུང་ལ་གསོལ་བ་འདེབས་པར་རིགས་སོ། །གཞན་ཡང་ཡིད་བཞིན་ནོར་བུ་སོགས་ནི་སྙིགས་མའི་དུས་སུ་འབྱུང་དཀའ་མོད། སེམས་ཅན་ལ་ཕན་པའི་ཆ་ཡི་རིན་པོ་

It would be reasonable that the splendor and wealth of the
teaching in general and the Nyingma School in particular
would increase,
So why are they and their followers in such decline?

Oh, Oh! If the Treasure revealer has not really received the Treasure teaching from the Guru or perceived it by clairvoyance but discovered the words from dualistic mind and if, furthermore, that person is not a great and authentic spiritual teacher, then it will be hard to feel confidence simply by hearing him say, "this is my Treasure teaching" and then showing some eloquent writings or something hewn from a rock. If, however, he could reveal authentic tantras such as the *Kālacakra Root Tantra* or the *Hevajra Tantra in Five Hundred Thousand Verses* that do not exist in Tibet; texts that truly possess important knowledge such as the *Eight Examinations;* previously non-existent wonderful textbooks that are certain to benefit crucial aspects of science such as the remaining calculations of philosophical astrology; scriptures that lay bare all the unknown difficult points of the tantra and sūtra sections; or precise and undeceiving prophecies that foretell the changing times and so forth—in short, a text of important knowledge that agrees with the sūtras and tantras and gives rise to joy in intelligent people, then that would be a truth to preserve.

Furthermore, if he could reveal a Buddhist scripture such as the *Great Treasury of Detailed Exposition* or a non-Buddhist text that could be temporarily useful, such as a treatise on art, then that would be very wonderful and something to protect. Also, could he reveal some or all of the remaining chapters of the *Jewel Mound Sūtra* or all the remaining parts of the *Sūtra on the Application of Mindfulness* then that would be wonderful too. Likewise, if he received a prophecy from the ḍākinīs and based on that could reveal a Tibetan treatise that previously existed in several copies but now has disappeared, such as Nubchen Sangye Yeshe's sūtra commentaries, then that would also be nice. But as the saying goes, "except for dead dogs, anything is revealed as Treasure," so no useful teachings whatsoever appear and it is pointless.

Still, if a medicine that would heal sickness by mere smell or an amazing medical scripture could be discovered as Treasure, or even if such a text were to just fall into one's hands, that would be something by which a worthy being could benefit others. So that is what the Treasure revealers should supplicate Padmasambhava for. Moreover, while it is hard for wish-fulfilling jewels to appear in degenerate times, if all kinds of wonderful jewels, helpful to sentient

ཆེ་ཅི་རིགས་ངོ་མཚར་ཅན་སུས་བལྟས་ཀྱང་ཡིད་མཚར་བ་བྱུང་ན་རང་གཞན་ཀུན་ལེགས་པར་འདུག་པས་དེ་ལྟར་ཐུགས་བཞག་མཛོད།

པདྨའི་བྱིན་རླབས་ཟབ་ཆོས་ངེས་སྤྱོད་ན། །རྟག་ཏུ་དེ་སྒྲུབ་དངོས་གྲུབ་ཐོབ་རིགས་མོད། །
ནོར་ཕྱིར་རྟག་ཏུ་ཚུལ་བཞིན་རང་གི་ཆོས། །གཞན་ལ་ཚོང་བཞིན་ཁྱིམ་པ་མ་མཐོང་ངམ། །

ཆོས་ཀྱི་ཆེ་བ་བཤད་པས་ཅི་ཞིག་བྱ། །ཁྲིད་རང་དངོས་གྲུབ་ཐོབ་ན་ཁྲིད་ཀྱི་ཆོས། །
ཕར་འཚོང་མི་དགོས་ཕྱུར་ལ་འདོད་མཁན་འོང་། །འོན་ཀྱང་ཁྲིད་རང་ཆོས་ཀྱིས་ཅི་ཞིག་ཐོབ། །

ཡི་གེ་བྲིས་ནས་ཆེ་གྲགས་ནོར་ཅན་རྣམས། །གར་ཡོད་ཁྲིད་རང་ང་ཡི་ཆོས་བདག་ཅེས། །
ཚོལ་ཞིང་སྙན་གྲགས་འབའ་ཞིག་བསམ་པས་གཡེངས། །
ཆོས་དེ་བསྒྲུབས་ཀྱང་ངེས་ཕན་ཅི་ཞིག་མཐོང་། །

བུད་མེད་གཟུགས་བཟང་མཐོང་ན་མཁའ་འགྲོ་ཟེར། །མི་དད་ཁ་ཟེར་ཅན་ཚོ་བདུད་དུ་འབོད། །
རང་ཉིད་རྡོ་རྗེ་འབངས་གྲུབ་པའི་སྤྲུལ་པར་འཛིན། །བསྒྲགས་རྒྱུ་མང་ལ་ཕན་རྒྱུ་ཅི་ཡང་མེད། །

སངས་རྒྱས་བསྟན་པའི་གནད་རྣམས་གང་ཡིན་དང་། །སྙིང་པོའི་བསྟན་པའི་ཆེ་བ་འདི་ཡིན་ཞེས། །
ཅུང་ཟད་ཙམ་ཞིག་རང་གིས་མ་ཤེས་ཀྱང་། །ང་ཡི་ཆོས་འདི་ཀུན་ལ་འཕགས་ཞེས་སྒྲོམ། །

བསྟན་པ་སྤྱི་དང་རྒྱལ་དབང་པདྨ་ཡི། །བསྟན་པ་སྙིང་ལ་གཅེས་སྤྲས་མི་ཤེས་ཀྱང་། །
གངས་ཅན་རྒྱུད་པ་སློག་བྱེད་ང་ཡིན་ཞེས། །ཁས་འཆེ་འགགས་ལ་ཐུག་ན་གཞན་ལས་དམན། །

beings and astonishing to whoever would see them, should appear it would be good for both oneself and everyone else. So please keep that in mind.

If it truly is a profound teaching of Padma's blessing,
Then it makes sense to practice it continuously and attain
accomplishment.
But have you not seen how some people, for the sake of wealth,
Always roam about spreading their teaching by selling it to others?

What is the use in extolling the greatness of your teaching?
If you gain accomplishment you will not have to sell your
teaching to others.
People wishing it will come to you!
Even so, what have you achieved from the dharma?

Having written letters, you search out the famous and rich
wherever they are,
And tell them "You are the sovereign of my teaching."
You are distracted by only thinking of fame.
Even if practicing that teaching, what benefit do you see thereby?

When you see a good-looking girl you call her a ḍākinī.
Suspicious people who criticize you are called demons.
You consider yourself a perfect reincarnation of the disciples of
Padmasambhava.
You announce a lot but do no good at all.

Without yourself knowing anything whatsoever
About the key points of the Buddha's teaching,
Or the greatness of the essential teaching,
You conceitedly say, "My teaching is superior to all others."

Although you do not know how to cherish in your heart the
general teachings
And the teachings of Padma, King of the Conquerors,
You say, "I am the one who will reverse the degeneration in the
Snowy Land."
When your pretense is exposed, you are worse than a commoner.

རང་དོན་གླང་དོར་ཕྲ་མོའང་ཅི་བཞིན་དུ། །ཤེས་པ་དཀོན་ན་གངས་ཅན་རྒྱལ་ཁམས་ལ། །
ཕན་འདོགས་གླང་དོར་སྟོན་པའི་ལུང་བསྟན་རྣམས། །ལྷ་འདྲེས་བསླུས་པའི་བརྫུ་བགམ་ཡིན་ནམ། །

བསྟན་ལ་དད་དང་འགྲོ་ལ་ཕན་པའི་བློ། །ལེགས་པར་འབྱོངས་པའི་ལག་རྗེས་ཅི་མེད་པར། །
སྙིང་རྗེས་གངས་ཅན་སྐྱོབ་ཕྱིར་སྤྲུལ་ཞེས་སྨྲ། །བློ་ལྡན་གཞན་གྱིས་བལྟས་ན་གད་མོ་འཚོར། །

ན་ཆུང་སེམས་རྩ་འགྱུལ་བ་འི་མཐུ་མེད་པར། །འདོད་པས་བསྐམ་པའི་རྫུན་ལུང་སྒྲོགས་པ་སོགས། །
ཡིད་བརྟན་ཡེར་བའི་ནུས་པ་ཙུང་ཟད་ཞིག །མེད་པ་དེས་ཀོ་རྒྱལ་ཁམས་ཇི་ལྟར་སྐྱོབས། །

ཇི་ལྟར་བྱས་ཀྱང་གྲུབ་པའི་མཛད་སྤྱོད་ཞེས། །རློམ་ཞིང་གཞན་མགོ་སྐོར་བའི་ཟོག་པོ་རྣམས། །
གཏེར་ལ་ཁྲུངས་འབྱིན་རྒྱལ་དབང་པདྨ་ལ། །རྫུན་གྱི་རྒྱབ་བརྟེན་བཅོལ་བ་འི་ལས་ངན་བསགས། །

འགའ་ཞིག་ལྷ་འདྲེ་མཐུ་བོ་ཆེས་རློམ་པའི། །གཏེར་མིན་གཏེར་འདྲ་སྣ་ཚོགས་འདོན་མོད་ཀྱི། །
རང་གིས་རང་རློམ་གྲུབ་པའི་གྲལ་ལ་བསྒྲིགས། །བདུད་ཀྱིས་བསླུས་པར་ཙུང་ཟད་མ་འཁྲིག་མང་། །

རྒྱལ་དབང་པདྨས་བསྟན་པའི་ཆོས་ཡིན་ན། །ང་ཡི་ཆོས་འདི་གཏེར་མ་ཡིན་ནམ་མིན། །
ཅི་འདྲ་སྙམ་ཞིང་གཞན་ལ་འདྲི་བ་དེ། །འགལ་རྟགས་ཡིན་ནམ་བློ་ལྡན་རྣམས་ཀྱིས་ཤེས། །

རང་གིས་རང་ཆོས་སྒྲུབ་ལ་སྤྲོ་བ་ཡིས། །ནན་ཏན་ཉམས་སུ་ལེན་པར་མ་བྱས་ན། །

When it is rare to know correctly what is good and bad for
oneself, even in the slightest,
Are not all the "helpful" predictions,
Stating what is good and bad for the Snowy Country,
The deceiving lies of gods and demons?

With no sign at all of having thoroughly trained
In the attitude of trusting the teachings and helping others,
You say, "I have emanated to protect the Snowy Land with
compassion."
When intelligent people see you they break into laughter.

Not having the power to stir the minds of young women,
You proclaim lustful, deceiving prophecies out of desire.
Without the slightest capacity to inspire trust,
How could you protect a kingdom?

The conceited charlatans who fool others, saying,
"Whatever I do is the activity of accomplishment,"
Produce documents for their Treasures and gather the negative
karma
Of attributing a false reference to Padma, King of the
Conquerors.

There are surely some people who chant various Treasure-like false
teachings
Produced by the deceit of powerful gods and demons.
There are many who fool themselves by pursuing the rank of an
accomplished master
Not suspecting at all that they are fooled by demons.

If it truly is a teaching taught by Padma, King of the Conquerors,
Intelligent people will know that it is a contradiction
To wonder, "This teaching of mine, is that a Treasure or not?"
And then ask others for advice.

If one does not earnestly practice
One's own teaching with joy,

དེ་ལ་གཞན་དག་བློ་ལྡན་སུ་ཞིག་གིས། །ནན་ཏན་འཇུག་པ་རྒྱུ་མཚན་ཅི་ཡིས་ཡིན། །

བླུན་པོས་ཅི་ཟེར་བདེན་པར་འཛིན་པ་ལ། །འདི་ཟབ་འདི་ཉིད་ཉམས་སུ་ལོངས་ཞེས་སུ། །
གདམས་པས་དེས་ཀྱང་དེ་ལྟར་འཛིན་མོད་ཀྱི། །ཆོས་ཀྱི་སྨུ་གུ་དེ་ལ་བྱུང་བར་ཟད། །

འདོན་རྒྱུས་དབུལ་བའི་སྨུ་གུ་སུ་ལའང་མེད། །བརྟོན་ན་ཕན་འབྲས་འཕགས་ན་ལེགས་མོད་ཀྱི། །
དངོས་གྲུབ་ཆུང་ལ་བར་ཆད་ཆེ་བ་དང་། །ཡིད་གཉིས་ཟ་བཞིན་མ་བརྟོན་དེ་བརྟོན་ཅི། །

ཆོས་ལ་བལྟས་ན་ལེགས་ལེགས་འདོན་སྒྲོ་འདྲ། །དད་བཞིན་ནན་ཏན་བརྩོན་པ་ཇི་སྲིད་འགྲོ། །
ཉམས་གླང་གསོལ་བཏབ་ལག་རྗེས་འབབ་ཞིག་གིས། །
ཐེ་ཚོམ་བསླང་སྙེ་ཐམས་ཅད་འདྲ་ཕྱིར་སླམ། །

མདོར་ན་བོན་པོ་འཕེལ་ཀ་རྟོལ་མནན་ལྟར། །བོན་གཤིས་ཅན་གྱི་གཏེར་ཆོས་དེ་དང་འདྲ། །
དེ་ལ་ཐེ་ཚོམ་ཟ་བའི་དུས་བྱུང་ན། །མཐུ་ལྡན་ཡོད་ན་ཡིད་གཉིས་སེལ་བར་རིགས། །

ཅེས་པའང་འཕྲལ་དྲན་མི་ཕམ་པས་སོ།། །།

Then why would any other intelligent person
Earnestly engage in it?

The fool believes everything that is said.
And when advised, "This is profound. Practice just this!"
He will surely do that.
But for him that is a spiritual famine.

There is no one at all who experiences the famine of lacking texts to chant.
Surely, when recited, if there is a superior beneficial effect, then great.
But if accomplishments decrease and obstacles increase,
And you experience doubt, then do not recite such texts. What is the point?

When looking at the teaching it seems impressive and delightful to chant.
So why do things get worse when persevering diligently with faith?
If doubt becomes the only sign of your practice and prayers
You may think that all Treasures are the same.

In short, as the Bönpos were suppressed at the time they spread,
The same applies to the Treasures founded in Bön.[140]
If you should ever feel doubt in this regard,
It is best to resolve your hesitation in the presence of a powerful person.

Composed by Mipham suddenly as it came to mind.

Part Two

The New Treasures of Chokgyur Lingpa

4

An Auspiciously Curling Tune

Few Treasures of the Nyingma School have left a larger imprint on contemporary Tibetan Buddhism than those of the famed nineteenth century master Chokgyur Dechen Shigpo Lingpa (1829-1870). Since the time of his revelations a century and a half ago, Chokgyur Lingpa's Treasures have become popular not only within the Nyingma School but also in the Kagyu lineage where they have been actively promulgated by such prominent figures as Jamgön Kongtrul, the Dazang and Situpa Tulkus, and, above all, several Karmapa hierarchs. The Treasures of Chokgyur Lingpa together with their commentaries are known collectively as the *New Treasures of Chokgyur Lingpa*.[141] Today they comprise an extensive collection in 39 volumes including more than 1000 individual titles[142] and several genres that, prior to the time of Chokgyur Lingpa, had never been revealed as Treasure but only existed in the older lineage of Transmitted Precepts.[143]

In addition to his role as a Treasure revealer, Chokgyur Lingpa was an influential figure in the ecumenical (*ris med*) movement that arose in eastern Tibet during the nineteenth century around the figures of Jamgön Kongtrul Lodrö Thaye and Jamyang Khyentse Wangpo. It was in large part the close relationship that Chokgyur Lingpa enjoyed with these two extraordinary masters that helped the *New Treasures* to become a widespread and popular tradition. Considering its significant impact on nineteenth and twentieth century Tibetan thought and society, it is surprising that the ecumenical tradition so far has received little scholarly attention.[144] Still, although the ecumenical tradition is only peripheral to our topic here, given the active involvement of Kongtrul and Khyentse in the revelations of Chokgyur Lingpa, future studies of the *New Treasures* will doubtless yield significant information on the workings of that movement.

The features of the *New Treasures* that make it so valuable—its vastness, visionary variety, and philosophical complexity—are at the same time also the greatest challenge to engaging with this collection and getting a basic overview of Chokgyur Lingpa's revelations. As a result, the *New Treasures* have previously remained almost unnoticed by Western research.[145] In this light, the present study aims to provide a general introduction to Chokgyur Lingpa and his tradition by outlining the major events, features, and people related thereto and so create a preliminary platform from which future, in-depth studies may proceed. For this, we first turn to the rich hagiographical literature concerned with the spiritual life and visionary achievements of Chokgyur Lingpa himself.

We are fortunate to find in the *New Treasures* a wealth of information collected and composed by several central figures of the lineage, including Chokgyur Lingpa himself. In colophons throughout the *New Treasures* Chokgyur Lingpa writes about the nature of his Treasures and the way they were discovered, often noting the details of time and place and thereby providing valuable information for a chronological reconstruction of his career. Besides the information supplied in colophons, Chokgyur Lingpa also composed a brief autobiography (predominantly in verse) written sometime during 1867 or early 1868 that later was joined with various accounts of Treasure revelation likewise recounted by Chokgyur Lingpa himself. This compilation was included in the *New Treasures* under the title *Basic Account of the Emanated Great Treasure Revealer's Biography Combined with a Few Treasure Chronicles*.[146] These writings of Chokgyur Lingpa are of great value for understanding his role within the ecumenical movement, especially a section in the autobiography in which he expounds on the philosophical values of the ecumenical tradition and the role of the Treasure tradition within this movement.[147] It is generally well known that Chokgyur Lingpa was a prominent figure within the ecumenical tradition,[148] but little is known about his specific views on ecumenicalism. In this chapter, Chokgyur Lingpa encourages spiritual practitioners to abandon one-sided critique of other traditions and instead to appreciate the commonalities between the many Tibetan religious traditions while still remaining respectful of their individual unique features. Specifically in relation to the Treasure tradition, Chokgyur Lingpa admonishes the followers of the Nyingma School to abandon attachment to the revelations of individual revealers and, instead, to focus on the relationship between all Treasures and the general Buddhist tradition and so acknowledge that the philosophical roots of the Treasures are firmly planted in the general teachings of sūtra and tantra.[149]

Besides Chokgyur Lingpa's own writings, the *New Treasures* contain several early writings by his foremost teachers, Jamgön Kongtrul and Khyentse Wangpo. These sources form the basis for all the subsequent hagiographical works on Chokgyur Lingpa. Most central is a short praise to the career of Chokgyur Lingpa composed by Jamgön Kongtrul under the title *Auspiciously Curling Tune: A Supplication to the Life of the Emanated Great Treasure Revealer Chokgyur Lingpa.*[150] In this work Kongtrul outlines the most significant events in Chokgyur Lingpa's life, listing his most prominent teachers, students, Treasures, and visions. The supplication is augmented with numerous annotations (*mchan 'grel*) in which Kongtrul provides a commentary on the events of the supplication. In the colophon Kongtrul notes that he composed the supplication at the request of Chokgyur Lingpa's consort Dechen Chödrön and several other devoted students.[151] As with so many works in the *New Treasures* the text is undated, but it was most likely composed soon after the death of Chokgyur Lingpa.[152] Later, at the request of Chokgyur Lingpa's famed scholar-student, Karmey Khenpo Rinchen Dargye (nineteenth century), Khyentse Wangpo composed an outline (*sa bcad*) of this praise, which he named *Divisions of the Auspicious Tune: The Condensed Meaning of the Supplication to the Great Treasure Revealer Chokgyur Lingpa.*[153]

On the past lives of Chokgyur Lingpa, Dazang Karma Ngedön Tenpa Rabgye (1808-1864), another of Chokgyur Lingpa's foremost teachers, composed a supplication to the past existences that Chokgyur Lingpa previously had occupied. This work, entitled *Rosary of Red Pearls: a Supplication to the Past Lives of the Vidyādhara Master—The Great Treasure Revealer Chokgyur Lingpa,*[154] was composed while Chokgyur Lingpa was still alive. It presents the details of his past lives predominantly based on information found in Treasure literature but also, to a lesser degree, on information accessed through meditative visions. As an elaboration on this supplication, Khyentse Wangpo composed a slightly longer text; *Lapis Lazuli Drama: General Notes on the Rosary of Red Pearls Past Lives Supplication.*[155] The main source for both works (and other subsequent descriptions of Chokgyur Lingpa's past lives) is a Treasure text revealed by the visionary Shigpo Lingpa Gargyi Wangchuk (1524-1583) named *Radiant Lamp*, which recounts Shigpo Lingpa's past lives in great detail.[156] These previous existences of Shigpo Lingpa are relevant for Chokgyur Lingpa as well since Shigpo Lingpa came to be regarded as one of Chokgyur Lingpa's previous incarnations, whereby the *Radiant Lamp* became an account of Chokgyur Lingpa's past lives as well.[157] Khyentse's work, which consists almost entirely of a lengthy quotation from the *Radiant Lamp*, establishes the authority of this prophesized account by categorizing the past lives experienced in meditative visions as merely an appendage (*kha skong*) to the revealed descriptions.[158] The past lives of Chokgyur Lingpa are presented below as they are recounted in these two sources.

Khyentse Wangpo composed yet another biographical text entitled *Breeze of Requesting the Auspicious Tune: Replies to Questions Arising from the Hagiography of the Great Treasure Revealer*,[159] which is a series of answers to questions posed by Chokgyur Lingpa's students regarding the life of their master. This text forms the basis for the subsequent hagiographies of Chokgyur Lingpa by both Kongtrul and Dudjom where longer passages often are quoted verbatim.[160] Khyentse presents events central to Chokgyur Lingpa's life and career in a structured manner that gives an excellent overview of the identity of Chokgyur Lingpa's main teachers,[161] the divisions of his Treasures,[162] his sevenfold transmission of teaching,[163] and the major group practice sessions over which Chokgyur Lingpa presided.[164]

Apart from the works of famed authors like Khyentse, Kongtrul, and Dazang, we find another important source of information in the so-called "general hagiography" (*phyi'i rnam thar*) of Chokgyur Lingpa entitled *Melody of the Fifth Auspicious Birth: A General Outer Biography of the Great Treasure Revealer Chokgyur Lingpa*[165] composed by Pema Yeshe (nineteenth/twentieth century)—a student of Chokgyur Lingpa and an important chant master (*dbu mdzad*) within his tradition. This hagiography, written at the request of the first Chokling reincarnation in the Neten lineage, Pema Gyurme Thegchok Tenpel (1873-1927), builds on the themes raised by Kongtrul and Khyentse but also gathers information from several smaller manuscripts in the *New Treasures*. In addition to this formal hagiography, Pema Yeshe also composed a lengthy description of Chokgyur Lingpa's journey to central Tibet at the end of his life.[166] Elsewhere in the *New Treasures* we find a brief account by an anonymous author describing Chokgyur Lingpa's revelation of *Seven Profound Cycles*.[167]

The richest source for information on Chokgyur Lingpa is surely the 600 page hagiography *A Clarification of the Branches of the Auspicious Tune: The Life of the Great Treasure Revealer Chokgyur Dechen Lingpa*[168] composed by the first Chokling reincarnation in the Kela lineage, Könchog Gyurme Tenpey Gyaltsen (nineteenth/twentieth cent.). This text offers a wealth of information regarding both the outer events in Chokgyur Lingpa's life and his inner experiences and meditative realizations. It was composed in 1921 and draws heavily on the above mentioned early works, but also incorporates new sources in the form of previously unpublished notes and manuscripts related to the life of Chokgyur Lingpa. Curiously, the works of Pema Yeshe are not mentioned in this text, and it seems possible that Könchog Gyurme might not have been aware of them.[169] Like the earlier works, Könchog Gyurme's biography is also structured along the framework previously established by Khyentse and Kongtrul.

The Tibetan hagiographical genre is unique in that it does not limit itself to a single life but often recounts the saint's existence within a framework of past, present, as well as future lives. Not only does Könchog Gyurme provide descriptions of all such lives of Chokgyur Lingpa, he also uses several biographical sub-genres that lend further uniqueness to the hagiographical literature of Tibet. The main body of the text is structured into three sections: 1) a brief teaching on the definitive and the provisional hagiographies,[170] 2) an expanded explanation by means of ten amazing accounts,[171] and 3) a conclusion by means of supplication and aspirations.[172] The definitive and the provisional hagiographies introduce two variant modes of hagiography: 1) the ultimate and essential hagiography[173] and 2) the symbolic, provisional hagiography.[174] The first of these divisions is a brief philosophical chapter that presents Chokgyur Lingpa as primordially inseparable from the basic nature of all phenomena. In spite of this being a condensed hagiographical exposition this chapter is nevertheless billed as the essential and true way to appreciate the actual being of Chokgyur Lingpa:

> In reality, his nature, all-pervading like the sky, is primordially the supremely luminous dharmakāya of great bliss, the indivisibility of ground and fruition.[175]

This chapter is termed "ultimate" and "essential" even though it barely covers two full pages, supporting the position that underneath the detailed historical narrative of the Treasure cosmos lies a reality of timelessness (*dharmakāya*), which gives historical events a relative quality and frees them from the confines of a strictly linear historical consciousness. Thus, similar to the historical narratives of Treasure revelation that rely on the backdrop of timeless reality, the acts of a Buddhist saint such as Chokgyur Lingpa are likewise to be viewed with a hermeneutic that acknowledges their occurrence in the world as reflections of this "ultimate and essential" way of being.

The following explanation of the symbolic provisional hagiography is a one-page listing of the topic for the main part of the text—Chokgyur Lingpa's achievements as perceived from the framework of relative existence. This leads into a more formal historical narrative structured on a three-fold division of Chokgyur Lingpa's past existences, present life, and his activity in future lives for the continuous benefit of sentient beings. The chapter devoted to his past lives consists of two divisions: 1) a general explication of the hagiography of the three kāyas[176] and 2) a particular division of the way that Chokgyur Lingpa appeared in this world.[177] The first of these categories once again highlights the importance of approaching the Tibetan hagiographical genre with sensitivity to the general Mahāyānist metaphysical conception of rūpakāya emanations emerging from the underlying dharmakāya matrix. Here Könchog Gyurme describes the manner in which buddhas and bodhisattvas take birth in the world without ever moving from the reality of dharmakāya and how they engage in the benevolent actions of converting sentient beings through the activities of "the fourfold taming" (*'dul ba bzhi*) of body, speech, mind, and miracles. Having reminded the reader of Chokgyur Lingpa's inherent affiliation with the basic nature of existence itself, Könchog Gyurme has prepared the ground for the ensuing detailed discussion of the events in Chokgyur Lingpa's "garland of lives"—the numerous preambulary existences preceding his feats in nineteenth century eastern Tibet. Below, we shall return to a closer look at these past lives.

In spite of the various hagiographical sub-categories presented up to this point, the main part of Könchog Gyurme's work is, after all, devoted to the life and career of Chokgyur Lingpa. In presenting his life, Könchog Gyurme follows Khyentse Wangpo's ten chapter outline that describes 1) Chokgyur Lingpa's youth, 2) the awakening of his karmic potential, 3) teachers, 4) spiritual development, 5) meditative realization, 6) visionary experiences, 7) Treasure discoveries, 8) students, 9) his sanctification of the environment, and 10) his passing into nirvāṇa.[178] Since Könchog Gyurme, like Pema Yeshe, bases his presentation on the early sources, there is a great deal of duplication found in his hagiography, but as his narrative is otherwise richly adorned with quotations from both Treasure texts and classical scriptures, the repetitiveness is not as pronounced as one could expect. Könchog Gyurme also incorporates several oral accounts into his narrative, but considering the vulnerability of the oral tradition in the turbulent social upheavals of the twentieth century, an even greater number of such reports would have been desired. Still, as Könchog Gyurme begins to unravel anecdotes of Chokgyur Lingpa's visionary life and the many extraordinary events connected thereto, we obtain a valuable look into the inner workings of the Treasure tradition. In these chapters (6 – 9), we not only receive a tour into the fascinating world of Treasure discovery with its rich symbolic language and ritual but also encounter the main protagonists in the ecumenical tradition as they relate to Chokgyur Lingpa's revelations. Previously, the main figures of the ecumenical tradition such as Khyentse, Kongtrul, and Chokling have been studied only little, but here valuable data on their work and relationship are presented.[179] Finally, having covered the main events of Chokgyur Lingpa's life, the author completes his work with a brief description of Chokgyur Lingpa's future lives (silent on the fact that he himself was one of them!).[180]

Apart from the hagiographical material of the *New Treasures,* Jamgön Kongtrul also included a hagiography of Chokgyur Lingpa in his survey of the Treasure revealers.[181] This in turn formed the basis for Dudjom's chapter on Chokgyur Lingpa in his history of the Nyingma School, which is mostly a verbatim copy of Kongtrul's writing.[182] It is also said that a longer and more detailed biography was written by Chokling's student Karmey Khenpo Rinchen Dargye (nineteenth century), but it is uncertain whether this work still exists.[183] Now, before we consider the life of Chokgyur Lingpa any further, let us first look closer at some of the many lives leading up to the birth of our Treasure revealing protagonist.

The past lives of Chokgyur Lingpa are recounted on the basis of the *Radiant Lamp*, a text revealed in the sixteenth century by the visionary Shigpo Lingpa as testimony to his own previous lives. As this scripture is a Treasure revelation, these past existences are not presented as if narrated by Shigpo Lingpa himself but instead by Padmasambhava back in the eighth century as a prophesy of what is yet to come. In Tibet it was standard practice that Treasure revealers discover this kind of *ex post facto* prophecy in which Padmasambhava foretells, as Ratna Lingpa puts it, "even the moles and physical marks on their body"[184] although, not surprisingly, this was a type of writing often looked upon with suspicion by many, even among the followers of the Nyingma School.[185]

In any case, Shigpo Lingpa's revelation lists his many past lives in India, China, Tibet, and elsewhere his karma and aspirations are said to have taken him. Since Chokgyur Lingpa is considered the reincarnation of Shigpo Lingpa this text is extensively quoted throughout the biographical texts of the *New Treasures,* where it becomes the primary source for retelling the past lives of Chokgyur Lingpa.[186] Here we are told how he (Shigpo Lingpa/Chokgyur Lingpa), in a distant past, first connected with the dharma in general, and especially with the all-important figures of the Treasure lineage: Padmasambhava and his royal disciple Trisong Detsen.

The *Radiant Lamp* begins in the early days of this aeon with the well-known story of Padmasambhava, Trisong Detsen, and Śāntarakṣita (in their former lives) building the stūpa called *Mistakenly Granted Permission*.[187] Here we are told that the future Trisong Detsen witnessed a black bird landing on the stūpa and made a wish that, in the future it would become his son. As the bird was none other than the Chokgyur Lingpa-to-be, the original karmic connection was thus established between him and the Buddhist dharma. The seed having been planted in the mind of the future Treasure revealer, he embarked on a series of rebirths predominantly unfolding in India and Tibet. As the fortunate black bird passed away it was, according to the *Radiant Lamp*, first born in Bodhgaya as Kīrti Jñāna, son of the elder Dharmabhadra. At that time he jokingly offered flowers to a representation of a buddha, thus sowing the seeds for liberation.[188] This act in turn led to rebirth in the Tuṣita Heaven as a divine being. Thereafter he was born as Aniruddha, the Buddha's cousin and one of the ten close disciples. In that existence he attained the state of an arhat and, even though he had perceived the truth of dharmatā, he still wished to enter the resultant vehicle. Thus, he continued in existence and assumed a series of animal and human existences in various regions of India, Nepal, China, and Tibet.[189]

Finally, however, the obscurations of the future Chokgyur Lingpa were purified during his life as a prince from the Indian kingdom of Bedar. From this point onwards, all subsequent reincarnations are said to be conscious and voluntary. This is also the time when he enters the Tibetan religious scene as well-known historical personae such as the famed minister Garwa at the court of King Songtsen Gampo (ca. 617-649/650). Then follows a life as the prince of Entse before we arrive at the all-important birth as Murub Tsenpo, the second son of King Trisong Detsen.[190]

In describing this life the text shifts to present tense as Padmasambhava (who in the Treasure text is recounting the lives of Shigpo Lingpa) now speaks in person directly to his Tibetan disciples. Padmasambhava lists the various names given to Murub Tsenpo and tells of the karmic bond between this prince and his wife Bumcham who, upon death, according to Padmasambhava's prophecy, will be united in the pure buddha fields.[191] Chokgyur Lingpa's life as Murub Tsenpo is of central importance as it is during that existence he comes into contact with Padmasambhava, receives empowerment and is prophesized as a major Treasure revealer. Now, once again, Padmasambhava changes his narrative and speaks in future tense as he prophesizes the future lives of Murub Tsenpo.

As this prince passes away, Padmasambhava predicts, he will be born as a king in the country (pure land?) of Urgyen Zangling from which he will continuously send out emanations, working for the welfare of all beings.[192] Padmasambhava then briefly describes a series of other births as various tantric practitioners of mixed prominence including, notably, two lives as female Treasure revealers.[193] Then follows a description of his life as the great Treasure revealer Sangye Lingpa (1340-1396), known for his revelation of the influential *Embodiment of the Realization of the Master* Treasure cycle. Having prophesized the life of Sangye Lingpa in detail, mentioning his birthplace, looks, name, etc., Padmasambhava continues by predicting Murub Tsenpo's subsequent birth as the female Treasure revealer Bummo Cham from Nyang in upper Tsang,[194] as an unnamed minister also from the Tsang region, and finally, the life as Shigpo Lingpa whose virtues are extolled in considerable detail.[195] As the *Lamp* is a revelation by Shigpo Lingpa, the account goes no further. Still, it is surprising that the *New Treasures* contains no attempt to recount the interim existences that presumably would have followed from the time of Shigpo Lingpa up until his rebirth as Chokgyur Lingpa—leaving a period of roughly 250 years unaccounted for.

Having in this way considered the traditional recounting of Chokgyur Lingpa's genealogy of past lives, we may now turn to some of the events of his life as they occurred in the nineteenth century, in particular his numerous revelations that secured him such fame and influence with a number of the greatest religious figures of his time.

5
Seven Descents

Chokgyur Lingpa was born on August 10, 1829[196] at the practice center of Gomde Dranang in Yertö[197] in the southern part of the eastern Tibetan region of Do Kham. His father, whose family had strong ties to the local Nangchen aristocracy, was the tantric adept Pema Wangchuk, who is described as having perfect qualities of power and capacity. His mother, Tsering Yangtsho, was also a virtuous being who had unchanging faith in the Three Jewels and was known for her generosity of giving away her possessions to the needy.[198] According to the texts, Chokgyur Lingpa was born without any pain to his mother amidst wonderful signs such as rainbow lights and a rain of flowers.[199] Despite these unusual signs and the existence of a Treasure discovered by Drime Lingpa (eighteenth century) foretelling the birth of a great Treasure revealer in the Yertö area named Ratna Urgyen, the child apparently was not recognized as a special being and his childhood years were spent in anonymity.[200]

A defining event in the life of the young Chokgyur Lingpa, or Norbu Tenzin as he was known at the time, occurred in the spring of 1841 when he was just 11 years old.[201] As he was playing alone in a place called Maṇikha, he came across an odd-looking yogin who was wearing a lotus crown, red dharma robes, blue boots, and using a skull staff for a walking stick. The yogin asked for the boy's name and the name of the place, and when Chokgyur Lingpa had answered, gave the following prophesy, "Well then, since this place is called Maṇikha, and your name is Norbu Tenzin, and the place up there is Ārya Nang, you will become someone especially noble in this world."[202] By this prophesy we are told that Chokgyur Lingpa "received a blessing to master the storehouse of profound Treasures."[203] Having uttered this prediction the yogin, who was actually Padmasambhava in person, dissolved into light and was gone.

Having met Padmasambhava in this way, Chokgyur Lingpa began his Treasure revealing career. In systematizing the various teachings that passed through or originated with Chokgyur Lingpa, his followers adopted a particular system known as "the seven descents" (*bka' bab bdun*). By means of these seven descents, or religious transmissions, all teachings handed down to Chokgyur Lingpa, as well as his own visionary revelations, are presented according to their manner of reception since, although Chokgyur Lingpa is considered an indispensable factor for the manifestation of his visionary teachings, he is nevertheless not considered their author but rather their transmitter.[204] The notion of seven descents has old roots in the Nyingma School where it can be traced to the writings of Rongzom Chökyi Zangpo (1012-1088) in the eleventh century. In its classical formulation this system refers to seven transmissions of tantric material passing from India into Tibet during the latter half of the eighth century and first half of the ninth century.[205]

In the nineteenth century, however, Chokgyur Lingpa and Jamyang Khyentse Wangpo both revealed Treasures that radically reinterpreted this system. The classical seven descents of Rongzom were only concerned with various lineages of the Transmitted Precepts, but the reinterpretation of this system included the lineages of Treasure and Pure Vision to the extent that the Transmitted Precepts only came to occupy a single transmission among the seven. The earliest source for this new system is a prophetic scripture from Chokgyur Lingpa's foremost Treasure, *Three Sections of the Great Perfection*, which declares that both Chokgyur Lingpa and Khyentse Wangpo will come to receive seven spiritual descents of 1) Transmitted Precepts (*bka' ma*), 2) Earth Treasures (*sa gter*), 3) Rediscovered Treasures (*yang gter*), 4) Mind Treasures (*dgongs gter*), 5) Recollected Treasures (*rjes dran gter*), 6) Pure Vision (*dag snang*), and 7) Oral Lineage (*snyan brgyud*).[206] As these transmissions traditionally provide the framework for the presentation of both Chokgyur Lingpa's life and his spiritual heritage, we too shall follow these seven descents in tracing the events of Chokgyur Lingpa's visionary career.

1. The Transmitted Precepts

Chokgyur Lingpa received the transmission for the Transmitted Precepts of the Nyingma School on several occasions and took an active part in propagating this ancient literary collection. Kongtrul gives the earliest description of Chokgyur Lingpa's receiving this transmission, writing that during his life Chokgyur Lingpa received most of the Transmitted Precepts still existing in

Tibet and in turn passed on many of them, including instructions on all three traditional divisions of the Transmitted Precepts.[207] Pema Yeshe further explains that Chokgyur Lingpa granted the empowerment of the *Sūtra that Gathers the Intention of All Buddhas* at the Pal Riwoche monastery; to the senior figures of both Evaṃ Chögar and Urgyen Mindrol Ling monasteries he conferred the empowerment and instructions of *Peaceful and Wrathful Magical Net*; and at Samye Chimpu he passed on many teachings of the Great Perfection.[208] Furthermore, Kongtrul notes that several of Chokgyur Lingpa's Mahāyoga and Anuyoga Treasures actually belong to the category of Transmitted Precepts in terms of both word and meaning.[209]

II. Earth Treasure

Even though tradition considers all Treasures of Chokgyur Lingpa as revealed truth, his earth Treasure revelations are given special importance. On the advice of Tai Situpa Pema Nyinche Wangpo (1774-1853), Chokgyur Lingpa kept most of his mind Treasures secret and instead focused on the propagation of his earth Treasure revelations.[210] As noted earlier, the category of earth Treasure covers both actual earth Treasures and rediscovered Treasures. Khyentse Wangpo states that Chokgyur Lingpa revealed altogether 37 major actual earth Treasures, but the various commentators do not uniformly agree on their exact identification. The difficulty of accurately identifying Chokgyur Lingpa's Treasures is noted by Khyentse Wangpo, who states:

> Regarding the origin of the approximately 37 successive earth Treasure revelations, it is difficult to explain them in detail since, in general, some had a seal of secrecy and still others were concealed as rediscovered Treasures.[211]

In spite of such obstacles, Khyentse Wangpo, with the assistance of Kongtrul and other close students of Chokgyur Lingpa, nevertheless composed a Treasure inventory identifying the following 37 earth Treasures:[212]

1) In the year that Chokgyur Lingpa first had his visionary meeting with Padmasambhava (1841) he discovered his first Treasure, which was revealed at Drakkar Dzongchung. On this occasion Chokgyur Lingpa discovered a vajra that had once belonged to Prince Murub Tsenpo, a mirror, and 24 sādhanas.[213] Later, Chokgyur Lingpa offered the mirror to Kongtrul and the vajra to Khyentse.[214] Around this time Chokgyur Lingpa received his novice vows from

Taklungma Ngawang Tenpey Nyima (b. 1788), but apparently did not receive any personal guidance from this master.[215] This period of Chokgyur Lingpa's life, in which he had not yet established a personal relationship with spiritual teachers who could advise him on his visionary experiences, seems to have been a time of some spiritual uncertainty. Chokgyur Lingpa himself speaks of several unreliable visions occurring during this period and describes how he struggled to establish whether they were positive signs for Treasure revelation or negative obstacles to his spiritual development. Finally he decided on the latter and ignored these early visions.[216]

2) The following year, when he was just 12 or 13 years old (1842-1843), Chokgyur Lingpa discovered his second Treasure at a white stūpa at Samye.[217] However, as circumstances were not right, he decided to conceal it again.[218]

3) The third earth Treasure was revealed on November 7, 1848 when Chokgyur Lingpa in secrecy discovered the cycle of *Guru's Heart Practice: Dispeller of All Obstacles*—one of his most influential Treasures—from the site of Danyin Khala Ronggo.[219] This Treasure, which belongs to the Mahāyoga cycle of *Magical Net*, contains practices for accomplishing the trikāya guru deities of Amitayus, Avalokiteśvara, and Padmasambhava in combination with 12 manifestations of Padmasambhava.[220] Chokgyur Lingpa did not immediately make this Treasure public but kept it a secret for eight years until he showed the yellow scrolls to Khyentse Wangpo, who enthusiastically told Chokling that he himself had revealed an almost identical Treasure. It is said that by comparing the two Treasures and finding them to be almost identical in both word and meaning, Khyentse and Chokling developed great confidence in each other and from this point onwards they collaborated closely on the establishment and propagation of this and many other Treasure cycles.[221]

4) On September 26, 1849 the Avalokiteśvara cycle of *Lotus Crowned Great Compassionate One* was discovered at Bundzong.[222] Accompanying this revelation were, among other unspecified objects, a small Avalokiteśvara statue said to have been crafted from a bone of Trisong Detsen.[223] In the prophecy of the *Lotus Crowned* cycle, Situ Pema Nyinche Wangpo is prophesized as an emanation of Padmasambhava himself and the main doctrine holder of the *Lotus Crowned* cycle:

> When the prince turns 25 he will meet
> My speech emanation known as Pema Nyinche—
> A regent of the Jina who holds high the victory banner of practice

And is like a torch in the dense darkness of the final days.
Without secrecy he will place his trust in him,
Where after many obstacles will be spontaneously cleared away.[224]

Accordingly, in 1853, Chokgyur Lingpa went to the monastery of Palpung where he met Situpa Pema Nyinche Wangpo. The meeting was important for Chokgyur Lingpa, as Situpa advised Chokling to keep his mind Treasures secret and instead focus on propagating earth Treasure revelations. 1853 was surely an important year for Chokgyur Lingpa, as he came into contact with all his closest teachers in the space of just a few months. Soon after meeting Situpa, on the day commemorating the Buddha's first teaching (July 10, 1853), Chokgyur Lingpa received bodhisattva vows from Khenchen Dazang, the second of his major spiritual friends, and in the same month (July 30, 1853) Jamgön Kongtrul Lodrö Thaye initiated him into the tantric vehicle by an empowerment ceremony of *Great Compassionate One Who Embodies All Sugatas,* whereby Kongtrul became the third of Chokgyur Lingpa's gurus.[225] Shortly thereafter, on October 10, 1853, Chokgyur Lingpa first met Jamyang Khyentse Wangpo, who offered him the empowerment of *Most Secret Blade Kīla* together with many instructions, including teachings on the Great Perfection, whereby he became Chokgyur Lingpa's fourth and most significant teacher, responsible for introducing him to the recognition of the nature of mind.[226]

5) The next Treasure revelation was a secret discovery of auxiliary texts belonging to the cycle of *Dispeller of All Obstacles* from a rock at the foot of the Riwo Wangzhu Mountain. These auxiliary practices focus on four deities who clear away obstacles: Tārā, Acala, Vajradaṇḍa, and Bhurkuṃkūta. Among these four, most texts focus on the practice of Tārā and the exercise of yogic heat (*gtum mo*) centered on the deity Acala.[227] The date for this Treasure is uncertain, but most likely it should be between November 21 and December 6, 1854.[228]

6) The sixth earth Treasure revelation was *Seven Profound Cycles* revealed at Karmey Damchen Drak on May 19, 1856.[229] These ritual cycles focus on seven deities (or groups of deities), each having a particular advantageous specialty: Māyājāla—profound tantra; Viśuddha—profound eminence; Hayagrīva—profound empowerment; Mañjuśrī Yamāntaka—profound fierce mantra; Kīlaya—profound wrathful activity; Guru, Deva, Ḍākinī—profound long life; and Mamo—profound dispeller of obstacles and creator of realization.[230]

7) On July 12, 1856, the seventh Treasure was revealed from Yegyal Namkha Dzö. This Treasure contained auxiliary texts related to *Seven Profound Cycles* as well as two statues and various sacred substances.[231]

8) On October 9, 1856 Chokgyur Lingpa returned to Danyin Khala Ronggo where previously he had revealed the *Dispeller of All Obstacles* cycle. This time he revealed a guide book for Danyin Khala Ronggo as well as a brief history of the *Dispeller of All Obstacles* cycle. He also revealed several secret sacred items (*dam rdzas bka' rgya ma*).[232]

Chokgyur Lingpa recounts that sometime during the following month (October 29 – November 28, 1856) he revealed a Brahmin skull from the site of Kham Mig Yedrak. He also mentions that, although a dharma Treasure (*chos gter*) was present at that location, he left it untouched.[233] Khyentse, however, does not classify this skull as an earth Treasure but instead as a material Treasure (*rdzas gter*).[234]

9) On January 28, 1857 Chokgyur Lingpa revealed his foremost Treasure, the *Three Sections of the Great Perfection*, from the Lotus Crystal Cave (*padma shel phug*) in Meshö Dzam.[235] As the teachings of the Great Perfection are considered to be the pinnacle of the nine vehicles, the exalted nature of this Treasure is evident from its title alone. According to Tulku Urgyen, this cycle is considered Chokgyur Lingpa's foremost Treasure because it is the only Tibetan Treasure to reveal all three sections of the Great Perfection.[236] It contains many subdivisions and has, according to Khyentse, no less than seven different individual "heart essence" (*snying thig*) teachings, such as the *Heart Essence of Pema Garwang*, the *Heart Essence of the Three Families*, and the *Heart Essence of Vairocana*. In revealing the *Three Sections of the Great Perfection* Chokgyur Lingpa was intimately assisted by both Khyentse and Kongtrul; especially by Khyentse who helped as the scribe while Chokgyur Lingpa dictated the teachings from the yellow scrolls.[237] Until then Chokgyur Lingpa's revelations had all taken place in secret and were only later made public. However, from this time onward there is a shift in his revelatory style, with more Treasures being revealed in public, often with large gatherings witnessing the events—the so-called "public revelations" (*khrom gter*).[238]

10) On February 4, 1857, one week after discovering the *Three Sections of the Great Perfection*, Chokgyur Lingpa revealed, at the same place,[239] the cycle of *Heart Essence of Garab Dorje* as well as a Garab Dorje reliquary (*gdung rten*).[240]

11) On May 24, 1857, at Pawo Wangchen Drak, a descriptive inventory (*mdo byang*) of the 25 sacred places of Do Kham was revealed. These 25 places

are divided into five main sections of body, speech, mind, quality, and activity with each section further divided into the same five groupings, thus totaling 25.[241]

12) Only nine days after the discovery of the Do Kham inventory Chokgyur Lingpa discovered a secret revelation of the *Heart Essence of Mañjuśrīmitra* taken from the Great Secret Cave (*gsang phug chen mo*) at Drinyen Dong on June 2, 1857.[242]

13) Six days later, on June 8, 1857, Chokgyur Lingpa revealed the *Heart Essence of Tsogyal* together with an unidentified inventory from Sengchen Namdrak.[243]

14) The next of Chokgyur Lingpa's earth Treasures was the cycle of *Six Scrolls of the Sacred Teaching*, revealed together with a secret manuscript, a crown belonging to Padmasambhava, a seal belonging to prince Murub Tsenpo, robes belonging to the Buddha, and spiritual medicine prepared by Garab Dorje. The revelation took place in the vicinity of Sengchen Namdrak on June 12, 1857.[244]

15) The next day at Drak Rinchen Barwa (also in the area of Sengchen Namdrak), Chokgyur Lingpa revealed a container with spiritual medicine prepared by the 25 disciples of Padmasambhava together with an unspecified cycle of teachings.[245]

16) On June 15, 1857 at Mengyal Drawey Drak (likewise in the Sengchen Namdrak area), medicinal substances and a yellow scroll were discovered. Khyentse records that Chokling distributed the medicine but kept the yellow scroll secret.[246] All the Treasures revealed in the vicinity of Sengchen Namdrak were public revelations.

17) The seventeenth earth Treasure is undated but was revealed at the Ḍākinī Crystal Cave (*mkha' 'gro shel phug*)[247] in lower Dzi where Chokgyur Lingpa discovered a guide to the place written on the robes of Śāntarakṣita as well as, among other things, earrings belonging to Gyalwa Chokyang.[248]

18) At the Vajra Bell Cave (*rdo rje cong phug*) in Kerong, Chokgyur Lingpa revealed a substance of longevity blessed by Padmasambhava and Yeshe Tsogyal together with an onyx box and several Treasure inventories.[249] Chokgyur Lingpa further mentions that in the surrounding area he revealed several wealth Treasures.[250]

19) On December 12, 1857, at Karmey Bumdzong, the four cycles of *Great Compassionate One Who Stirs the Depth of Samsāra* together with several sacred substances were revealed.[251]

20) Later, Chokgyur Lingpa revealed the yellow scrolls for the *Embodiment of the Realization of the Dharma Protectors* from Bumdzong Lake. It is said that amidst a gathering of people he received the yellow scrolls in a stone container from a nāga demon who brought the Treasure to the surface of the lake holding it between its teeth.[252]

21) Likewise at Bumdzong, Chokgyur Lingpa revealed the six cycles of *Realization of Zurza*,[253] an inventory for Bumdzong, and the cycle of *Magical Net of Pema Garwang* together with a Tārā statue and blessed pills made from the body of the Indian master Prabhahasti.[254] The *Realization of Zurza* Treasure is a set of Mahāyoga practices meant for the accomplishment of six *ḍākinīs*: Vajravārāhī, Wrathful Tārā, Guhyajñāna, Maṇḍarava, Yeshe Tsogyal, and Ekajaṭī.

22) Sometime during 1858, Chokgyur Lingpa revealed the *Congregation of Mamos* Treasure together with blessed pills at Ogmin Karmey Palgyi Deu.[255]

23) On November 16, 1858 at Kela Norbu Punsum Drak the inner guru cycle of *Guru's Heart Practice: Wish-fulfilling Jewel Spontaneously Accomplishing Intentions* was revealed together with a statue of Padmasambhava.[256] The *Wish-fulfilling Jewel* cycle, which is the inner division among the nirmāṇakāya guru practices contained in the *New Treasures*, is focused on the accomplishment of Padmasambhava in the form of Guru Chemchok with a retinue of emanations.[257]

24) Shortly thereafter, at the Cliff of Blazing Light (*'od 'bar brag*) in Gotö, Chokgyur Lingpa revealed an account of the historical origins of sacred medicine and a statue said to liberate by sight as well as a short Treasure text of Mahārāja Vaiśravaṇa.[258]

25) On August 8, 1859 the three cycles of *Inner Secret Essence* were revealed from Tsādra Rinchen Drak, the upper retreat center at Palpung Monastery. These three cycles focus on the practice of the deities Vajrasattva, Yangdak Heruka, and Vajrakīlaya. He also revealed a guide to that place and sacred pills made from "all buddhas."[259]

After this Chokgyur Lingpa revealed two short, undated, Bön sādhanas from a protruding rock at Lhado, though Khyentse does not include them in his enumeration. The sādhanas focus on the Bön deities Wangdrak Barwa and Magyal Pomra. Könchog Gyurme mentions this revelation but describes it as an auxiliary revelation to Chokgyur Lingpa's 25th revelation.[260]

26) During the early winter of 1859 Chokgyur Lingpa revealed inventories for many Treasure sites as well as several descriptions of such sites from the

Jewel Crystal Rock (*rin chen shel brag*) at Gatö Meseng. He also revealed a clay figure containing a tooth of Padmasambhava.[261]

27) According to Khyentse, the next earth Treasure revelation took place from the Turquoise Rock (*g.yu brag*) at Gatö where Chokgyur Lingpa brought forth a statue of white Tārā made by Vimalamitra, together with substances for long life and (the text?) of *Inner Heart Essence*. We are told that this revelation was kept in utmost secrecy.[262]

According to the catalogue of the *New Treasures,* however, the 27th Treasure was a series of short rituals entitled *Four Dharma Protector Cycles of Ten Qualities That Bring Happiness to Tibet and Kham*. These rituals, which were revealed at Yegyal Namkha Dzö, concern the four protectors Yamāntaka, Hayagrīva, Kīlaya, and Gönpo.[263]

28) Chokgyur Lingpa did not reveal another earth Treasure until May 30, 1864, from the Turquoise Dragon Rock (*g.yu bal brag*) at Yegyal Namkha Dzö. It contained the cycles of *Embodiment of the Sugatas of the Eight Pronouncements* (the famous Mahāyoga eight-deity practice originally revealed by Nyangral Nyima Özer),[264] *Vajra Bridge of Acala* (a short cycle of Anuyoga scripture focused on the deity Acala), and *Heart Essence of Samantabhadra* (an Atiyoga cycle based on the maṇḍala of the peaceful and wrathful deities), accompanied by an unidentified statue and various sacred substances.[265]

29) To the west[266] of Namkha Dzö, and presumably around the same time, at the cliff known as Countenance of Life (*tshe zhal brag*), or Cliff of Longevity (*tshe rgyas brag*), Chokgyur Lingpa revealed a longevity substance blessed by Padmasambhava and Yeshe Tsogyal together with the cycles of *Vajra Garland Accomplishing Longevity* and *Tantra of Longevity: Confluence of Immortality Nectar*.[267]

30) On November 4, 1866 in the Secret Cave (*gsang phug*) of Rongme Chime Karmo Taktsang the Treasure of *Five Cycles of the Essential Sacred Dharma* was revealed.[268]

31) Later, on November 16, 1866, at Chime Karmo Taktsang, Chokgyur Lingpa discovered the instruction manual of Padmasambhava entitled *Wisdom Essence of Oral Instructions on the Stages of the Path* that belongs to the innermost guru cycle of *Powerful Vajra Wrath*.[269] This text, which is one of the most important Treasures of Chokgyur Lingpa, was transcribed from the yellow scroll by Khyentse Wangpo and later elaborated on in a highly regarded commentary by Jamgön Kongtrul.[270] Könchog Gyurme mentions that this was the only text that could be established from the *Powerful Vajra Wrath* cycle, as circumstances did not allow for further revelations. Even so, he claims that

the value of this single text alone is immense since it contains not only the essence of the tantras, explanatory scriptures, and oral instructions of all Treasure teachings in general, but in particular all four cycles of accomplishment of the guru principle.[271] Könchog Gyurme continues to praise Kongtrul's commentary and even classifies it as a Treasure in its own right:

> Just hearing the name of this profound teaching puts existence in tatters. To study and reflect upon it gives rise to undefiled wisdom. To put it into practice grants the result of buddhahood. This commentary is also a Treasure that burst forth from the expanse of genuine wisdom; certainly no ordinary person, no matter how learned he might be, will be able to write like this.[272]

So respected is Kongtrul's commentary that it has come to be regarded as *the* exposition on the paths and practices of the *New Treasures* and the single most authoritative explanation of the intent of Chokgyur Lingpa's Treasures.

32) On the following day Chokgyur Lingpa revealed a Treasure from the lake called Mapham Senggö Yutsho.[273] Khyentse does not mention what the Treasure consisted of, but Pema Yeshe says it contained jewels and "similar objects."[274]

33) On April 2, 1867 at Dzongshö Deshek Dupey Phodrang Chokgyur Lingpa discovered a clay figure (*sāccha*) made by Padmasambhava, Śāntarakṣita, and Trisong Detsen together with an inventory to Dzongshö Deshek Dupa.[275]

34) On April 15, 1867 at Pema Shelri sacred pills were revealed together with an inventory for that site.[276]

35) The following day, and presumably likewise at Pema Shelri, Chokgyur Lingpa revealed a stone container for *Heart Essence of All Knowledge-holders* together with sacred substances and a Treasure container, shaped like a curved knife, for *Heart Essence of the Gathering of Herukas* from the Garuda Nest Cliff (*khyung tshang brag*).[277] According to Könchog Gyurme, this was a material Treasure (*rdzas gter*), so it must be assumed that there were no texts in the containers.[278]

36) Khyentse lists the thirty sixth as the cycle of *Union with Buddha Samvara,* a guide to Rudam Ganggyi Rawa, and sacred substances all revealed on May 20, 1867[279] from three stone containers at Rudam Gangtrö Dewa Chenpo.[280]

Könchog Gyurme (whose list includes 38 major earth Treasures) counts another Treasure, not listed by Khyentse, as the thirty sixth, but aside from classifying it as a material Treasure, gives no information about it. He then counts the revelation from Rudam Gang as the thirty seventh.[281]

37) At Kela Norbu Punsum Drak, on August 13, 1867, Chokgyur Lingpa revealed his last major earth Treasure. This was the *Seven Cycles of the Sacred Dharma* together with ornaments belonging to Guru Senge Dradrok and a statue of that master.[282] According to the catalogue of the *New Treasures*, an inner accomplishment of the ḍākinīs and an offering ritual to the Treasure protectors Nordak Chesum were established from the yellow scrolls; however, no teachings of this cycle remain.[283]

This completes Khyentse's description of the 37 major earth Treasures. He adds that Chokgyur Lingpa also revealed numerous smaller Treasures such as inventories and material Treasures, and mentions the revelations of seven different kinds of inventories from a single earth Treasure at Sengchen Namdrak.[284] To illustrate the many material Treasures that Chokgyur Lingpa revealed, Khyentse mentions the revelation of relics of the Buddha and soil from the sacred place of Maratika in Nepal that took place at Riwo Wangphuk after Chokgyur Lingpa had revealed the auxiliary material for the *Dispeller of All Obstacles* cycle. He also includes in this category the revelation of the Brahmin skull described above (no. 8), bodhicitta pills of Padmasambhava and Yeshe Tsogyal revealed at Paog Burmo, and relics of the Buddha Kāśyapa revealed from the Gyamgyal Yutsho Lake.[285]

It was prophesized that Chokgyur Lingpa would reveal more than one hundred Treasures representing enlightened body, speech, mind, and activity, but according to Khyentse, it is almost impossible to put an exact number on his Treasures since some of those representing enlightened body—such as statues—were multiplied while other revelations of enlightened speech—such as the teachings of *Seven Profound Cycles* and *Three Sections of the Great Perfection*—contain numerous individual teachings. Furthermore, Khyentse says, Chokgyur Lingpa performed innumerable revelations of sacred substances but to derive an overview of these revelations one needs to refer to the colophons of his individual Treasures.[286] It is therefore clear that the mention of 37 Treasures is merely a representative and auspicious number that the tradition has adopted as a basis for discussing Chokgyur Lingpa's visionary output.

The vast majority of the revelations that Chokgyur Lingpa made public belong to the category of "actual earth Treasures that were destined for himself" (*rang skal sa gter dngos*). Nevertheless, he also revealed a small number of Treasures of the remaining three categories (rediscovered Treasure, actual mind Treasure, and recollected Treasure). For the most part these have been listed in works already translated,[287] but as some details of the revelations are omitted in those sources they will be listed in full in the following sections.

III. Rediscovered Treasure

According to Khyentse, there are two kinds of rediscovered Treasure: 1) those concealed by previous Treasure revealers and now revealed either in actuality or through the power of blessing, and 2) Treasures that appear merely as a transmission. This latter form occurs in cases where the texts of previous revelations still remain but the transmissions of empowerment, reading, explanation, and study have been cut.[288] Chokgyur Lingpa revealed both these forms of rediscovered Treasure.

To the former category belongs the *Heart Essence of Guru Drakpo: The Red Hūṃ* that was revealed through the power of blessing as a Treasure of Sangye Lingpa—Chokgyur Lingpa's past existence.[289] Könchog Gyurme informs us that although many texts were revealed for this cycle they were all subsequently lost.[290] He also mentions another set of revelations not reported by Khyentse, the *Seven Cycles of Pacifying Goddesses* discovered at Drakyang Dzong. These Treasures had originally belonged to the Treasure revealer Lhatsun Ngönmo (eleventh century) and were now re-revealed from the combined efforts of Chokling and Khyentse. Chokgyur Lingpa discovered the yellow scroll and offered it to Khyentse for translation of the coded signs.[291] The dual ownership of this revelation might be why Khyentse does not list the cycle of the *Pacifying Goddesses* as one of Chokgyur Lingpa's Treasures. Interestingly, Kongtrul does list it as an earth Treasure of Chokgyur Lingpa though not as one of the 37 major Treasures.[292] None of these sources give a time or date of revelation, but the colophon for the Treasure text itself states that this was a secret revelation occurring some time in 1868 or early 1869 (a male dragon year).[293]

The cycle of *Mother Tantra that Brings the Ḍākinīs' Secret Onto the Path* represents the second category of rediscovered Treasure. It had originally been revealed by the female Treasure revealer Khandroma Kunga Bum (thirteenth century), whose spiritual transmission now fell to Chokgyur Lingpa.[294] Könchog Gyurme, however, classifies this Treasure as a recollected Treasure and explains that Chokgyur Lingpa remembered this teaching from his past life as Dungtsho Repa the younger (thirteenth century), who was the chief lineage holder of the teachings of *Mother Tantra that Brings the Ḍākinīs' Secret Onto the Path*.[295] Elsewhere Kongtrul explains the reason for this dual classification noting that Chokgyur Lingpa received this teaching twice, as both a rediscovery and a recollection.[296]

IV. Actual Mind Treasure

The only recorded actual mind Treasure is the cycle of *Profound Essence of Tārā* that was revealed on the basis of a vision in which the deity Tārā appeared and spoke to Chokgyur Lingpa.[297] The hagiographies give no detail of time or place, but in a longer commentary to this cycle, Jamgön Kongtrul mentions that the revelation occurred while Chokgyur Lingpa sat in the Lotus Crystal Cave (*padma shel phug*) of Meshö Dzam. It is said that in the early morning, Tārā appeared to him and whispered "excellent, excellent, excellent" into his ear, which provoked the Treasure to "naturally burst forth from the expanse of realization." Later Chokling dictated the teaching to Khyentse, who in turn passed it on to Kongtrul.[298]

V. Recollected Treasure

Having remembered his past existence as Nub Khulungpa Yönten Gyatso (ninth century), Chokgyur Lingpa revealed the Anuyoga instructions of *Vajra Arrayed Scripture* that had originally been taught by Nub Sangye Yeshe (eighth-ninth century) and passed to Nub Khulungpa.[299]

In a similar fashion Chokgyur Lingpa revealed the teaching of *Statement of Nub* together with four ways of reciting the *ru lu* mantra as well as many steps for sacred dances that he likewise recollected from his life as Nub Khulungpa.[300]

Remembering his past existence as Sangye Lingpa, Chokgyur Lingpa revealed instructions on yogic exercise for the *Embodiment of Realization* cycle.[301] Könchog Gyurme further mentions that these revelations merely illustrate Chokgyur Lingpa's recollected Treasures and that many others were revealed without being propagated.[302]

VI. Actual Pure Vision

The most prominent of Chokgyur Lingpa's teachings received as actual pure vision is *Vimalamitra's Guru Practice*.[303] He received this teaching in the practice cave of Vimalamitra at Riwo Wangzhu, where Chokgyur Lingpa met the Indian paṇḍita dwelling in a sphere of light, who offered him instruction.[304]

Another less-known pure vision teaching is a brief sādhana for meditation on Gesar, the legendary Tibetan king. This text is not mentioned in any of the early sources but is included in the latest edition of the *New Treasures* following *Vimalamitra's Guru Practice*. The text does not directly identify itself as a pure vision teaching but rather states that it "burst forth from the expanse of realization of Chokgyur Dechen Lingpa."[305] Elsewhere, however, the contemporary master Dilgo Khyentse (1910-1991) mentions that this teaching indeed belongs to the pure vision category.[306] Khyentse Wangpo also notes that apart from these two teachings many other visions appeared to Chokgyur Lingpa in which he saw various masters, deities, and syllables and heard the dharma being taught.[307]

VII. Hearing Lineage

Chokgyur Lingpa is said to have visited Padmasambhava's celestial realm of the Copper Colored Mountain on several occasions. During these visionary journeys he reportedly received numerous oral instructions but the only recorded teaching is the *Heart Essence of the Profound Meaning of Ati* that he received directly from Padmasambhava.[308] A detailed account of the first visit by Chokgyur Lingpa to the Copper Colored Mountain is given by Könchog Gyurme.[309] The difference between the two divisions of pure vision (actual pure vision and hearing lineage) is subtle, but Khyentse defines the two in the following manner: *actual pure vision* is a vision that, as a result of past aspirations combined with present auspicious circumstances, appears directly to the senses in the ordinarily perceived environment; while a *hearing lineage* involves either actual travel to the pure lands in a subtle body of "wind mind" (*rlung sems*) or a complete cessation of ordinary experience, in which buddhas and deities are met and their instruction is received.[310]

This completes the survey of the seven descents of dharma transmission that flowed through Chokgyur Lingpa as his spiritual heritage. As should be evident by now, the issue of authorship is not always determinable within a fixed schema. This is particularly true when Treasure teachings are traced back to a matrix of inspired personae acting in the world as conveyors of enlightened messages rather than as individual authors acting out of their own creative experience. Furthermore, as we have seen that commentators have often classified various teachings differently, we can conclude that these systems of enumeration are illustrative rather than prescriptive.

Besides the teachings listed within the seven descents, the *New Treasures* contain numerous additional texts attributed to Chokgyur Lingpa though not received as Treasure or in visions. These writings are found throughout the *New Treasures* and cover a wide variety of genres and topics. A common form of writing is a re-arrangement of the original Treasure material to facilitate its application in a ritualized format. Other genres include descriptions of visions and Treasure revelations as well as commentaries on specific Treasures and the three inner yogas.

Finally, we must mention another group of texts: the cycle of *Profound Essence that Embodies the Families of the Three Kāyas*, which was received by Jamyang Khyentse in a vision on December 7, 1870 shortly after the death of Chokgyur Lingpa on June 29, 1870. In this vision Khyentse perceived Chokgyur Lingpa to have taken birth in the Lotus Covered Realm (*padmas khebs pa'i zhing khams*) as the bodhisattva Pemey Nyugu. In this form he appeared to Khyentse and bestowed on him empowerment and instruction. Khyentse later dictated these teachings to Kongtrul, who wrote them down.[311] It is interesting to note in this context that while he was alive the vast majority of teachings produced by Chokgyur Lingpa were attributed to others (such as Padmasambhava) while a teaching that emerged only after he had passed away came to be seen as genuinely his. Such is, however, the nature of the Treasure literature in its relativity of time and matter where common conventions are stretched and molded to fit the special and unique worldview of visionary Buddhism.

Other Authors in the *New Treasures*

Although Chokgyur Lingpa was the dominant force behind the rituals and practices contained in the *New Treasures*, the close relationship he enjoyed with some of the most outstanding masters of nineteenth century, especially Jamyang Khyentse Wangpo and Jamgön Kongtrul, was a major factor for the success and renown of his revelations and the effect of these two exceptional masters on the formation and propagation of the *New Treasures* can hardly be overestimated. Chokgyur Lingpa counts Kongtrul and Khyentse as his foremost teachers, responsible for introducing him to the secret Mantrayāna vehicle and the most profound and essential realization of the nature of mind.[312]

The relationship of these three masters was, however, more than a traditional student-teacher connection. Not only did both Kongtrul and Khyentse also consider Chokling as one of their own teachers, treating him with respect and veneration, they actively assisted him in his career by lending him all the weight of their status and credibility and were the first to publicly recognize Chokling as a genuine Treasure revealer, thus opening other peoples' eyes to his revelations. More significantly, both took an active part in Chokling's revelations, so that several of his Treasures were revealed through the collective effort of all three teachers.

The colophons of the *New Treasures* show ample evidence of the close collaboration among the three masters. No fewer than 74 colophons mention Chokling and Khyentse working together either on the revelation or the establishment of a scripture, while similar collaboration between Chokling and Kongtrul is mentioned on 23 occasions.[313] The nature of the partnership varies from text to text but typically involves Chokling revealing the Treasure and subsequently dictating it to either Khyentse or Kongtrul. Another, somewhat less common form of collaboration is Chokling revealing the yellow scroll and passing it on to Khyentse for both decoding and transcription. At times the colophons are elaborate and descriptive, while at others they may be omitted altogether. The longer colophons often contain useful information regarding authors, dates, places, and circumstances. The colophon for the Amitayus ritual of *Seven Profound Cycles* provides a good example:

> The royal emanation of the prince, the great Treasure revealer, Chokgyur Lingpa revealed this red copper scroll in front of seven karmic friends in his twenty eighth year, at sunrise on the tenth day of the sixth month in the fire male dragon year at the upper practice cave at Yeldrak Namkha Dzö in the middle of the Zalmo range in southern Do Kham—a site where the knower of the three times, the precious one from Oḍḍiyāna, meditated. Later that year, at the waning half of the eleventh month on the perfect day of the festival when ḍākinīs gather, it was established and the scribe, Jamyang Khyentse Wangpo Kunga Tenpey Gyaltsen, a fortunate one who enjoys the nectar of the master's speech, put it into writing. May the lotus feet of the supreme holders of the doctrine remain firm for a hundred aeons and may the profound Treasure teachings spread and increase in all directions, times, and situations and remain for long.[314]

On several occasions all three masters collaborated on the revelation of Treasures, the most famous such event being the revelation of the *Three Sections of the Great Perfection*.[315] There is little doubt that Chokgyur Lingpa's affiliation with Khyentse and Kongtrul was crucial for the recognition and prestige of his Treasures at a time when dubious claims of Treasure revelation abounded to the extent that large parts of the population seem to have been losing faith in the tradition.[316] In spite of such challenges, figures like Khyentse and Kongtrul still commanded sufficient respect that their mere approval of Chokgyur Lingpa would have provided him with instant recognition and credibility. Once these two masters accepted Chokling as their spiritual teacher and actively assisted him in his work, little else was needed for him to gain universal respect and acceptance.

Khyentse and Kongtrul invested considerable effort in assisting Chokgyur Lingpa, and given that they were already well-established religious figures who would have had nothing to gain by supporting Chokgyur Lingpa's career, their words of praise must have come from the heart. Their efforts in propagating the *New Treasures* clearly go beyond mere courtesy and, apart from Chokling himself, Khyentse and Kongtrul are the two most prolific contributors to this collection.[317] At the same time we have no reason to believe that Chokgyur Lingpa was not a charismatic and powerful master in his own right who, once endorsed by the established clergy, must have impressed people with his abundant public display of spiritual powers.

The list of further authors contributing to the *New Treasures* is long and counts several prominent masters of the Kagyu and Nyingma schools, such as both the fourteenth and fifteenth Karmapa hierarchs Thegchok Dorje (1799-1864) and Khakyab Dorje (1871-1922), Dazang Karma Ngedön Tenpa Rabgye, a number of the subsequent Chokling reincarnations, Dilgo Khyentse (1910-1991), and many others.[318] Judging from the list of authors alone, we can see that the *New Treasures* almost immediately gained a prominent following among both Kagyu and Nyingma lineages. In particular, because of the propagation by Kongtrul and the Karmapa hierarchs, the *New Treasures* became popular within the Karma Kagyu School, which up to this day includes several of Chokgyur Lingpa's Treasures in its standard schedule of meditative rituals.[319]

From Chokgyur Lingpa the *New Treasures* have been transmitted in two lineages—a family lineage (*rigs brgyud*) and a religious lineage (*chos brgyud*). These lineages (and the lineages of Chokgyur Lingpa's incarnations) have already been discussed in some detail by Urgyen Tobgyal and Tulku Urgyen and will not be restated here.[320] Tulku Urgyen, in his commentary on the lineage-supplication to the masters of the *New Treasures*, composed by Chokgyur Lingpa's grandson Tersey Tulku with later additions by Dilgo Khyentse, comments on the lineage of masters responsible for transmitting the collected *New Treasures* starting with Jamyang Khyentse Wangpo and Jamgön Kongtrul.[321] This list accounts for the primary lineage holders of Chokgyur Lingpa's Treasures. Extant catalogues of transmission (*thob yig* / *gsan yig*) reveal that in the early days distinct lineages for each Treasure revelation flourished before a uniform collection was compiled by the second Chokling incarnation of the Kela lineage, Könchog Gyurme Tenpey Gyaltsen, who commissioned the woodblocks for the first edition of a collected *New Treasures*.[322] With Chokgyur Lingpa's Treasures gathered into a single body, the various lineages were united and subsequently passed down as a whole collection, thus considerably easing the task of tracing the subsequent genealogy of the transmitted lineage.

This concludes our survey of Chokgyur Lingpa and his Treasure tradition. In the following chapters, we shall look closer at two specific texts from the *New Treasures* sharing a theme that often has been misunderstood and misinterpreted—the so-called wrathful practices of tantric Buddhism, here centering on the deity Vajrakīlaya as contained in the Treasure of the *Seven Profound Cycles* revealed by Chokgyur Lingpa.

Part Three

Practice & Accomplishment of Vajrakīlaya

6

Introduction to the Translations

The deity Vajrakīlaya[323] occupies a special place in the heart of the Nyingma School where he is renowned as the personal deity of Padmasambhava and considered among the most efficacious deities for swiftly attaining enlightenment and, in particular, destroying all obstacles preventing this goal. In this capacity Vajrakīlaya has come to occupy a central role in the Mahāyoga pantheon of the Treasure tradition as well as in the older system of the Transmitted Precepts. Vajrakīlaya is, however, not exclusively a Mahāyoga deity but is practiced in all three inner tantric divisions of the Nyingma School. Although the historical origins of this deity still remain unclear, the last decade has witnessed a considerable increase in studies focusing on Vajrakīlaya. Most notably, the Indian roots for this deity seem no longer in doubt.[324] In Tibet the practice of Vajrakīlaya was initially a concern for the Nyingma and Sakya schools, but over time this deity gained acceptance within all four major Tibetan Buddhist schools.[325]

As for the Vajrakīlaya revelations of Chokgyur Lingpa, three separate cycles, each corresponding to the three sections of Mahāyoga, Anuyoga, and Atiyoga, were revealed and included in the *New Treasures*. The texts presented here belong to the Mahāyoga practice of *Vajrakīlaya of the Seven Profound Cycles*.[326] This cycle in turn belongs to the larger collection of *Seven Profound Cycles* that Chokgyur Lingpa revealed at Karmey Damchen Drak on May 19, 1856.[327] The practice of *Vajrakīlaya of the Seven Profound Cycles* is arranged as the fifth of the seven cycles. Among all Chokgyur Lingpa's Treasures this particular practice has become one of one of the most widely practiced, especially within the Kagyu School where its rituals have become an important part of the yearly ceremonial schedule.[328] Although the practices related to this cycle contain 32 individual texts and span more than 1000 pages, the main Treasure text (*gter zhung*) itself, originally revealed by Chokgyur Lingpa as the foundation for this practice, is relatively brief.[329] The remaining texts in the cycle include a wide variety of genres that each fulfills a specific purpose in the appropriation of the core Treasure. This may include aspects of the practice that are not fully developed in the main Treasure text, such as prayers to the lineage, the refuge ritual, and engendering the awakened mind, or explanatory scriptures intended to initiate the devotee into the practice presented by Padmasambhava in the original Treasure. Finally, several texts have been extracted from the main Treasure text to facilitate easy use and access, and now appear as distinct works on their own.[330]

The texts translated here illustrate only some of the developments that a Treasure traditionally is said to undergo as it passes through various stages of hermeneutical assimilation within a lineage. The first of the texts, the practice manual (*las byang*), is a meditation liturgy, or sādhana (*grub thabs*), belonging to the core Treasure text, while the second, the deity guidance (*lha khrid*), represents the later commentarial tradition. According to tradition, although the practice manual belongs to Padmasambhava's original Treasure, this text is itself an adaptation, made by Padmasambhava, of a much earlier tantra delivered by the buddha Vajrakīlaya himself. As noted earlier, the Treasures are not said to originate in the individual Treasure revealer or even in Padmasambhava but are traced to a dharmakāya realm where a buddha teaches the Treasure-to-be to a devotional retinue that is no different from himself. From this initial teaching the Treasure is then gradually transmitted through various lineages of decreasing spiritual subtlety until it arrives in the physical world inhabited by ordinary men and women. At this stage the Treasure is subject to the skillful modification of awakened propagators, such as Padmasambhava, who present the central message of the Treasure in a practical way that is suited for ordinary devotees unable to accommodate the scope and profundity of the initial tantra.

In the case of *Vajrakīlaya of the Seven Profound Cycles*, the initial root tantra is the *Sacred Tantra of the Great Purpose of the Four Kīlas*. This tantra, whose authorship is credited to the buddha Vajrakīlaya, is a condensed text of a mere five pages but nevertheless functions as the basis for all the other texts contained in the cycle.[331] In this tantra Vajrakīlaya, surrounded by a retinue that he himself has emanated, teaches in a language highly charged with the symbols of semiotic ambiguity so characteristic of tantric literature. The opening reads:

PLACE
STAMP
HERE

SNOW LION
PUBLICATIONS

P.O. Box 6483
Ithaca, NY 14851
USA

Śrī Vajrakumāra namo.

The one who, in the perfect language, is called Youthful Vajra arose from dharmadhātu in the form of wrathful compassion. His terrifying main face was dark blue, his right face white and the left one red. In a terrifying dance he brandished nine- and five-pronged vajras, a mass of fire, a khaṭvāṅga, and a kīla. His infuriated body was adorned with the eight charnel ground ornaments, his wings were spread, and his four legs apart. He appeared in the desire realm, like a bolt of lightning, and liberated Rudra of the desire realm. He blessed the skandhas to be a charnel ground palace and resided within it without moving. He then spoke these words:

HŪṂ
The supremely secret essence of mind,
The blissful vajra of permanent purity,
Is planted in the space of the primordially pure all-ground.
I am indivisible space and awareness.
OṂ VAJRAKĪLI KĪLAYA HŪṂ PHAṬ

Having thus spoken, all intelligent people were liberated into the state of unified space and wisdom. This was the first chapter teaching the kīla of primordially pure awareness from the *Sacred Tantra of the Great Purpose for the Four Kīlas*.[332]

The following three chapters consist of equally brief and esoteric instructions given by Vajrakīlaya on the nature of "the kīla of the drop of great bliss" (*thig le bde ba chen po'i phur pa*), "the kīla of the rescue rope of loving compassion" (*snying rje thugs rje'i dpyang thag gi phur pa*) and "the final perfection of the material kīla" (*rdzas kyi phur pa mthar rdzogs*).[333] Then the text concludes with the following postscript by Padmasambhava:

Samaya. Seal. Seal. Seal. Previously, I Padma have used this tantra of the four kīlas, which is the root section of the 100,000 sections of the *Vidyottamatantra*, as a splendid waist amulet. Now, for the benefit of future generations it is placed and hidden as a terrifying Treasure. May it meet with a worthy being. Profound Seal.

> Strict Seal. Treasure Seal. Hidden Seal. Secret Seal. Secret Seal. Seal. Seal. Seal.[334]

Even though (or perhaps because) the text has prominent origins in the much hailed (but obscure) *Vidyottamatantra* collection, it is directly approachable only by someone of the highest spiritual caliber, as the meditation techniques taught in this tantra are only implicitly expressed within the abstract and symbolic language employed. In this way the Treasure must undergo some form of transformation before it can function as a suitable means for the salvation of an ordinary practitioner. Padmasambhava is crucial in this hermeneutic metamorphosis, for he not only transmits and conceals the original tantric scripture but also composes a method by which an ordinary practitioner can bring its message into actual experience—the sādhana of Vajrakīlaya. In the cycle of *Vajrakīlaya of the Seven Profound Cycles* this text is called the *Practice Manual of Combined Activity* and is the first of the texts translated here.[335] In the root Treasure text, the compilation of which is attributed to Padmasambhava, this ritual is included in an abridged form that allows the aspiring practitioner to assume the identity of Vajrakīlaya through a series of visualizations that transform ordinary experience into a direct perception of enlightenment as formulated in the Mahāyoga scriptures. In this way the genre of sādhana literature manifests as the central genre of Treasure literature as it becomes the medium that represents the direct method for awakening—more so than even the original and fundamental tantra itself.

The second translation is a commentary on Padmasambhava's practice manual explaining the way to perform the prescribed ritual. As such, this commentary is not a Treasure text and does not claim ancient roots. It is entitled *Instructions of the Knowledge-holders—Clearly Arranged Deity Guidance for the Single Form of the Most Secret Kīla of Mind* and was composed by Tsawa Bhande Karma Rinchen Namgyal (nineteenth century), a close student of Chokgyur Lingpa's.[336] In this text Rinchen Namgyal elaborates on the import of the complex meditative visualizations that are only implicitly contained in Padmasambhava's practice manual. Although this ritual is generally classified as a "wrathful" (*khro bo*) practice, Rinchen Namgyal's commentary demonstrates how the sanguinary and seemingly antinomian rituals described in the Vajrakīlaya scriptures should not be seen in isolation from the peaceful achievement of enlightenment.[337] In this way these two Treasure genres illustrate how enlightened intent is processed in the visionary literature from its raw form in the original tantra, through the skilled interpolation of Padmasambhava, into the practical pedagogy of explaining the actual application of the ritual to the ordinary devotee in search of the transformative experience of awakening.

༄༅། ཡང་གསང་ཐུགས་ཀྱི་ཕུར་གཅིག་ལས༔
ལས་བྱང་ཕྲིན་ལས་འདུས་པ་བཞུགས་སོ༔

ཧྲཱི་བཛྲ་ཀུ་མཱ་ར་ན་མོ༔
སྙིང་པོ་ཡེ་ཤེས་དབྱིངས་ནས་བཞེངས༔ རྡོ་རྗེ་གཞོན་ནུར་ཕྱག་བགྱིས་ནས༔
བྱི་ཏོ་ཏ་མ་འབུམ་སྡེ་ཡི༔ སྙིང་པོ་དོན་བསྡུས་ཕྲིན་ལས་བསྡེབས༔

དེ་ལ་སྔོན་འགྲོ་དངོས་གཞི་རྗེས༔ སྔོན་འགྲོ་སྦྱོར་བ་ཚོགས་བསགས་པ༔
དང་པོ་དབེན་པའི་གནས་དག་ཏུ༔ སྐུ་གསུང་ཐུགས་ཀྱི་རྟེན་བཀྲམ་ཞིང༔
དཀྱིལ་འཁོར་བཞེངས་ལ་སྒྲུབ་རྫས་བཀོད༔ ཕྱི་ནང་གསང་བའི་མཆོད་པ་བཤམས༔
རྣལ་འབྱོར་པ་རྣམས་སྟན་བདེར་འདུག༔

གཉིས་པ་གནས་བདག་མཆོད་པ་དང༔ ཕྱོགས་བཅུའི་རྒྱལ་བ་མདུན་དུ་བསྒོམ༔
སྐྱབས་འགྲོ་སེམས་བསྐྱེད་ཡན་བདུན་འབུལ༔ བཀའ་བསྒོ་མཚམས་བཅད་བཛ་ཕྱག་འཚལ༔
སྐུ་གསུང་ཐུགས་ཀྱི་བཤགས་པ་བྱ༔ བསྒྲུབ་པར་དམ་བཅའ་བྱིན་ཆེན་དབབ༔
མཆོད་པ་བྱིན་གྱིས་བརླབས་པ་རྣམས༔ སྤྱི་ཆིངས་བཞིན་དུ་བལྟ་བར་བྱ༔

7

The Practice Manual of Combined Activity

From the Single Kīla of Innermost Mind

Śrī Vajrakumāra namo,
Having paid homage to the Youthful Vajra,
Essential wisdom arising from space,
Here is the combined activity—the condensed essential meaning
Of the hundred thousand sections of the Vidyottamatantra.

For this there are preliminaries, main part, and conclusion.
The preliminaries consist of preparations and gathering the accumulations.
First, in a secluded and pure place,
Arrange the supports of enlightened body, speech, and mind.
Erect the maṇḍala and arrange the practice materials.
Arrange the outer, inner, and secret offerings.
The yogins should then take a pleasant seat.

Second, make offerings to the local lords,
And visualize the conquerors of the ten directions in front of you.
Take refuge, arouse the enlightened mind, and offer the seven branches.
Issue the command, establish the boundaries, and make symbolic salutations.
Perform the apologies of body, speech, and mind.
Make the pledge to practice and bring down great resplendence.
Then consecrate the offering articles.
These should be studied as they appear in the general outlines.

གཉིས་པ་དངོས་གཞི་ཏིང་གསུམ་ནི༔

ཧཱུྃ་

རྡོ་རྗེ་འཁྲོས་པས་ཞི་སྡང་གཅོད༔ མཚོན་ཆ་སྔོན་པོ་འབར་བ་ནི༔

ནམ་མཁའི་དཀྱིལ་ནས་ཐིག་པ་ཤར༔ ཛྙ་ཌྷཱ་ཏུ་ཤྲཱི་ཨཱཿ

མ་ཧཱ་སུ་ཁ་ཨཱཏྨ་ཀོ་ཧཾ༔ བོ་དྷི་ཙི་ཏྟ་ཧཱུྃ༔

ཨཿ ཡཾཿ རཿ སུཾཿ ཀཾཿ ཪཾཿ ཧཱུྃཿ ཏྲིཿ བཾཿ ཏཿ ཧྲཱུྃཿ

ཧཱུྃ་

འབྱུང་བ་ཆེན་པོ་མཁའ་ལས་བབ༔ ཀུན་ཁྱབ་ནམ་མཁའ་སྟོབས་ཆེན་རླུང་༔

ཁྲག་མཚོ་ཞིང་གི་ས་གཞི་གདལ༔ ཀེང་རུས་རི་རབ་མེ་ཆེན་འབར༔

ཧཱུྃ་ལས་བསྐྱུང་བའི་གུར་ཆེན་དང་༔ དུར་ཁྲོད་རབ་འཇིགས་ས་གཞིའི་དབུས༔

སྣ་ཚོགས་པདྨ་རྒྱ་གྲམ་སྟེང་༔ ཧྲཱུྃ་ལས་དུར་ཁྲོད་གཞལ་ཡས་ཁང་༔

ཕྱི་ནི་རིན་ཆེན་རྒྱན་དང་ལྡན༔ ནང་ནི་དུར་ཁྲོད་ཆས་ཀྱིས་བརྗིད༔

བཛྲ་རཏྣ་རྡོ་རྗེའི་བྲག༔ ཧྲཱུྃ་ལས་རིན་ཆེན་འབར་བའི་གདན༔

ལྷ་ཆེན་ཕྱོགས་སྐྱོང་བསྒྱལ་བའི་ཁྲིར༔ ཐབས་ཤེས་ཉི་ཟླ་པདྨའི་སྟེང་༔

དབུས་སུ་ཧཱུྃ་གི་འཕྲོ་འདུ་ལས༔ ཨོཾ་བཛྲ་ཀཱི་ལི་ཀཱི་ལ་ཡ་སརྦ་བིགྷྣཱན་བཾ་ཧཱུྃ་ཕཊ༔

ངང་ཉིད་རྡོ་རྗེ་ཆོས་དབྱིངས་ལས༔ འབར་བའི་ཁྲོ་བོ་མི་བཟད་པ༔

མཐིང་ནག་གཡས་དཀར་གཡོན་དམར་ཞལ༔ དབུ་སྐྲ་སྤྱིར་བཅིངས་རྡོ་རྗེའི་ཏོག༔

Second, the main part of the three samādhis:

HŪṂ
Vajra wrath cuts through aggression.
The blazing blue weapon,
Arises as a drop in the center of space.
DHARMADHĀTU ŚUDDHE ĀḤ
MAHĀ SUKHA ĀTMAKO 'HAṂ BODHICITTA HŪṂ
E YAṂ RA SUṂ KEṂ RAṂ HŪṂ TI BAṂ HA BHRŪṂ

HŪṂ
The great elements descend from space—
The all-pervading sky, the wind of great force,
The ocean of blood, the ground of outstretched human skin,
And Mount Sumeru made of skeletons blazing in a great fire.

From HŪṂ appears the great protective dome
And the supremely terrifying charnel ground.
In the middle of the area, on a multicolored lotus and a vajra cross,
Is a BHRŪṂ from which the charnel ground palace appears.

Outwardly it is adorned with precious stones.
Inwardly it is resplendent with charnel ground ornaments.
Vajrarati is the vajra rock.
From BHRŪṂ appears the blazing jewel seat.

On a throne of the suppressed great gods who guard the directions
Are the sun and moon of means and knowledge, and a lotus.
Centered thereon is a HŪṂ from whose emanation and absorption appears:
OṂ VAJRAKĪLI KĪLAYA SARVAVIGHNĀN BAṂ HŪṂ PHAṬ

From the state of dharmadhātu,
The overwhelming Blazing Wrathful One is present.
He is deep blue with a white face to the right and a red to the left.
His hair is tied on top of his head and has a vajra top-ornament.

ཐོད་སྐམ་རིན་ཆེན་རྩེ་བྲན་ཅན༔ དང་པོས་རྩེ་དགུ་སྡིགས་མཛུབ་ཕྲུར༔
བར་པས་རྩེ་ལྔ་ཁ་ཊྭཱཾ་གསོར༔ འོག་མས་རི་རབ་ཕུར་པ་བསྒྲིལ༔

ཞབས་བཞིས་ལྷ་ཆེན་ཕོ་མོ་མནན༔ གཡོན་བརྐྱངས་དུར་ཁྲོད་ཆས་ཀྱིས་འཇིགས༔
ཡུམ་ཆེན་འཁོར་ལོ་རྒྱས་འདེབས་མ༔ ཨུཏྤལ་དུང་དམར་སྐྱོབ་པས་འཁྱུད༔

མེ་དཔུང་འབར་བའི་ཀློང་དུ་བཞུགས༔ ཕུར་བུའི་ཙྭ་ཙྭ་སྐར་ལྟར་འཁྲུགས༔
ཐུགས་ཀར་འོད་ཀྱི་གུར་ཁྱིམ་ནང༔ རྡོ་རྗེ་སེམས་དཔའ་ཚོན་གང་བའི༔

ཐུགས་ཀར་རིན་ཆེན་ཉི་ཟླའི་སྟེང༔ རྡོ་རྗེའི་ལྟེ་བར་ཧཱུྃ་སྔོན་པོ༔
ཉི་མར་འབྲུ་དགུ་གཡོ་མེད་བསྐོམ༔ རྟ་མགྲིན་པདྨ་འཛིན་པས་སྲུངས༔

ཡབ་ཡུམ་གསང་བ་རྡོ་རྗེ་དང༔ པདྨ་མཉམ་པར་སྦྱོར་བ་ཡི༔
རྗེས་ཆགས་བྱང་སེམས་ཧཱུྃ་ཡིག་བཅུ༔ སྙིང་འོག་ཕྱོགས་མཚམས་འཕྲོས་པ་ལས༔

སྙིང་དུ་ཧཱུྃ་ཀར་སྒྲ་འབྲིན་མ༔ སྤྲུལ་པ་ཕག་དང་ཟིག་བྱུའི་མགོ༔
ཤར་དུ་རྣམ་རྒྱལ་སླིམས་མ་ཉིད༔ སྤྲུལ་པ་སྟག་དང་བྱ་རྒོད་མགོ༔

ཤར་ལྷོ་དབྱུག་སྔོན་སྤྱིར་མོ་ཉིད༔ སྤྲུལ་པ་གཡག་དང་བྱ་རོག་མགོ༔
ལྷོ་ཕྱོགས་གཤིན་རྗེ་དུར་ཁྲོད་བདག༔ སྤྲུལ་པ་ཤ་བ་ཙུག་པའི་མགོ༔

He is adorned with dry skulls and jewel crest ornaments.
The upper hands raise up a nine-pronged vajra and display the threatening posture,
The middle hands wave a five-pronged vajra and a skull staff,
And the lower hands roll the kīla of the central mountain.

His four feet suppress Mahādeva and Mahādevī.
With his wings out-stretched and in the charnel ground attire he is fearsome.
The mighty consort is Dīptacakra,
Who embraces the lord and offers him an utpala flower and a blood-filled skull.

They dwell in a sphere of flaming fires
And kīla sācchas shoot out like stars.
Inside a dome of light in his heart center
Is Vajrasattva, the size of a finger joint.

In whose heart center, on a jewel, sun, and moon,
Is a vajra with a blue HŪṂ in its center.
On the sun, visualize the nine unmoving syllables.
Hayagrīva protects holding a lotus.

Ten bodhicitta HŪṂ syllables from the passion
of the union of the secret vajra
And lotus of the lord and consort
Radiate upwards, downwards, and in-between.

Thereby appears in zenith Hūmkāra and Resounding Vajra,[338]
And the Pig- and Lizard-headed emanations.
To the east are Krodhavijaya and Haughty Vajra,[339]
And the Tiger and Vulture headed emanations.

In the southeast are Nīladaṇḍa and Vajra Claw,[340]
And the Yak- and Crow-headed emanations.
In the southern direction are Yamāntaka and the Lady of the Charnel Ground,[341]
And the Deer- and Owl-headed emanations.

ལྷོ་ནུབ་མི་གཡོ་གཏུན་ཁུང་མ༔ སྤྲུལ་པ་གཟིག་དང་ཁྭ་ཏའི་མགོ༔
ནུབ་ཕྱོགས་རྟ་མགྲིན་གཏུམ་མོ་ནི༔ སྤྲུལ་པ་བྱི་ལ་པུ་ཤུད་མགོ༔

ནུབ་བྱང་འདོད་རྒྱལ་མདའ་སློམས་ནི༔ སྤྲུལ་པ་སྤྱང་ཀི་ཁྲ་ཡི་མགོ༔
བྱང་དུ་བདུད་རྩི་ཀླུང་འབྱིན་ནི༔ སྤྲུལ་པ་སེང་གེ་ཕ་ཝང་མགོ༔

བྱང་ཤར་ཁམས་གསུམ་གསོད་བྱེད་ནི༔ སྤྲུལ་པ་དོམ་དང་སྲེ་མོང་མགོ༔
འོག་ཕྱོགས་སྟོབས་ཆེན་སྐྲུལ་མ་ནི༔ སྤྲུལ་པ་དྲེད་དང་བྱི་བའི་མགོ༔

སྤྲུལ་པའི་ཁྲོ་ཆེན་ཡབ་ཡུམ་རྣམས༔ ཞལ་གསུམ་ཕྱག་དྲུག་མཚོན་ཆ་འཕྱེན༔
དུར་ཁྲོད་ཆས་བརྒྱད་མི་གློང་བཞུགས༔ བསྐལ་པའི་མེ་ལྟར་གསལ་བར་བསྒོམ༔

ཀླ་གམ་ནང་དུ་སྤྲུལ་པའི་སྲས༔ སྐུ་སྟོད་ཁྲོ་བོ་འཛིགས་པ་ལ༔
སྐུ་སྨད་ཕུར་བུ་འབར་བའི་དཔལ༔ མི་དཔུང་དབུས་སུ་སྐར་ལྟར་འཁྲུགས༔

སྒོ་བཞིར་སྤྲུལ་པའི་ཁྲོ་མོ་བཞི༔ ཕྱི་རོལ་དམ་ཅན་ཚོགས་རྣམས་གསལ༔
ཨོཾ་བཛྲ་ཀཱི་ལི་ཀཱི་ལ་ཡ་སརྦ་བིགྷྣཱན་བཾ་ཧཱུྃ་ཕཊ༔

ཧཱུྃ༔
དམ་ཚིག་ཆེན་པོའི་དཀྱིལ་འཁོར་འདིར༔ ཡེ་ནས་དག་པའི་སྐུ་གསུང་ཐུགས༔
ཡེ་ཤེས་ལྷ་ཡི་བདག་ཉིད་དུ༔ བྱིན་གྱིས་བརླབས་ཤིང་དབང་བསྐུར་རོ༔
ཨོཾ་ཨཱཿ ཧཱུྃ༔ ཨོཾ་ཧཱུྃ་ཏྲཱཾ་ཧྲཱིཿ ཨཱཿ ཨོཾ་བཛྲ་ཀཱི་ལི་ཀཱི་ལ་ཡ་ས་པ་རི་ཝཱ་ར་བཛྲ་ས་མ་ཛཿ

In the southwest are Acala and Vajra Mortar,[342]
And the Leopard- and Raven-headed emanations.
In the western direction are Hayagrīva and Fierce Vajra,[343]
And the Cat- and Hoopoe Bird-headed emanations.

In the northwest are Aparājita and Haughty Arrow Vajra,[344]
And the Wolf- and Hawk-headed emanations.
In the north are Amṛtakuṇḍalin and Wind Blowing Vajra,[345]
And the Lion- and Bat-headed emanations.

In the northeast are Trailokyavijaya and Vajra Slayer,[346]
And the Hyena- and Weasel-headed emanations.
In the nadir are Mahābala and Vajra Exhortation,[347]
And the Brown Bear- and Rat-headed emanations.

All the great emanated wrathful lords and consorts
Have three faces, six arms, and hurl weapons;
Possess the eight charnel ground ornaments and dwell in a sphere of fire;
And are visualized as brightly as the fire ending an aeon.

Inside a crescent are the emanated sons.
Their upper bodies are wrathful and frightening,
And the lower bodies are the blazing blades of kīlas.
Amidst a heap of fire they shoot out like stars.

At the four gates are the four emanated wrathful females,
And outside gatherings of oath-bound beings are visualized.
OṂ VAJRAKĪLI KĪLAYA SARVAVIGHNĀN BAṂ HŪṂ PHAṬ

HŪṂ
In this great samaya maṇḍala,
The primordially pure enlightened body, speech, and mind
Are blessed and empowered
As the identity of the five wisdoms.
OṂ ĀḤ HŪṂ OṂ HŪṂ TRĀṂ HRĪḤ ĀḤ OṂ VAJRA KĪLI KĪLAYA SAPARIVĀRA VAJRA SAMĀJAḤ

ཧཱུྃ༔
ཆོས་ཀྱི་དབྱིངས་ཀྱི་ཞིང་ཁམས་ནས༔ སྲིད་པ་རྡོ་རྗེ་ཕུར་བུའི་ལྷ༔
དམ་ཚིག་དཀྱིལ་འཁོར་འདི་ལ་དགོངས༔ ཡེ་ཤེས་དཀྱིལ་འཁོར་འགྲུབ་པར་མཛོད༔
བཛྲ་ས་མ་ཛཿ

ཡེ་ཤེས་དཀྱིལ་འཁོར་མདུན་བྱོན་བསམ༔

ཧཱུྃ༔
སྲིད་པ་ཕུར་བུའི་དཀྱིལ་འཁོར་འདིར༔ ཡེ་ཤེས་ཁྲོ་བོ་གཤེགས་སུ་གསོལ༔
ཡེ་ཤེས་ཁྲོ་བོ་གཤེགས་ནས་ཀྱང་༔ རྟགས་དང་མཚན་མ་བསྟན་པ་དང་༔
ཀཱི་ལ་ཡ་ཡི་དངོས་གྲུབ་སྩོལ༔ ཨོཾ་བཛྲ་ཀཱི་ལི་ཀཱི་ལ་ཡ་ས་པ་རི་ཝཱ་ར་བཛྲ་ས་མ་ཛཿ ཛཿ ཧཱུྃ་བཾ་ཧོཿ

ཧཱུྃ༔
དུར་ཁྲོད་རབ་འཇིགས་གཞལ་ཡས་འདིར༔ རུ་དྲ་བསྒྲལ་བའི་གདན་སྟེང་དུ༔
ཧེ་རུ་ཀ་དཔལ་ལྷ་ཚོགས་རྣམས༔ དགྱེས་ཤིང་བརྟན་པར་བཞུགས་སུ་གསོལ༔ ས་མ་ཡ་ཏིཥྛ་ལྷན༔

ཧཱུྃ༔
ཆོས་ཀྱི་དབྱིངས་ལས་སྐུར་བཞེངས་པའི༔ ཧེ་རུ་ཀ་པའི་ཚོགས་རྣམས་ལ༔
གུས་པའི་ཡིད་ཀྱིས་གར་དང་བཅས༔ བརྒྱང་བསྐུམ་སྟབས་ཀྱིས་ཕྱག་བགྱིའོ༔
ཨ་ཏི་པཱུ་ཧོཿ པྲ་ཏཱི་ཙྪ་ཧོཿ

ཧཱུྃ༔
རུ་དྲ་བསྒྲལ་བ་ལས་བྱུང་བའི༔ མེ་ཏོག་བདུག་སྤོས་མར་མེ་དྲི༔ ཞལ་ཟས་རྐང་གླིང་ཐོད་རྔའི་སྒྲ༔
ཧེ་རུ་ཀ་ཡི་ཚོགས་ལ་འབུལ༔ མ་ཧཱ་པུཥྤེ་དྷཱུ་པེ་ཨཱ་ལོ་ཀེ་གནྡྷེ་ནཻ་ཝི་ཏྱ་ཤབྡ་པཱུ་ཛ་ཧོཿ

HŪṂ
Deities of Vajrakīlaya of Existence!
From the pure realm of the basic space of phenomena
Consider this samaya maṇḍala
And fulfill it as a wisdom maṇḍala!
VAJRA SAMĀJAḤ

Imagine the wisdom *maṇḍala* has arrived before you.

HŪṂ
To this maṇḍala of the kīla of Existence,
Wrathful Wisdom, please arrive!
Wrathful Wisdom, when you arrive,
Manifest the signs and marks
And grant the accomplishments of Kīlaya.
OṂ VAJRAKĪLI KĪLAYA SAPARIVĀRA VAJRA SAMĀJAḤ JAḤ HŪṂ VAṂ HOḤ

HŪṂ
Gatherings of divine glorious herukas!
Please delight and take your seat
In this palace of the utterly terrifying charnel ground
On a cushion of subjugated Rudra
SAMAYA TIṢTHA LHAN

HŪṂ
To the gatherings of herukas
Who manifest in form from the basic space of phenomena,
Dancing with a devoted attitude,
In the dancing posture, I pay homage.
ATI PŪ HOḤ PRATIŚA PŪ HOḤ

HŪṂ
The flowers, incense, lights, perfume,
Food, and sound of bone trumpets and skull drums
That arise from the liberation of Rudra,
I offer to the gathering of herukas.
MAHĀ PUSHPE DHUPE ĀLOKE GHANDHE NAIBIḌYA ŚABDA PŪJĀ HOḤ

ཧཱུྃ༔

གཏི་མུག་བསྒྲལ་བའི་ཤ་ཆེན་དང༔ འདོད་ཆགས་བསྒྲལ་བའི་ཁྲག་ཆེན་དང༔
ཞེ་སྡང་བསྒྲལ་བའི་རུས་ཆེན་རྣམས༔ དཔལ་ཆེན་འཁོར་དང་བཅས་ལ་འབུལ༔
མ་ཧཱ་མཱཾ་ས་རཀྟ་ཀཱིཾ་ནི་རི་ཏི་ཁཱ་ཧི༔

རང་བྱུང་གདོད་ནས་དག་པའི་རྫས༔ རྩ་བརྒྱད་སྟོང་ལ་སྦྱར་བའི་སྨན༔
ཡེ་ཤེས་ལྔ་རྫོགས་སྒྲུབ་པའི་རྫས༔ ཧེ་རུ་ཀ་ཡི་ཚོགས་ལ་འབུལ༔ སརྦ་པཉྩ་ཨ་མྲྀ་ཏ་ཁཱ་ཧི༔

མཆན་དོན་སྦྱར་ཞིང་དངོས་གྲུབ་བླངས༔

ལྷ་ཡི་དམ་ཚིག་རྡོ་རྗེ་ལ༔ རྣལ་འབྱོར་ཅན་གྱི་ཧཱུྃ་བསྒོམ་ཞིང༔
ཨོཾ་ཨཱཿ ཧཱུྃ་གིས་དངོས་གྲུབ་བླངས༔ ལྷ་ལ་ཐིམ་པས་མཆོག་ཐོབ་འགྱུར༔ སརྦ་སིདྡྷི་ཧཱུྃ༔

ཧཱུྃ༔

དུང་ཆེན་སྣོད་དུ་རུ་དྲ་བསྒྲལ༔ དམར་ཆེན་ཐ་རླབས་མཁའ་ལ་འཁྱིལ༔
འཁོར་བ་སྟོང་པའི་རཀྟ་འདི༔ དཔལ་ཆེན་འཁོར་དང་བཅས་ལ་འབུལ༔ མ་ཧཱ་རཀྟ་ཁཱ་ཧི༔

ཧཱུྃ༔

ཛྭ་ལ་འབར་བའི་སྣོད་ནང་དུ༔ སྲིད་གསུམ་བསྒྲལ་བའི་བ་ལིཾ་ཏ༔
དཔལ་གྱི་གཏོར་མ་ཆེན་པོ་འདི༔ ཧེ་རུ་ཀ་ཡི་ཚོགས་ལ་འབུལ༔ མ་ཧཱ་བ་ལིཾ་ཏ་ཁཱ་ཧི༔

ཧཱུྃ༔

ཆོས་དབྱིངས་ཡུམ་གྱི་བྷ་གའི་ཀློང༔ བདེ་ཆེན་ཐབས་ཀྱིས་རྡོ་རྗེས་སྦུབ༔

HŪṂ
To the Great Glorious One and his retinue I offer
The great flesh of liberated dullness,
The great blood of liberated desire,
And the great bones of liberated anger.
MAHĀMĀṂSA RAKTA KIṂ NI RI TI KHĀHI

The self-existing, primordially pure substance
Is the medicine applied to the eight thousand channels.
The substance that perfects the five wisdoms
I offer to the gathering of herukas.
SARVA PANCA AMṚTA KHĀHI

Combine the words and the meaning and receive the accomplishments.

The yogin visualizes the HŪṂ
On the samaya vajra of the tongue
And receives the accomplishments with OṂ ĀḤ HŪṂ.
By dissolving into the tongue they become supreme attainment.
SARVA SIDDHI HŪṂ

HŪṂ
Rudra is liberated in the vessel of the human skull.
The deep red waves wash through the sky.
This rakta that empties saṃsāra
I offer to the Great Glorious One and his retinue.
MAHĀ RAKTA KHĀHI

HŪṂ
Inside the vessel of the blazing bhanda,
Is the baliṇgta of the liberated threefold existence.
This glorious great bali
I offer to the gathering of herukas.
MAHĀ BALIṄGTA KHĀHI

HŪṂ
The expanse of the bhaga of the dharmadhātu consort
Is opened by the vajra through the method of great bliss.

བདེ་སྟོང་འདུ་འབྲལ་མེད་པ་འདི༔ དཔལ་ཆེན་འཁོར་དང་བཅས་ལ་འབུལ༔
མ་ཧཱ་སུ་ཁ་ཤཱུནྱ་མོ་ཀྵ་པཱུ་ཛ་ཧོ༔

ཧཱུྃ་
ང་ལ་བར་ཆད་བྱེད་པའི་བགེགས༔ སྣའམ་འོན་ཏེ་བདུད་ཀྱང་རུང་༔
ཨེ་ཡི་དཀྱིལ་འཁོར་ཆེན་པོར་བསྒྲལ༔ དཔལ་ཆེན་འཁོར་བཅས་ཞལ་དུ་བསྟབ༔ མ་ཧཱ་རཀྟ་ཁཱ་ཧི༔

འཇིགས་པའི་དབྱངས་དང་རོལ་མོ་ཡིས༔

ཧཱུྃ་
ཡེ་ཤེས་སྐུ་ནི་གཟི་བརྗིད་འབར༔ གྲགས་སྟོང་གསུང་གིས་འཇིག་རྟེན་གཡོ༔
སྙིང་རྗེའི་ཐུགས་ཀྱིས་སྟོང་གསུམ་བསྒྲལ༔ ཧེ་རུ་ཀ་ལ་ཕྱག་འཚལ་བསྟོད༔

མི་དགེ་བཅུ་བསྒྲལ་ཁྲོ་ཆེན་བཅུ༔ ཕར་ཕྱིན་བཅུ་ལས་བཞེངས་པའི་ཡུམ༔
ཐབས་ཤེས་སྐུ་སྦྲུལ་ཟ་གསོད་ཚོགས༔ ཕྱོགས་བཅུའི་ལྷ་ལ་ཕྱག་འཚལ་བསྟོད༔

བསད་ཅིང་མནན་པ་མ་ཡིན་ཏེ༔ ཐུགས་རྗེའི་ཐབས་ཀྱིས་བསྒྲལ་བའི་ཕྱིར༔
སྙིང་རྗེ་འདུས་པའི་ཀཱི་ལ་ཡ༔ སྲས་མཆོག་རྣམས་ལ་ཕྱག་འཚལ་བསྟོད༔

དཔལ་གྱི་སྲུན་ཐུར་ཁས་བླངས་པའི༔ ཚད་མེད་རྣམ་བཞིའི་སྒོ་མ་བཞི༔
ཕྱི་འཁོར་སྐྱོང་བ་ཕོ་ཉའི་ཚོགས༔ ཕྲིན་ལས་སྒྲུབ་ཕྱིར་ཕྱག་འཚལ་བསྟོད༔

དེ་ནས་ཛཔ་ཀྱི་རིམ་པ་ནི༔

ཨོཾ་བཛྲ་ཀཱི་ལི་ཀཱི་ལ་ཡ་ཧཱུྃ་ཕཊ༔

This empty bliss free from meeting and parting,
I offer to the Great Glorious One and his retinue.
MAHĀMUDRĀ BHAÑJA MOKSHA PŪJĀ HOḤ

HŪṂ
The obstructing spirits who create obstacles for me,
Whether they are gods or demons,
Are liberated in the great maṇḍala of the E
And offered as food to the Great Glorious One and his retinue.
MAHĀ RUDRA KHA HI

Sing the following in a fearsome tune accompanied by cymbals:

HŪṂ
Their wisdom body is ablaze with majestic brilliance.
Their speech of empty sound moves the world.
Their compassionate mind liberates the one billion worlds.
I salute and praise the herukas.

The ten Great Wrathful Ones liberate the ten unvirtuos actions.
The consorts arise from the ten pāramitās.
The gatherings of Devourers and Slayers are bodily emanations of means and knowledge.
I salute and praise the deities of the ten directions.

Killing while not being suppressed
Is done in order to liberate with the means of compassion.
I salute and praise the Supreme Sons
Of Kīlaya who embodies compassion.

In front of the Glorious One the four female gate keepers
Took the pledge of the four boundless contemplations.
The gathering of messengers protects the outer perimeter.
I salute and praise them in order to accomplish the activities.

Now follows the stages of the recitation:

OṂ VAJRAKĪLI KĪLAYA HŪṂ PHAṬ

དྲག་པོ་སྤྱི་དྲིལ་སྙིང་པོ་ནི༔

ཨོཾ་བཛྲ་ཀཱི་ལི་ཀཱི་ལ་ཡ་སརྦ་བིགྷྣཱན་བཾ་ཧཱུྃ་ཕཊ༔

སྐབས་སུ་འཇབ་བསྟོད་མཆོད་པ་བྱ༔ རྗེས་ཀྱི་བྱ་བ་ཚོགས་བསྐང་དང༔
བསྒྲལ་བསྡུབ་ལོངས་སྤྱོད་ལྷག་མ་གཏང༔ བསྐུལ་ཞིང་ཚད་མདོ་བརྟན་མ་སྐྱོང༔
བྲོ་བརྡུང་ཚེ་འགུགས་མཆོད་བསྟོད་བསྡུ༔ ལྷར་ལྷུང་སྨོན་ལམ་བཀྲ་ཤིས་དང༔
རྒྱུན་སྤྱོད་སྤྱི་ཆིངས་བཞིན་དུ་བྱ༔

ས་མ་ཡ་རྒྱ་རྒྱ་རྒྱ༔

སྤྲུལ་པའི་གཏེར་ཆེན་མཆོག་གྱུར་གླིང་པས་ཀརྨའི་དམ་ཅན་བྲག་ནས་སྤྱན་དྲངས་པའི་གནམ་ལྕགས་ཕུར་སྒྲོམ་རྒྱ་མདུད་གྲུ་གསུམ་ནང༌། ལྕགས་ཀྱི་བྱང་བུ་གུ་རུའི་ཕྱག་བྲིས་ལ་ངོ་མཚར་བའི་བཀོད་པ་དང་བཅས་ལེགས་པར་ཕབ་པའི་ཡི་གེ་པ་ནི་པྲཛྙཱ་ཛྙཱ་ཛའོ།།

The essence of the general wrathful recitation is:

OṂ VAJRAKĪLI KĪLAYA SARVAVIGHNĀN BAṂ HŪṂ PHAṬ

At times, perform praises and offerings of recitation.
The ensuing activities are: the feast, the mending,
Enjoying the liberation offering, giving residuals,
Requesting, issuing commands, nurturing the Tenma goddesses,
Performing dances, summoning life, and completion by offerings
and praises.
Then, arise as the deity, make aspirations, and benedictions,
And perform the daily activities according to the general outlines.

Samaya. Seal. Seal. Seal.

At the Karma Vow-holders' Rock the incarnated great Treasure revealer Chokgyur Lingpa revealed a meteorite kīla chest marked with a triangular seal. Inside was an iron plate inscription in the handwriting of the guru containing this wonderful arrangement. The scribe for the proper decoding was Prajñā Dhvaja.

༄༅། །ཡང་གསང་ཐུགས་ཀྱི་ཕུར་གཅིག་གི་ལྷ་ཁྲིད་གསལ་བར་བཀོད་པ་
རིག་པ་འཛིན་པའི་ཞལ་ལུང་ཞེས་བྱ་བ་བཞུགས་སོ།།

ན་མོ་ཤྲཱི་གུ་རུ་བཛྲ་ས་ཏྭ་ཡེ།
བདེ་སྟོང་དབྱེར་མེད་བླ་མ་རྡོ་རྗེ་སེམས། །འབར་བའི་སྐུར་བཞེངས་བཛྲ་ཀུ་མ་ར། །
ཡབ་ཡུམ་སྲས་དང་སྤྲུལ་འཁོར་བཅས་པ་ལ། །གུས་པས་འདུད་དོ་བཀའ་གནང་མཐུ་ནུས་སྩོལ། །
བྱང་ཆུབ་སྒྲུ་གུ་བསྐྲེད་མཛད་སྙིང་རྗེའི་སྤྲིན། །གཟུང་འཛིན་རྣམ་རྟོག་འཇོམས་པ་རྡོ་རྗེའི་ཆར། །
མ་རུང་དགྲ་སྡེ་སྡིག་པ་དུས་མཐའི་ཤུགས། །ཕྲིན་ལས་འདུས་པ་དཔལ་ཆེན་ཧེ་རུ་ཀའི། །
ཚིག་ཁྲིད་རིག་པ་འཛིན་པའི་ཞལ་ལུང་འདི། །སྐལ་ལྡན་ཐར་འདོད་རྣམས་ཀྱི་དྭངས་བས་ལོངས། །

དེ་ཡང་སྐུ་བཞི་ཡེ་ཤེས་ལྔའི་བདག་ཉིད། །ཁྱབ་བདག་རྡོ་རྗེ་སེམས་དཔའི་གོ་འཕང་ཆེ་འདི་ཉིད་ལ་འགྲུབ་ཅིང་། ས་ལམ་གྱི་བར་ཆད་ཐམས་ཅད་ཆར་གཅོད་པར་བདེ་གཤེགས་ཐམས་ཅད་ཀྱི་ཕྲིན་ལས་འདུས་པ་དཔལ་ཆེན་རྡོ་རྗེ་གཞོན་ནུའི་ཏིང་ངེ་འཛིན་བསྒོམ་པར་བྱ་སྟེ། དེ་ལའང་རྒྱུད་དང་སྒྲུབ་ཐབས་མཐའ་ཡས་པ་ཞིག་མཆིས་པ་ལས་འདིར་བསྟན་དང་འགྲོ་བ་ཡོངས་ཀྱི་དཔུང་གཉེན། མཁས་དང་གྲུབ་པ་ཀུན་གྱི་གཙུག་གི་ནོར་བུ། སྤྲུལ་པའི་གཏེར་ཆེན་རྒྱ་མཚོ་ཡོངས་ཀྱི་འཁོར་ལོས་སྒྱུར་བ་

8

Instructions of the Knowledge-holders

Clearly Arranged Deity Guidance for the Single Form of the Most Secret Kila of Mind

Namo Śrī Guru Vajrasattvāye,
Guru Vajrasattva—indivisible bliss and emptiness—
Arises in the blazing form of Vajrakumāra.
To the lord, the consort, and the offspring, together with the emanated retinue,
I bow down with devotion—bestow your permission, power and capacity.
The clouds of compassion make the sprout of enlightenment grow.
Vajra rain destroys dualistic thought.
The intensity of the fire at the final age burns the hordes of vicious enemies.
This instruction of the knowledge-holders, the ritual guidance
To the Great Glorious Heruka who is the embodiment of activity,
Should be applied with delight by those fortunate ones seeking liberation.

That is, one should meditate on the samādhi of the great glorious Vajrakumāra that accomplishes, in this very life, the identity of the four kāyas and the five wisdoms, the state of the pervasive lord Vajrasattva, thoroughly eliminates all obstacles to the levels and paths, and embodies the activity of all sugatas. Regarding this, among the limitless tantras and sādhanas in existence, here is the essence of the ocean-like profound teachings revealed as Treasure by he who is a protector of the dharma and all beings, the crown jewel of all learned and accomplished ones, and the universal monarch of all incarnated

མཆོག་གྱུར་བདེ་ཆེན་ཞིག་པོ་གླིང་པ་ཕྲིན་ལས་འགྲོ་འདུལ་རྩལ་གྱིས་གཏེར་ནས་སྤྱན་དྲངས་པའི་ཟབ་ཆོས་རྒྱ་མཚོ་ལྷ་བུའི་སྙིང་པོ། གྲུབ་པའི་སློབ་དཔོན་ཆེན་པོ་པདྨ་སཾ་བྷ་ཝའི་ཐུགས་དམ་ཟབ་པ་སྐོར་བདུན་གྱི་ནང་ཚན། ཕྲིན་ལས་ཀྱི་ཟབ་པ་ཡང་གསང་ཐུགས་ཀྱི་ཕུར་གཅིག་གི་ཁྲིད་ཀྱི་རིམ་པ་གསལ་བར་བཀོད་པ་ལ་གསུམ། བསྐྱེད་པ་སྐུ། བཟླས་པ་གསུང་། ཏིང་ངེ་འཛིན་ཐུགས་ཀྱི་རྣལ་འབྱོར་རོ། །

དང་པོ་ལ་རྣམ་པ་གསལ་བ།

རྣམ་དག་དྲན་པ། ང་རྒྱལ་བརྟན་པ་སྣེ་གསུམ་གྱི་དང་པོ་ཏིང་ངེ་འཛིན་གསུམ་གྱིས་གཞི་བཟུང་བར།

དེ་བཞིན་ཉིད་ཀྱི་ཏིང་ངེ་འཛིན་ནི། ཆོས་ཉིད་སྐྱེ་མེད་ངོ་རྗེས་ཕར་མཚན་མའི་རྣམ་རྟོག་ཀུན་འཇོམས་ལ། ཚུར་གང་གིས་ཀྱང་མི་བཤིག་པ། ཆོས་རྣམས་དངོས་པོ་སྟོང་ཞིང་བདག་མེད་པ་མཉམ་ཉིད་དུ་བསྒོམ་པའོ། །ཀུན་སྣང་ནི། དོན་དམ་དེ་བཞིན་ཉིད་མ་རྟོགས་པའི་འཁོར་བ་ལ་སྙིང་རྗེའི་རྩལ་གཡོས་ཏེ། ཁྲོས་པ་ལྟར་སྣང་བའི་རིག་པའི་ཡེ་ཤེས་ཀྱིས་ཞེ་སྡང་གཙོ་བོར་གྱུར་པའི་ཉོན་མོངས་པའི་ལས་རྒྱུན་གཅོད་པའོ། །རྒྱུ་ནི། དེ་ལྟ་བུའི་སྟོང་ཉིད་སྙིང་རྗེ་དབྱེར་མེད་མཚོན་པའི་ཡི་གེ་ཧཱུྃ་ཆེན་པོ་འོད་འབར་བ། ནམ་མཁའ་ནས་རང་བྱུང་ཐིག་ལེའི་རྣམ་པར་ཤར་བའོ། །དེ་ཡང་རིམ་པ་བཞིན། དྷརྨ་དྷཱ་ཏུ་ཛྙཱ་ཨཱཿ ནི་ཆོས་ཀྱི་དབྱིངས་སྤྲོས་པའི་མཚན་མ་ལས་འདས་པའི་ཆོས་ཉིད་རྣམ་པར་དག་པ་དབྱིངས་ཡེ་ཤེ་བཞིན་པ་ཀུན་ཏུ་བཟང་མོའི་དཀྱིལ་འཁོར། མ་ཧཱ་སུ་ཁ་ཨཱཏྨ་ཀོ྅ཧཾ། སྟེ། ཐབས་བདེ་བ་ཆེན་པོའི་བདག་ཉིད་ཡེ་ཤེས་ལྷུན་གྱིས་གྲུབ་པ་ཀུན་ཏུ་བཟང་པོའི་དཀྱིལ་འཁོར། བོ་དྷི་ཙིཏྟ་ཧཱུྃ་ནི། བདེ་སྟོང་གཉིས་མེད་སྤྲུས་བདེ་བ་ཆེན་པོ་རྩ་བ་བྱང་ཆུབ་སེམས་ཀྱི་དཀྱིལ་འཁོར་རྒྱུའི་ཧཱུྃ་ཡིག་ལས་འཕྲོས་པའི་རྟེན་འབྱུང་བའི་རིམ་བརྩེགས་གཞལ་ཡས་ཁང་གདན་དང་བཅས་པ་དང་། བརྟེན་པ་ལྷ་བསྐྱེད་པ་གཉིས། དང་པོ་ནི། རྒྱུའི་ཡི་གེ་ལས་ཨེ་མཐིང་ནག་ཆད་པ་ལས། ཀུན་ཁྱབ་ཀྱི་ནམ་མཁའ་མཐིང་ནག་གྲུ་གསུམ་རྒྱ་ཚད་འབྱམས་ཀླས་པ། དེའི་སྟེང་དུ་ཡཾ་ལྗང་ནག་ལས་སྟོབས་ཆེན་རླུང་གི་དཀྱིལ་འཁོར་རྒྱ་གྲམ་གྱི་དབྱིབས་ཅན་སྟོང་ཆེན་བར་མའི་མཐའ་དང་མཉམ་པ། དེའི་སྟེང་དུ་ར་ཡིག་དམར་ནག་ལས་ཁྲག་མཚོ་དམར་རླུམ་འཁྱིལ་བ།

great Treasure revealers—Chokgyur Dechen Shigpo Lingpa Thinley Drodul Tsal. Within the divisions of the *Seven Profound Cycles*—the realization of the accomplished Padmasambhava—the profound activity is the *Single Form of the Most Secret Kīla of Mind.* A clear arrangement of the gradual instructions for this consists of the following three topics: the physical yoga of creation, the verbal yoga of recitation, and the mental yoga of samādhi.

The Physical Yoga of Creation

The first of these is divided into clear appearance, recollection of purity, and stable pride. In the first of these the foundation is laid with the three samādhis.

Clear Appearance

The samādhi of suchness is to train in the equality that all phenomena and objects are empty and without a self—the unborn vajra of the natural state which outwardly annihilates all conceptual thoughts and inwardly is utterly indestructible.

The all-illuminating samādhi is to be moved by the power of compassion towards those in saṃsāra who do not realize the suchness of the ultimate and to cut the karmic continuity of disturbing emotions, headed by anger, with seemingly wrathful awareness-wisdom.

As for the seed samādhi, the seed is a radiant great blue letter HŪṂ that arises from space in the form of a self-existing sphere symbolizing this kind of indivisible emptiness and compassion. Then follows gradually: DHARMADHĀTU ŚUDDHE ĀḤ, which is the basic space of phenomena, the perfectly pure natural state beyond mental constructs, primordial basic space as it is, the maṇḍala of Samantabhadrī. MAHĀ SUKHA ĀTMAKO 'HAṂ is the identity of the means of great bliss, spontaneously present wisdom, the maṇḍala of Samantabhadra. BODHICITTA HŪṂ is the great-bliss-son of non-dual bliss and emptiness, the root maṇḍala of the awakened mind. From the HŪṂ seed syllable radiate the support—the gradually piled elements, the palace, and the seats—and the supported—the deities.

From the seed syllable radiates a dark blue E, from which the all-pervading dark blue space arises as a triangle of infinite dimensions. On top of that is a dark green YAṂ, from which the forceful wind maṇḍala arises in the shape of a cross, equal to the limits of the million-fold universe. On this is a dark red RA syllable, from which the red ocean of blood appears, round and swirling.

དེ་སྟེང་སྦུ་སེར་ནག་ལས་ཞིང་ཆེན་བརྡལ་བའི་ས་གྲུ་བཞིར་མཉམ་པ། དེ་སྟེང་དུ་ཀཾ་སྔོན་པོ་ལས། ཀེང་རུས་འཛོམས་ཐབས་སུ་བརྩེགས་པའི་རི་རབ་བང་རིམ་བཞི་པ། རཾ་དམར་པོ་ལས་ཡེ་ཤེས་ཀྱི་མེ་དཔུང་འབར་བའི་དབུས། ཧཱུྃ་སྔོན་པོ་ལས་མཚོན་ཆ་རྣམ་ལྔའི་སྲུང་བའི་གུར་ཁང་ནང་འཁོར་ལོ་རྩིབས་བཅུའི་སྟེང་དུ་ཧཱུྃ་ཀཱ་ར་སོགས་ཁྲོ་ཆེན་བཅུ་དང་། སྤྲུལ་པའི་ཁྲོ་ཚོགས་དང་མཚོན་ཆ་འཚུབ་པས་བར་མེད་དུ་གཏམ་པའི་ནང་དུ་ཧི་དམར་སྐྱ་ལས་དུར་ཁྲོད་ཆེན་པོ་བརྒྱད། དེ་ཡང་གལ་པོ་ལས། བསིལ་བ་ཚལ་དང་སྐྲུ་ལ་རྫོགས། ཧེ་ཆེན་རོལ་དང་གསང་ཆེན་རོལ། །པདྨ་བརྩེགས་དང་ཡ་མ་ཁ། །ཁྲུ་བྲུག་གློང་དང་མངོན་རྫོགས་ཡིན། །ཞེས་གསུངས་པའི་ནང་དུ། བདེ་བྱེད་བརྩེགས་ལ་སོགས་པའི་མཆོད་རྟེན་བརྒྱད། དེར་གནས་པའི་ཧཱུྃ་ཀཱ་ར་སོགས་གྲུབ་ཆེན་བརྒྱད། ཀེང་རུས་རབ་ཏུ་འབར་སོགས་མེ་ཕུང་བརྒྱད། རབ་ཏུ་འཁྲུགས་པ་ལ་སོགས་པའི་འཐོར་རླུང་བརྒྱད། ཛཾ་བུ་པ་ལ་སོགས་ཤིང་བརྒྱད། དེར་གནས་པའི་ཞིང་སྐྱོང་བརྒྱད། ཏ་ཏར་གཏོད་པའི་རོ་ལང་བརྒྱད་དང་བཅས་པའི་དུར་ཁྲོད་ཕྱོགས་བཞི་པདྨ་དང་། མཚམས་བཞི་གཞུ་ཡི་དབྱིབས་ལྟ་བུའི་བར་མཚམས་མཚོ་བརྒྱད་ལ་ཀླུ་ཆེན་བརྒྱད་བཅས་གནས་སོ། །དུར་ཁྲོད་དང་པདྨའི་བར་འཇིག་རྟེན་པའི་འཁོར་ཡུག་ཡིན་པས་ཀླུམ་སྐོར་ཁོན་དང་། རྒྱ་ཆུང་ངུ་རང་ནི་ཡོད་པར་སློབ་དཔོན་དག་བཞེད་པར་མི་མཛད་དོ། །དེ་དབུས་པཾ་དམར་པོ་ལས་སྣ་ཚོགས་པདྨ་འདབ་མ་འབུམ·····སྙེག་རྡོར་བཞིན་གཞུང་ལྟར། ལྡན་གྱི་སྟེང་དུ། ཏ་ལྗང་གུ་ལས་རྡོ་རྗེ་རྒྱ་གྲམ་ར་བཅུ་གཉིས་པ། ཤར་དཀར་སོགས་ཕྱོགས་མདོག་ལྟེ་བ་ལེབ་ཆགས་གྲུ་བཞི་མཐིང་ནག་གི་སྟེང་། ཧཱུྃ་ཁ་དོག་ལྗ་ལྡན་ལས་གཞལ་ཡས་ཁང་གཉིས་རིམ་གྱི། ཕྱི་རིན་པོ་ཆེའི་ནང་ནས་མཐིང་དཀར་སེར་དམར་ལྗང་བའི་བརྩེགས་པ་སྣ་ལྔ་ལ་རྩ་བར་འདོད་སྣམ་དམར་པོ་མཆོད་ལྷས་བརྒྱན་པ། སྒོ་བཞིར། ཏ་རྐང་། ཆུ་སྲིན། སྒྲོམ། ཟར་ཚག སྒྲོས་འཕྱང་། ཆུན་འཕྱང་། ཤར་བུ། ཁྲུང་མགོ་སྟེ་ཏ་བབ་སྣམ་བུ་བརྒྱད་དང་ལྡན་པ། རྩེར། ཕ་གུ། བྲེ་ཕུལ། དྲ་བ་ཤར་བུ། མདའ་ཡབ་སོགས་རྒྱན་གྱིས་མཛེས་པའི་ནང་ཀ་བ་བརྒྱད་ཀྱིས་བཏེགས་པའི་གདུང་འཁོར་མོའི་སྟེང་དུ་རིན་པོ་ཆེའི་ཕ་གུ་བརྩེགས་པའི་བུམ་པའི་དབྱིབས་ལྟ་བུ་དང་།

On top of that is a dark yellow SUṂ, from which arises the square ground of an outstretched human skin. On top of that is a blue KEṂ from which appears the four levels of the Sumeru mountain made of stacked skeletons. From a red RAṂ emerges a blazing mass of fire of the five wisdoms. In the middle of this, from a blue letter HŪṂ, appears a protection dome containing the five kinds of weapons. Inside is a ten-spoked wheel on which are the ten wrathful ones such as Hūmkāra and the gatherings of wrathful emanations who fill the entire space swirling their weapons. Within this, from a pink letter TI, the eight great charnel grounds manifest. According to the *Galpo Tantra* they are:

> The Cool Grove and Perfection in Form,
> Play of Great Bliss and Play of the Great Secret,
> Lotus Mound and Yamakha,
> Expanse of the Cuckoo Bird and Complete Perfection.

Inside the charnel grounds are eight stūpas, such as the Enchanting Mound; the eight mahāsiddhas living there, such as Hūmkāra; the eight bonfires, such as the Fully Blazing Skeleton; the eight hurricanes, such as the Most Turbulent; the eight trees, such as the jambu tree; the eight local guardians living there as well as the eight zombies with hostile laughter. In between the charnel grounds are eight oceans where the eight great nāgas live. The four oceans in the cardinal directions are shaped like lotuses and the four in the intermediate directions are shaped like bows. Since what is between the charnel grounds and the lotuses is the enclosure of the universe, the teachers only mention that it is round without stating its measure.[348]

In the middle of this is a red PAṂ from which arises a multicolored lotus with 100,000 petals (as explained in the scriptures of Līlāvajra). On top of that, from a green HA, appears a double vajra with 12 prongs. It has the colors of the cardinal directions, such as being white in the east, and the middle is flat, square, and dark blue. On top of that is a five colored BHRUṂ from which a two storied palace arises. On its outside are five layers of blue, white, yellow, red, and green precious stones. Its base is a red protruding foundation that is ornamented with offering gods. At the four gates are the eight architraves—the horse ankle, lotus, casket, lattice, cluster ornament,[349] garlands, rain spouts, and garuda head. The gates are beautified at the top[350] with ornaments such as the border, top border, rainspout, web, and ledge. Inside eight pillars support the encircling beam on top of which are jewel borders shaped like a vase. On top of this is a feature which is like a square

དེའི་སྟེང་དུ་གྲུ་བཞི་གྲི་འདྲ་བའི་སྟེང་པདྨ་ལ་གནས་པའི་ཆོས་ཀྱི་འཁོར་ལོ་ཏོག་དང་བཅས་པ་ཕྱི་དབྱིབས་མཆོད་རྟེན་ལྷ་བུའོ། །ནང་ནི་ཐོད་པ་སྐམ་རློན་རྙིང་གསུམ་བརྩེགས་པ་གནམ་ལྕགས་ཀྱི་གཟེར་གྱིས་བསྡམ་སྟེ། ཁྲག་ཞག་གི་འདམ་གྱིས་བརྒྱན་པར་ཤ་ཆེན་གྱི་སྤུམ་བུ་ལ་དུར་ཁྲོད་ཀྱི་མཆོད་པས་མཛེས་པ། རྩེར་མགོ་བོའི་ཕ་གུ། ཉི་ཟླའི་མཐོང་སྐར། རྐང་ལག་མཆོག་མ་བསྒྲོལ་བའི་གྲི་ཕྱུལ་ལ། སྦྲུ་མའི་སྐ་རགས་དང་། རུས་པའི་དྲྭ་བ། རྐང་ལག་གི་ཤར་བུ། རྒྱལ་ཚིག་གི་མདའ་ཡབ། ཞིང་གི་རྒྱལ་མཚན། ནང་ནས་ཚངས་པའི་གདུང་མ་དང་། སྦྲུ་སྐར་གྱི་དྲལ་ཕྱམ། ཀླུ་བརྒྱད་ཀྱི་ཀ་གདན། ལྷ་བརྒྱད་ཀྱི་ཀ་བ། གཟའ་བརྒྱད་ཀྱི་ཀ་ཞུ་ཅན། ཞིང་ཆེན་གྱི་ལྤགས་པས་ཐོག་བཀབ་སྐེ་རུ་དྲའི་མགོ་བོ་དང་། ཙཎྜའི་ཏོག་གིས་མཛེས་པ། ཞིང་ལྤགས་ཀྱི་སྒོ་ལེབ་དང་། སྦྲུལ་ནག་གི་སྐྱེས་བུ་བཙུག་པ་སོགས་དུར་ཁྲོད་ཀྱི་རྒྱན་གྱིས་བརྟེན་པའི་ནང་དུ་ཤ་ཆེན་གྱི་གྲུ་ཆད་སྤྱུག་ནག་རོ་ཚལ་གྱིས་བརྒྱན་པའི་སྟེང་དུ། ཧཱུྃ་ལས་རིན་ཆེན་མཐིང་ནག་ཆ་བརྒྱད་པའི་ལྟེ་བ་ཐོད་པའི་རབ་རྐྱང་པ་ཆ་ཕྲན་གྱི་ཚད་ཅན་གྱི་ཀླུམ་པོར་བསྐོར་བའི་དབུས་སུ། ཨེ་མཐིང་ནག་རྡོ་རྗེའི་འགྲེང་བུའི་དཔག་པ། བཛྲ་ར་ཀྲི་སྟེ་རྡོ་རྗེའི་བྲག་ཆེན་ཉི་ཟླ་པདྨ། གཙོ་བོ་ལ་ལྷ་ཆེན་པོ་ཁ་སྦྲུབ་ནག་པོ་རྩེ་གསུམ་ཐོད་ཁྲག་སྟག་ཤམས་ཅན། མོ་དམར་པོ་གན་རྐྱལ་རྩེ་གསུམ་ཐོད་ཁྲག་གཟིག་ཤམས་ཅན། ཁྲོ་བཅུར། ཤར་གྱི་ཐོད་རའི་རྩ་བར། ལྷ་ཚངས་པ། ཤར་གྱི་རིན་པོ་ཆེའི་འཛུམ་སྟེང་། དྲི་ཟ། ལྷོར་གཤིན་རྗེ། ནུབ་ཏུ་ཀླུ་དབང་། བྱང་དུ་གནོད་སྦྱིན། ཤར་ལྷོར་མེ་ལྷ། ལྷོ་ནུབ་ཏུ་སྲིན་པོ། ནུབ་བྱང་དུ་རླུང་ལྷ། དབང་ལྡན་དུ་བགེགས་རྒྱལ། ནུབ་ཀྱི་ཐོད་རའི་རྩ་རས་བདག་རྣམས་རང་རང་གི་ཆུང་མ་དང་བཅས་བྱི་ཆིངས་སུ་བསྡོལ་བ། ཟླ་གམ་ནང་དུ་དགྲ་བགེགས་བསྡོལ་བའི་གདན་ལྷ་གྲངས་དང་མཉམ་པ་སོགས་སོ། །ལར་གཞལ་ཡས་ཁང་དང་། གཙོ་འཁོར་གྱི་གདན་འདི་རྣམས་ཀྱི་ཐད། མན་ངག་དང་ཁྲུད་ཆོས་ཞིབ་པར་སློབ་དཔོན་གྱི་ཞལ་ལས་ཤེས་དགོས་སོ། །གཉིས་པ་བརྟེན་པ་ལྷ་བསྐྱེད་པ་ནི། ནམ་མཁར་གནས་པའི་རྒྱུའི་ཧཱུྃ་དེ་ཉིད་སྐར་མདའ་ལྟུང་བ་ལྟར་གདན་དབུས་མའི་སྟེང་དུ་བབ་པ་ལས། འོད་ཟེར་མཐའ་ཡས་པ་ཕྱོགས་བཅུར་འཕྲོས་རྒྱལ་བ་རྣམས་མཆོད་ཅིང་ཐུགས་དམ་བསྐུལ། སེམས་ཅན་རྣམས་ལ་ཕོག་པས་སྒྲིབ་པ་སྦྱངས། སླར་འོད་ཟེར་རྒྱལ་བ་རྣམས་ཀྱི་བྱིན་རླབས་དང་

pot. Thereupon is a lotus that supports the wheels of Dharma that, in combination with the top ornament, have the shape of a stūpa.

On the inside are three layers of dry, fresh, and rotten skulls fixed together with meteorite nails and graced with a smear of blood and fat. Streamers of human skin are beautified with charnel ground offerings. Above is a border made of human heads, as well as windows made of the sun and moon, and a top border of legs and arms, joined at the ends, and having ribbons of intestines and lattices of bone. There are cornices of feet and hands, a ledge of backbones, and a victory banner made of human skin. Within are beams of Brahmā and a roof woodwork of stars. The pillar bases are the eight nāgas, the pillars are the eight gods, and the pillar capitals are the eight planets. Covering the ceiling is a human skin that is adorned with a top-ornament of Rudra's head and heart. The doors are made of human skin and the door frames of black serpents. Within the splendor of such charnel ground ornaments is a brownish black square[351] of human flesh adorned with a grove of corpses, on top of which is a BHRUṂ. From that syllable appears a deep blue eight-sided jewel. In the middle of that jewel is a single, small and round skull enclosure. In the centre of that is a deep blue E shaped by vajras and vajrarati—the great vajra rock—a sun, a moon, and a lotus.

For the central deity the seat is Mahādeva who lies face down, is black, holds a trident and a blood-filled skull cup, and wears a tiger skirt, as well as Mahādevī who is red, lies on her back, holds a trident, a blood-filled skull cup, and wears a leopard skirt. The seats for the ten wrathful ones are placed in a half circle of subjugated enemies and demons equal in number to the deities. At the eastern skull enclosure is the god Brahmā, on the eastern tip of the jewel is Gandharva, to the south Yama, to the west the Lord of the Nāgas, to the north Yakṣā, to the southeast Agni, to the southwest Rākṣasa, to the northwest Yāyu, to the northeast Vināyaka, and right at the western skull enclosure Bhūmipati. All are in physical union with their wives. Moreover, the esoteric instructions and the particularly detailed explanations concerning the palace and the central and surrounding seats should be understood by being received orally from a master.

Second follows the creation of the deities:

The HŪṂ seed syllable that remained in space descends, like the fall of a shooting star, down onto the center of the central seat. Limitless light rays radiate out in the ten directions and make offerings to the Conquerors and invoke their vows. As they touch sentient beings their obscurations are purified. The rays then return together with the blessings of the Conquerors. As they

བཅས་པ་ཚུར་འདུས་ཏེ་ཧཱུྃ་ལ་ཐིམ་པས་རྡོ་རྗེ་མཐིང་ནག་ཧཱུྃ་གིས་མཚན་པར་གྱུར། སླར་འོད་ཟེར་འཕྲོ་འདུ་སྔར་བཞིན་བྱས། ཚོགས་གཉིས་ཡོངས་སུ་རྫོགས་པ་དཔལ་ཆེན་པོའི་སྐུར་གྱུར་པ་ནི། ཐུགས་ཀྱིས་བསྐྱེད་ཅིང་ཚིག་གིས་གསལ་གདབ་པའོ། །ཨོཾ་བཛྲ་ཀཱི་ལི་ཀཱི་ལ་ཡ་སརྦ་བིགྷྣཱན་བཾ་ཧཱུྃ་ཕཊ༔ ཅེས་བརྗོད་པས་གདོན་ནས་དག་པའི་ངང་ངམ་གཤིས་རང་བཞིན་སྟོང་པ་ཉིད་ཀྱི་དབྱིངས་ཆོས་ཀྱི་སྐུ་ལས་མ་གཡོས་བཞིན་དུ། ལོངས་སྤྱོད་རྫོགས་སྐུ་དཔལ་རྡོ་རྗེ་སེམས་དཔའི་སྐུ་གསུང་ཐུགས་མི་ཟད་པ་རྒྱན་གྱི་འཁོར་ལོ་འབར་བ་རྣམ་པར་སྤྲུལ་པའི་སྐུར་ཤར་བའི་ཁྲོ་བོ་ཤིན་ཏུ་མི་བཟད་པ་གཏུམ་པའི་ཚུལ་ཅན། དཔལ་ཆེན་རྡོ་རྗེ་གཞོན་ནུ། སྐུ་མདོག་མཐིང་ནག ཞལ་ཡས་དཀར། གཡོན་དམར། དབུས་མཐིང་བའི་ཞལ་རེ་རེ་ལ་སྤྱན་གསུམ་གསུམ་སྟེ་དྲག་པོའི་སྤྱན་དགུ་དང་ལྡན་པ། དབུ་སྐྲ་ནི་ཁྲི་ཆིག་སྟོང་སྤྱི་བོར་བཅིངས་ཏེ་རྡོ་རྗེ་ཕྱེད་པའི་ཏོག་དང་། ཐོད་པ་སྐམ་པོ་ལྔའི་དབུ་རྒྱན་རིན་པོ་ཆེའི་རྩེ་བྲན་དང་ལྡན་པ། ཕྱག་དྲུག་གི་དང་པོ་གཉིས་ཀྱི། རྩེ་དགུ་དང་སྡིགས་མཛུབ་དང་བཅས་པའི་མེ་ཕུང་། བར་པ་གཉིས་ཀྱི་རྩེ་ལྔ་དང་ཁ་ཊྭཱཾ། འོག་མ་གཉིས་ཀྱི་རི་རབ་ཀྱི་ཕུར་པ་བསྒྲིལ་བ། ཞབས་བཞི་གཡོན་བརྐྱང་བའི་གར་གྱི་ལྷ་ཆེན་ཕོ་མོ་མནན་པ། གཡས་རྡོ་རྗེའི་ཐེལ་ཕྲན་གྱིས་མཚན་པའི་སྤྱུ་གྲི་དང་། གཡོན་རིན་པོ་ཆེའི་མཚན་པའི་རྒྱ་གྲིའི་གཤོག་པ་བརྒྱངས་ཤིང་། འཁོར་ལོའི་མཚན་པའི་རལ་གྲིའི་མཛུག་མ་དང་ལྡན་པ། སྤྱི་བོར་རུས་པའི་འཁོར་ལོ། སྙན་རྒྱན། མགུལ་རྒྱན། ཐལ་བ། སྐ་རགས། ཕྱག་ཞབས་ཀྱི་གདུ་བུ་སྟེ་རྒྱན་དྲུག ཐོད་པ་སྐམ་རློན་རྙོན་གསུམ་གྱི་ཕྲེང་བ་ཚར་གསུམ། སྦྲུལ་རྒྱལ་རིགས་དཀར་པོའི་སྐ་ཆིངས། རྗེའུ་རིགས་སེར་པོའི་སྙན་རྒྱན། བྲམ་ཟེ་དམར་པོའི་མགུལ་ཆུ། གདོལ་པ་ནག་པོའི་སྐུ་རེག དམངས་རིགས་ལྗང་གུའི་ཕྱག་ཞབས་ཀྱི་གདུ་བུ་སྟེ། ཐོད་སྐམ་རྩེ་ཕྲན། དབུའི་རྒྱན་དང་། རུས་རྒྱན། མགོ་ཕྲེང་སྦྲུལ་ཆུན་སྐུའི་རྒྱན་ཏེ་གདགས་པའི་རྒྱན་གཉིས། གླང་ཆེན་གོ་ལྤགས་ཀྱི་སྟོད་གཡོགས། ཞིང་ལྤགས་སྨེད་དཀྲིས་སྟག་ལྤགས་ཤམ་ཐབས་སྟེ་བགོ་བའི་གོས་གསུམ། དཔྲལ་བར་ཐལ་ཆེན་ཚོམ་བུ་མཁུར་ཚོས་རཀྟའི་ཐིག་ལེ། ཨོག་མར་ཞག་གི་ཟོ་རིས་ཏེ་བྱུག་པའི་རྫས་གསུམ་བཅས་དུར་ཁྲོད་ཆས་བརྒྱད་དང་དེའི་སྟེང་དུ་མཐིང་ནག་ཅོད་པ་འཕུར་བ་རྡོ་རྗེ་གོ་ཁྲབ་ཀྱི་ཆས། མེ་ཕུང་ཀློང་ན་བཞུགས་པ་འབར་བ་མེའི་ཆས་ཏེ་དཔལ་གྱི་ཆས་བཅུ་དང་། སྐུ་སྒེག་པ་དཔའ་བ། མི་སྡུག་པ།

dissolve into the HŪṂ, it is transformed into a deep blue vajra marked with a HŪṂ. Once more, in the same fashion, light spreads out and returns, whereby the two accumulations become fully perfected and the vajra transforms into the form of the Great Glorious One. Perform the creation of this with the mantra and the visualization with the words.

Say, OṂ VAJRAKĪLI KĪLAYA SARVAVIGHNĀN BAṂ HŪṂ PHAṬ. Thereby, without moving from dharmakāya, the primordially pure state or nature that is the natural space of emptiness, sambhogakāya—glorious Vajrasattva—appears in the form of the blazing inexhaustible adornment wheel of enlightened body, speech, and mind as the great glorious Vajrakumāra, who is nirmāṇakāya in the ferocious form of absolutely overwhelming wrath. His body is deep blue and in each of his faces—of which the right is white, the left red, and the middle blue—are three eyes, so he is endowed with nine fierce eyes. His 21,000 strands of hair are tied together at the crown of his head where he has a top ornament of a half vajra. He wears a head ornament of five dry skulls and a bejeweled crest ornament. With the upper two of his six hands he holds a nine-pronged vajra and a mass of fire that he brandishes in the threatening posture. The two middle hands hold a five-pronged vajra and a skull staff. The lower two roll the kīla of the central mountain. His four feet, dancing with the left legs outstretched, stamp on Mahādeva and Mahādevī. His wings, the right a blade marked with a small vajra seal and the left a sharp celestial knife marked with jewels, are outstretched. He has a tail which is a sword marked with a wheel.

He has six ornaments: a bone wheel at the top of his head, earrings, necklace, ashes, a belt, and bracelets on the hands and feet. He has a triple garland of dry, rotten, and fresh skulls. A white rājakula snake holds his hair together, yellow vaiśya snakes are his earrings, a red brahman snake is his necklace, black caṇḍāla snakes are on his body, and green śūdra snakes function as bracelets on his hands and feet. Dry skulls are his head ornament.

He is also endowed with the eight charnel ground ornaments: the crown and bone ornaments, together with the garland of human heads and bundles of snakes ornamenting his body are the two fastened ornaments; the shirt of elephant hide, the underskirt of human skin, and the tiger skin skirt are the three worn garments; and the clot of ashes in his forehead, the drops of rakta on his cheeks, and the smears of fat on his neck are the three applied elixirs. On top he has a deep blue crown and a vajra coat of mail. That he stands in the expanse of a mass of fire is the ornament of fire. Thus the ten glorious ornaments are complete. He shows the nine aspects of dance, which are a playful, fearless, and repulsive body; an agitated, abusive, and frightening speech; and

གསུང་རྒོད་པ། གཤེ་བ། འཇིགས་སུ་རུང་བ། ཐུགས་སྙིང་རྗེ་བ། རྔམ་པ་ཞི་བའི་ཚུལ་ཏེ་གར་དགུ་སོགས་ཁྲོ་བོའི་ཆས་དང་ཚུལ་གྱིས་རྣམ་པར་འཇིགས་པ། ཡུམ་ཆེན་འཁོར་ལོ་རྒྱས་འདེབས་མ་སྐུ་མདོག་མཐིང་ནག་ལང་ཚོས་སྨིག་པ། ཞལ་གཅིག་ཕྱག་གཉིས་གཡས་རང་རྟགས་ཨུཏྤལ་དང་བཅས་པའི་ཡབ་ཀྱི་མགུལ་ནས་འཁྱུད་ཅིང་། གཡོན་པས་དུང་དམར་ཞལ་དུ་སྟོབ་པ། ཐོད་སྐམ་དང་རིན་པོ་ཆེའི་དབུ་རྒྱན་ཐལ་བ་སྤྱངས་པའི་ཕྱག་རྒྱ་ལྔ་དང་། གཟིག་པགས་ཀྱི་ཤམ་ཐབས་སོགས་དུར་ཁྲོད་ཀྱི་ཆས་ཀྱིས་བརྒྱན་པ། ཡབ་ཡུམ་གཉིས་མེ་ཕུང་འབར་བའི་ཀློང་དུ་བཞུགས་པའི་སྐུའི་བ་སྤུ་བྱེ་བ་ཐེར་འབུམ་རྡོ་རྗེས་གཏམས་ཤིང་། ཕུར་བུའི་ཙྭ་ཙྭ་སྐར་ལྟར་འཁྲུགས་པ། ཡབ་ཀྱི་ཐུགས་ཀར་འོད་ཨེཀྟ་ཏྲི་ལ་ལྟ་བུའི་གུར་ཁྱིམ་སྒོ་གཅིག་དང་ལྡན་པའི་ནང་ན་ཡེ་ཤེས་པ་རྡོ་རྗེ་སེམས་དཔའ་ཚོན་གང་བའི་ཐུགས་ཀར་རིན་པོ་ཆེ་ཆ་བརྒྱད་པའི་དབུས་ཉི་ཟླ་སྦྲན་གཞག་ཙམ་གྱི་གདན་ལ་གསེར་གྱི་རྡོ་རྗེ་ནས་འབྲས་ཙམ་གྱི་ལྟེ་བར་ཉི་མ་ལ་གནས་པའི་ཧཱུྃ་སྔོན་པོ་ཡུངས་འབྲུ་ཙམ་གྱི་མཐར་ཀཱི་ལ་ཡ་འབྲུ་དགུ་པ་སྤུས་བྲིས་པ་ཙམ་གྱིས་བསྐོར་བ་གཡོ་མེད་དུ་གནས་པར། གུར་ཁྱིམ་གྱི་སྒོ་སྲུང་རྟ་མགྲིན་དམར་པོ་པདྨ་དང་ཁཊྭཱཾ་འཛིན་པས་བསྲུང་བར་བསམ། འདིའི་སྒོ་ཡི་སྐབས་འདིར་མན་ངག་མི་འདྲ་བ་ཞིག་ཡོད་ཀྱང་བླ་མའི་ཞལ་ལས་མཉན་པ་ལས་དཀྱུས་སུ་འབྲིར་མི་འོས་པས་འདིར་མ་བཀོད་དོ།

།གཉིས་པ་ཕྱོགས་བཅུ་ཁྲོ་བོའི་དཀྱིལ་འཁོར་བསྐྱེད་པ་ནི། དཔལ་ཆེན་རྡོ་རྗེ་གཞོན་ནུ་ཡབ་ཡུམ་མཉམ་པར་སྦྱོར་བའི་རྗེས་སུ་ཆགས་པའི་བྱང་ཆུབ་སེམས་སྤྲིན་ལས་ཧཱུྃ་ཡིག་སྤྲེལ་མ་བཅུ་གདན་སོ་སོའི་སྟེང་དུ་འཕྲོས་པ་ལས། ཤར་གྱི་ཐོད་རའི་རྩ་བར་ཚངས་པའི་གདན་གྱི་སྟེང་དུ། ཁྲོ་བོ་ཧཱུྃ་ཀཱ་ར་མཐིང་ནག་གཡས་དཀར་གཡོན་དམར་བའི་ཞལ་ཅན། ཕྱག་དྲུག་དང་པོ་གཉིས་ཁྲོ་བཅུ་སྤྱིའི་རང་རྟགས་རྡོ་རྗེ་དང་དུང་ཁྲག བར་པ་གཉིས་མདའ་གཞུ་འགེངས་པ། འོག་མ་གཉིས་ཕུར་བུ་འདྲིལ་བ་ནི་ཁྲོ་བཅུ་ཀུན་ལ་འདྲ། ལུས་དང་གྲིབ་མའི་ཚུལ་དུ་ཡུམ་རྡོ་རྗེ་སྒྲ་འབྱིན་མ་སྔོ་སྐྱ། གཡས་རྡོ་རྗེ་དང་བཅས་པས་མགུལ་ནས་འཁྱུད་ཅིང་གཡོན་པས་བྷན་དམར་ཞལ་དུ་སྟོབས་པའི་ཕྱག་མཚན་ནི་ཡུམ་ཀུན་འདྲའོ། །གཡས་སུ་ཕྲ་མན་ཕག་གི་མགོ་ཅན་གཡས་མདའ་ཆེན་དང་གཡོན་འཁོར་ལོ། གཡོན་དུ་ཕྱག་བརྙན་སྦྲིག་བུའི་མགོ་ཅན་གཞུ་མཆོག་དང་ཏྲི་ཤུལ་འཛིན་པ། ཤར་དུ་རྣམ་རྒྱལ་དཀར་པོ་གཡས་སྔོ་གཡོན་དམར་བའི་ཞལ་ཅན། ཕྱག་བར་པ་གཉིས་འཁོར་ལོ་དང་

a compassionate, splendorous, and peaceful mind. With such wrathful ornaments and manners he is utterly terrifying.

The great consort Dīptacakra is dark blue and charming in her youth. She has one face and two hands. Her right hand embraces the neck of the lord holding her particular mark, the utpala flower. With the left she offers a blood-filled skull to his mouth. These, in combination with the dry skulls, the jewel head ornament and the ashes, are the five seals of renunciation. She is also adorned with charnel ground ornaments, such as a leopard skirt. On the bodies of the lord and consort, who are standing in a blazing mass of fire, are ten trillion vajra hairs, and kīla sācchas shoot out like stars.

In the heart center of the lord you should visualize a dome that appears like sapphire light. It has a single entrance and inside is the wisdom being Vajrasattva, the size of a finger. In his heart center is an octagon jewel in the middle of which is a seat of the sun and the moon, the size of a split pea. Here is a golden vajra the size of a barley grain. In its center, resting on a sun, is a blue letter HŪṂ the size of a mustard seed around which the nine Kīlaya syllables, as fine as if written by a hair, form an unmoving circle. The protector of the dome is the red Hayagrīva who protects while holding a lotus and a bhañja. Although there is a special instruction for the occasion of this gate I will not explain it here as it generally is unsuited for writing and so should be received directly from a master.

The second part concerns the creation of the maṇḍala of the wrathful ones of the ten directions. From the union of the great glorious Vajrakumāra and consort arise clouds of bodhicitta of passion from which appear ten joined HŪṂ letters. They disperse to their individual seats as follows:

Right at the eastern skull enclosure on a seat of Brahmā is the wrathful Hūmkāra. He is dark blue with three faces, of which the right is white and the left is red. Of his six hands the first two hold a vajra and a blood-filled skull, which are the particular mark of the Ten Wrathful Ones. The middle two hold a bow and arrow. The lower two roll a kīla, which is similar for all the Ten Wrathful Ones. The light-blue consort Resounding Vajra is like a shadow to his body. Her right hand, holding a vajra, embraces his neck while the left offers him a blood-filled skull cup. These hand-symbols are the same for all the consorts. To their right is a pig-headed hybrid holding a lance in the right hand and a wheel in the left. To their left is a lizard headed attendant holding a supreme bow and a trident.

In the east is the white Vijaya. He has three faces of which the right is blue and the left is red. His two middle hands hold a wheel and a skull staff. His

ཁ་ཊྭཾ་ག ཡུམ་རྡོ་རྗེ་སྙེམ་མ་དཀར་དམར། ཕྲ་མན་སྟག་གི་མགོ་ཅན་མདའ་ཆེན་དང་འཁོར་ལོ། ཕྱག་བརྙན་བྱ་རྒོད་མགོ་ཅན་གཞུ་མཆོག་དང་ཏྲི་ཤུལ་འཛིན་པ། ཤར་ལྷོར་དབྱུག་སྔོན་མཐིང་སྐྱ་ཞལ་གཡས་དཀར་གཡོན་དམར། བར་པ་གཉིས་མེ་ཕུང་དང་དབྱུག་ཐོ་ཡུམ་རྡོ་རྗེ་སྤྱིར་མོ་སྔོ་སྐྱ། ཕྲ་མན་གཡག་གི་མགོ་ཅན་མེ་ཕུང་དང་བེ་ཅོན། ཕྱག་བརྙན་བྱ་རོག་མགོ་ཅན་དབྱུག་ཐོ་དང་དགྲ་སྟ་འཛིན་པ། ལྷོར་གཤིན་རྗེ་སེར་ནག་གཡས་སྔོ་གཡོན་དམར་བ། བར་པ་གཉིས་བེ་ཅོན་དང་དགྲ་སྟ། ཡུམ་རྡོ་རྗེ་དུར་ཁྲོད་བདག་མོ་དམར་སེར། ཕྲ་མན་ཤ་བའི་མགོ་ཅན་མེ་ཕུང་དང་བེ་ཅོན། ཕྱག་བརྙན་འུག་པའི་མགོ་ཅན་དབྱུག་ཐོ་དང་དགྲ་སྟ་འཛིན་པ། ལྷོ་ནུབ་མི་གཡོ་བ་ལྗང་ནག་གཡས་དཀར་གཡོན་དམར་བ་བར་པ་གཉིས་རལ་གྲི་དང་ཞགས་པ། ཡུམ་རྡོ་རྗེ་གཏུན་ཁྲུང་མ་སྔོ་ནག ཕྲ་མན་གཟིག་གི་མགོ་ཅན་རལ་གྲི་དང་ཞགས་པ། ཕྱག་བརྙན་ཁྭ་ཏའི་མགོ་ཅན་ཞགས་པ་དང་སྤུ་གྲི་འཛིན་པ། ནུབ་ཕྱོགས་རྟ་མགྲིན་དམར་ནག་གཡས་དཀར་གཡོན་སྔོ་བ། བར་པ་གཉིས་སྐྱུལ་ཞགས་དང་སྤུ་གྲི། ཡུམ་རྡོ་རྗེ་གཏུམ་མོ་དམར་གསལ། ཕྲ་མན་བྱི་ལའི་མགོ་ཅན་རལ་གྲི་དང་ཞགས་པ། ཕྱག་བརྙན་སྤུ་ཤུད་ཞགས་པ་དང་སྤུ་གྲི་འཛིན་པ། ནུབ་བྱང་འདོད་རྒྱལ་དམར་སྐྱ་གཡས་དཀར་གཡོན་སྔོ་བའི་ཞལ། བར་པ་གཉིས་བ་དན་དང་རྫ་ཡབ། ཡུམ་རྡོ་རྗེ་མདའ་སྙེམ་མ་དམར་སྐྱ། ཕྲ་མན་སྤྱང་ཀི་བ་དན་དང་རྒྱ་གྲམ་ཕྱག་བརྙན་ཁྲ་མགོ་རྫ་ཡབ་དང་དྲིལ་བུ་འཛིན་པ། བྱང་དུ་བདུད་རྩི་འཁྱིལ་བ་ལྗང་ནག་གཡས་དཀར་གཡོན་དམར་བ། བར་པ་གཉིས་རྒྱ་གྲམ་དང་དྲིལ་བུ། ཡུམ་རྡོ་རྗེ་རླུང་འབྱིན་མ་ལྗང་ནག ཕྲ་མན་སེངྒེའི་མགོ་ཅན་བ་དན་དང་རྒྱ་གྲམ་ཕྱག་བརྙན་ཕ་ཕྱང་རྫ་ཡབ་དང་དྲིལ་བུ་འཛིན་པ། བྱང་ཤར་ཁམས་གསུམ་རྣམ་རྒྱལ་ནག་པོ་གཡས་དཀར་གཡོན་དམར་བ། བར་པ་གཉིས་ཐོ་བ་དང་བགེགས་མགོ། ཡུམ་རྡོ་རྗེ་གསོད་བྱེད་མ་ལྗང་སེར། ཕྲ་མན་དོམ་ཐོ་བ་དང་ཐོང་གཤོལ། ཕྱག་བརྙན་སྲེ་མོང་བགེགས་མགོ་དང་གཏུན་ཤིང་འཛིན་པ། ནུབ་ཀྱི་ཐོད་རའི་རྩ་བར་སྟོབས་པོ་ཆེ་ནག་པོ་གཡས་དཀར་གཡོན་དམར་བའི་ཞལ་ཅན། ཕྱག་བར་པ་གཉིས་ཐོང་གཤོལ་དང་གཏུན་གྱིས་བརྡུང་བ། ཡུམ་རྡོ་རྗེ་བརྟུལ་མའམ་བསྐུལ་བྱེད་མ་ནག་མོ་རྡོ་རྗེ་བྲན་དམར། ཕྲ་མན་དྲེད་ཀྱི་མགོ་ཅན་ཐོ་བ་དང་ཐོང་གཤོལ། ཕྱག་བརྙན་བྱི་བའི་མགོ་ཅན་བགེགས་མགོ་དང་གཏུན་ཤིང་འཛིན་པའོ། །

consort is the whitish-red Haughty Vajra. A tiger-headed hybrid holds a lance and a wheel, and a vulture-headed attendant holds a supreme bow along with a trident.

In the southeast is the light blue Nīladaṇḍa. His right face is white and the left is red. His two middle hands hold a mass of fire and a club. His consort is the light blue Vajra Claw. A yak-headed hybrid holds a mass of fire and a pestle and a crow-headed attendant holds a club and an ax.

In the south is the dark yellow Yamāntaka. His right face is blue and the left is red. His two middle hands hold a pestle and an ax. His consort is the orange Lady of the Charnel Ground. A deer-headed hybrid holds a mass of fire and a pestle and an owl-headed attendant holds a club and an ax.

In the southwest is the dark green Acala. His right face is white and the left is red. His two middle hands hold a sword and a lasso. His consort is the dark blue Vajra Mortar. A leopard-headed hybrid holds a sword and a lasso, and a raven-headed attendant holds a lasso and a blade.

In the west is the dark red Hayagrīva. His right face is white and the left is blue. His two middle hands hold a lasso made of snakes and a blade. His consort is the bright red Fierce Vajra. A cat-headed hybrid holds a sword and a lasso, and a hoopoe bird-headed attendant holds a lasso and a blade.

In the northwest is the light red Aparājita. His right face is white and the left is blue. His two middle hands hold a banner and a tail-fan. His consort is the light red Haughty Arrow Vajra. A wolf-headed hybrid holds a banner and a crossed vajra, and a hawk-headed attendant holds a tail-fan and a bell.

In the north is the dark green Amṛtakuṇḍalin. His right face is white and the left is red. His two middle hands hold a crossed vajra and a bell. His consort is the dark green Wind Blowing Vajra. A lion-headed hybrid holds a banner and a crossed vajra, and a bat-headed attendant holds a tail-fan and a bell.

In the northeast is the black Trailokyavijaya. His right face is white and the left is red. His two middle hands hold a hammer and the head of a demon. His consort is the greenish-yellow Vajra Slayer. A hyena-headed hybrid holds a hammer and a plough, and a bear-headed attendant holds the head of a demon and a wooden bat.

Right at the western skull enclosure is the black Mahābala. His right face is white and the left is red. His two middle hands strike with a plough and a bat. His consort is the black Vajra Activity, or Vajra Exhortation, who holds a vajra and a fresh skull. A brown bear-headed hybrid holds a hammer and a plough, and a rat-headed attendant holds the head of a demon and a wooden bat.

དེ་ལྟར་ཁྲོ་བོ་ཡབ་ཡུམ་ཀུན་དཔལ་དང་དུར་ཁྲོད་ཀྱི་ཆས་སོགས་གཙོ་བོ་ཡབ་ཡུམ་དང་མཚུངས་པ། ཕྲ་མན་དང་ཕྱག་བརྙན་རྣམས་ཀྱི་སྐུ་མདོག་ཁྲོ་བཅུ་ཡབ་ཡུམ་རང་རང་མཚུངས་པར་ཡང་བཤད། སྐུ་ལས་ཡེ་ཤེས་ཀྱི་མེ་ཕུང་དང་གཟི་བརྗིད་བསྐལ་པའི་མེ་ལྟར་འབར་ཞིང་བལྟ་བས་མི་བཟོད་པ་མ་འདྲེས་ཡོངས་རྫོགས་སུ་གསལ་བར་བསྒོམ་མོ། །གསུམ་པ་སྤྲོལ་བྱེད་ཕུར་བུ་རྫས་ཀྱི་དཀྱིལ་འཁོར་བསྐྱེད་པ་ནི། གཙོ་བོ་ཡབ་ཡུམ་གྱི་བྱང་སེམས་འོད་ཀྱི་གོང་བུ་ལས་ཧཱུྃ་ཡིག་ཉེར་གཅིག་ཟླ་གམ་རྣམས་སུ་སྤྲོས་ཏེ་འཕོད་པ་ལས་བྱུང་བའི་འོད་ཟེར་གྱི་རྩེ་ལས་ཕུར་བུ་ཕྲ་མོ་དཔག་ཏུ་མེད་པ་འཕྲོས། ཁམས་གསུམ་སེམས་ཅན་ཐམས་ཅད་ཀྱི་སྒོ་གསུམ་དང་རིགས་དྲུག་གི་བག་ཆགས་སྣང་ཞེན་ཐམས་ཅད་བསྒྲིགས་ཤིང་སྦྱངས། དཔལ་ཆེན་པོའི་རང་བཞིན་དུ་གྱུར། སླར་འདུས་ཧཱུྃ་ཡིག་རྣམས་ལ་ཐིམ་སྟེ་ཡོངས་སུ་གྱུར་པ་ལས། སྲས་མཆོག་ཉེར་གཅིག་སྐུ་མདོག་མཐིང་ནག་ཨུཏྤལ་རྒྱས་པའི་མདོག་འདྲ་བ་ཞལ་གཡས་དཀར། གཡོན་དམར་བའི་ཞལ་གསུམ་ལྷུགས་ཀྱི་རལ་པ་དང་ལྡན་པའི་སྐུ་སྟོད་ཁྲོ་བོ་འཛིགས་སུ་རུང་བ། གཡས་ཀྱི་སྲས་བདུན་གྱི་ཕྱག་དྲུག་གི་གཡས་དང་པོའི་རང་རྟགས་འཁོར་ལོ། བར་པས་རྩེ་ལྔ། གཡོན་དང་པོའི་མེ་ཕུང་། བར་པ་ཁ་ཊྭཱཾ། ཐ་མ་གཉིས་ཕུར་བུ་འདྲིལ་བ། གཡོན་གྱི་སྲས་བདུན་གྱི་ཕྱག་དང་པོའི་རང་རྟགས་པདྨ། རྒྱབ་ཀྱི་སྲས་བདུན་གྱི་ཕྱག་དང་པོའི་རང་རྟགས་རྒྱ་གྲམ། ཕྱག་གཞན་སྲས་མཆོག་ཀུན་ཕྱག་མཚན་འདྲ་བར། སྐུ་སྨད་རྒྱ་སྲིན་གྱི་ཁ་ནས་ཐོན་པའི་གནམ་ལྕགས་རྡོ་དབལ་ཟུར་གསུམ་དགྲ་བགེགས་ཀྱི་སྲོག་གི་གོར་བཙུགས་པ་དུར་ཁྲོད་ཀྱི་ཆས་ཀྱིས་བརྒྱན་ཅིང་འབར་བའི་འོད་ཙྭ་ཙྭ་སྐར་ལྟར་འཁྲུགས་པ། སྙིང་རྗེའི་སྤྲོལ་བའི་བདག་ཉིད་དུ་བསྐྱེད་དོ། །ཕོ་བྲང་ནང་མའི་སྒོ་བཞིར་སྤྲུལ་པའི་སྒོ་སྐྱོང་ཁྲོ་མོ་བཞི། ཤར་དུ་གནོད་སྦྱིན་པུ་ཤུད་ལྕགས་ཀྱུ་འཛིན་པ་དཀར་པོ། ལྷོར་འཇིགས་བྱེད་ཀང་ཀ་ཞགས་པ་འཛིན་པ་སེར་པོ། ནུབ་ཏུ་བདུད་རྩིའི་སྲིན་བྱ་ལྕགས་སྒྲོག་འཛིན་པ་དམར་པོ། བྱང་དུ་གསོད་བྱེད་ཁྲ་མགོ་དྲིལ་འཁྲོལ་འཁྱེད་པ་ལྗང་མོ་རྣམས། ཕྱག་གཡས་རང་རྟགས་ཕྱག་རྒྱ་བཞི་དང་། གཡོན་པ་རྣམས་ལས་བཞིའི་ཕུར་བུ་འདྲིལ་བ། གཞན་ཡང་བར་ཁྲམས་སུ་ཤར་དུ་ཤྭ་ན་མུ་ཁ་སོགས་ཕུར་སྲུང་བཅུ་གཉིས། ཕྱི་མའི་ཁྲག་ཁྲམས་སུ་ཤར་དུ་ཞི་མཛད་དཀར་མོ་བདུན་སོགས་དབང་ཕྱུག་ཉེར་བརྒྱད། ཕྱིའི་སྒོ་སྲུང་སྐྱེས་བུ་གིང་བཞི་ཕྱིའི་འཁོར་ཡུག་ཤར་དུ་ཕུར་པའི་ལྷ་མོ་དབུ་བརྒྱ་མ་དང་། ནུབ་ཏུ་འབྱུང་པོ་རྡོ་རྗེ་སྡེ་ཡོན་

In this way all the male and female wrathful ones are equal to the main lord and consort in terms of splendor, charnel ground ornaments, etc. It is also said that the body colors of the hybrids and attendants are identical to their respective male and female wrathful ones. The fire of wisdom and the majestic brilliance that blazes from their bodies, like the fire at the end of an aeon, are overwhelming to behold. Visualize this, clearly and distinctly without mixing it up.

Third follows the creation of the material liberating kīla maṇḍala:

The bodhicitta light sphere of the central lord and consort emanate 21 HŪṂ syllables into a crescent formation that emits light rays, from the tips of which innumerable small kīlas emanate. They burn and purify the body, speech, and mind of all sentient beings in the three realms together with their habitual tendencies of attachment to the appearances of the six classes of beings. Thereby they are transformed into the nature of the Great Glorious One. Gathering back, they dissolve into the HŪṂ syllables that transform into the 21 supreme sons. They are dark blue in color like the blossomed utpala flower with a wrathful and terrifying upper body. They have three faces, of which the right is white and the left is red, and they have thick matted iron hair. The seven sons to the right have six hands. The top right holds a wheel which is their particular mark and the middle right holds a five-pronged vajra. The top left holds a mass of fire and the middle left a skull staff. The two lower hands roll a kīla. The seven sons to the left hold in their top right hand a lotus, which is their particular mark. The top right hand of the seven sons behind holds a crossed vajra, which is their particular mark. In the other hands all the supreme sons hold the same hand implements. Their lower body, emerging from the mouth of Makara, is the three edged, sharp, meteoric blade that is planted in the location of the life force of enemies and obstructing forces. They are adorned with charnel ground ornaments and, in a light of a blazing fire, sācchas shoot out like stars. They are created as the liberating identity of compassion.

At the four inner gates of the palace are the four wrathful emanated gatekeepers. In the east is the white Yakṣā with a hoopoe-bird head, holding an iron hook. In the south is the yellow Bhairavī with magpie head, holding a lasso. In the west is the red Amṛtā with an owl head, holding an iron chain. In the north is the green Ghātakā with a hawk head, ringing a bell. They all hold their particular mark in their right hand and their left hand rolls the kīla of the four activities. Furthermore, in the middle courtyard are the 12 kīla protectors, such as Śvanmukhā in the east. In the last blood-courtyard are the 28 Īśvarīs, such as the Seven White Extinguishers in the east. The four kiṃkara

གྱིས་གཙོས། མཁའ་འགྲོ་སོ་གཉིས། མ་བདུན་སྲིང་བཞི། འབར་མ་དྲེགས་པ་བྲ་གཙན་སོགས་
ཕོ་ཉ་རྣམས་ཉི་མ་ལས་འོད་ཟེར་བཞིན་མགྲོན་ཐབས་ཀྱི་ཚུལ་དུ་གསལ་བར་བསྐྱེད་དོ། །དེ་ལྟར་
རིམ་གྱིས་བསྐྱེད་པ་དེ་ཉིད་བཛྲ་ཀཱི་ལ་ཡའི་སྔགས་ཀྱིས་གཅིག་ཆར་དུ་གསལ་གདབ་པའོ། །གཉིས་
པ་བྱིན་གྱིས་རླབས་ཤིང་དབང་བསྐུར་བ་སོགས་གསུམ་ལས། དང་པོ་ནི། བདག་དམ་ཚིག་
པའི་དཀྱིལ་འཁོར་ལ་ཡེ་ནས་དག་པའི་སྐུ་གསུང་ཐུགས་ཀྱི་བདག་ཉིད་བྱིན་གྱིས་བརླབས་ཤིང་།
གནས་གསུམ་དུ་སྐུ་གསུང་ཐུགས་ཀྱི་ལྷ་གསུམ་མམ་ཡིག་འབྲུ་གསུམ་གྱིས་མཚན་པར་བསམ་མོ།
།ཡེ་ཤེས་ལྷའི་བདག་ཉིད་དུ་དབང་བསྐུར་བས། དབང་རྟགས་དེ་བཞིན་གཤེགས་པ་རིགས་ལྔ་
ལས་སྤྱིར་རྡོ་རྗེ་གཞོན་ནུ་རྡོ་རྗེའི་རིགས་ཡིན་ནའང་། ཕྲིན་ལས་ཀྱི་ལྷར་བཞེངས་པས། དོན་གྲུབ་
གཙོ་བོར་གྱུར་པའི་རིགས་ལྷུས་དབུ་བརྒྱན་པར་བསམ་མོ། །གཉིས་པ་སྤྱན་དྲངས་པ་ལ་གསུམ་
ལས། དང་པོ་སྙན་གསན་དབབ་པ་ནི། ཆོས་ཀྱི་དབྱིངས་ནས་སྲིད་པ་རྡོ་རྗེ་ཕུར་བུའི་ལྷ་ཚོགས་
རྣམས། བསྐྱེད་པ་དམ་ཚིག་པའི་དཀྱིལ་འཁོར་འདི་ལ་དགོངས་ཏེ། ཡེ་ཤེས་ཀྱི་དཀྱིལ་འཁོར་དང་
དབྱེར་མེད་དུ་འགྲུབ་པར་མཛོད་ཅིག་པ་དང་། བཛྲ་ས་མ་ཛཿས་བསྐུལ་བས། དེ་བཞིན་གཤེགས་
པ་རྣམས་ཆོས་ཀྱི་དབྱིངས་ལས་གཟུགས་ཀྱི་སྐུར་བཞེངས་ཏེ་སྤྱན་དྲངས་པའི་དུས་སུ་འབྱོན་པར་མཛད་
དུ་གསོལ། ཞེས་བརྡའ་སྐུར་བའོ། །གཉིས་པ་སྤྱན་དྲངས་པ་དངོས་ནི། སྲིད་པ་གསུམ་གྱིས་
བསྡུས་པའི་ཕྱི་སྣོད་ནང་བཅུད་ཐམས་ཅད་རྡོ་རྗེ་གཞོན་ནུར་གསལ་བའི་དཀྱིལ་འཁོར་དུ། འོག་མིན་
གྱི་གནས་ནས་ཡེ་ཤེས་ཀྱི་ཁྲོ་བོ་དམ་ཚིག་གི་གནས་འདིར་གཤེགས་ནས་མཆོག་གི་དངོས་གྲུབ་ཡེ་
ཤེས་གྲུབ་པའི་རྟགས་དང་། ཐུན་མོང་དམ་ཚན་གྲུབ་པའི་མཚན་མ་རྣམས་དངོས་ཉམས་སྨི་ལམ་གྱི་
ཡུལ་དུ་བསྟན་པ་དང་། རྡོ་རྗེ་ཕུར་བུའི་མཆོག་ཐུན་གྱི་དངོས་གྲུབ་མ་ལུས་པ་སྩལ་དུ་གསོལ་ཞེས་
སྤྱན་དྲངས་པའི་སྔགས་བརྗོད་པ་དང་བཅས་པས། བདག་གཙོ་བོའི་ཐུགས་ཀ་ནས། ལྷ་མོ་བཞི་
འོག་མིན་དུ་སྤྲོས་པས་ཡེ་ཤེས་པ་དགུག། བཅིངས་སྡོམ། དགྱེས་པ་བསྐྱེད་དེ་སྤྱན་དྲངས་པས།
རྒྱལ་པོ་བསྐྱོད་ནས་འཁོར་ཤུགས་ཀྱིས་ཡོངས་བ་བཞིན་དུ། འཁོར་གཞལ་ཡས་ཁང་དང་བཅས་
པ་མདུན་གྱི་ནམ་མཁར་བྱོན་པར་བསམ། གསུམ་པ་བཞུགས་སུ་གསོལ་བ་ནི། དུར་ཁྲོད་ཀྱི་
གཞལ་ཡས་ཁང་པར། གཙོ་བོ་དབུས་སུ་རུ་དྲ་དང་། སྟེང་དུ་ཚངས་པ་ཕོ་མོ་བསྙོལ་བ་སོགས་

spirits protect the outer gates. At the outer wall is the hundred headed kīla goddess in the east. In the north, headed by the bhuta spirit Dorje Nayön, are servants, such as the 32 ḍākinīs, the seven mothers, the four sisters, the blazing ones, haughty spirits, and wild beasts. The attendants should be clearly developed in a welcoming manner, like rays from the sun. Furthermore, what has been gradually created here can be visualized in an instant by the mantra of Vajrakīlaya.

Blessing, conferring empowerment, and so forth contain three parts. The first, which is the descent of blessings and conferring of empowerment, is to visualize that the personal samaya maṇḍala is blessed as the identity of the primordially pure enlightened body, speech, and mind and that the three deities, or syllables, of enlightened body, speech, and mind manifest in the three places. Although in general, among the five families of tathāgatas, the empowerment insignia of Vajrakumāra's family is the vajra, he manifests as a deity of activity because of having been empowered as the identity of the five wisdoms. One should therefore conceive that his head is adorned with the five families headed by Amoghasiddhi.

Then follows the invitation. This in turn has three parts:

First one makes a request by saying, "Gatherings of deities of Vajrakīlaya of Existence, from the basic space of phenomena, please consider this arisen samaya maṇḍala and make it indivisible from the wisdom maṇḍala," and then, "VAJRA SAMĀJAḤ." Then, while applying the symbolic gestures say, "I pray that the tathāgatas may manifest as rūpakāya from the basic space of phenomena and arrive at this occasion of invitation."

Second is the actual invitation. Invite by saying, "I request you to arrive, from the abode of Akaniṣṭha, to this samaya place of the wrathful ones possessing wisdom, which is the maṇḍala in which all outer worlds and inner contents of the three-fold existence are visualized as Vajrakīlaya. Then, please display in actuality, visions, or dreams the signs of accomplishing wisdom—the supreme accomplishment—and the marks of accomplishing the vow-holders—the common accomplishments. Furthermore, please grant all supreme and common accomplishments of Vajrakīlaya without exception." While saying this, think that from the heart center of the central lord four goddesses emanate to Akaniṣṭha and summon the wisdom beings, bind, constrain, delight, and invite them. Thereby, like the retinue arriving by themselves once the king has moved, the retinue together with the palace arrives in the space before you.

Third is the request to remain. Request the main deity to joyfully remain in the charnel ground palace on a seat made of Rudra with Brahmā and Brāhmī

གདན་གྱི་སྟེང་དུ་དགྱེས་པར་བཞུགས་སུ་གསོལ་བ་ནི། ས་མ་ཡ་ཏིཥྛ་ལྷན། ཞེས་བརྗོད་པས་དམ་ཚིག་གི་དཔལ་ལ་ཡེ་ཤེས་ཀྱི་དཔལ། ཆུ་ལ་ཆུ་ཐིམ་པ་ལྟར་གཙོ་བོ་ལ་གཙོ་བོ། འཁོར་ལ་འཁོར། གཞལ་ཡས་ཁང་ལ་གཞལ་ཡས་ཁང་ཐིམ་སྟེ་དབྱེར་མེད་དུ་གྱུར་པར་བསམ། གསུམ་པ་མཆོད་པ་ལ་བདུན་ལས། དང་པོ་མཉེས་པ་ཕྱག་གི་མཆོད་པ་ནི་གཙོ་བོའི་ཐུགས་ཀ་ནས་བདག་ལས་ཀྱི་རྡོ་རྗེ་གཞོན་ནུའི་རྣམ་པར་ཐོན་ཏེ། དཀྱིལ་འཁོར་གྱི་ཤར་སྒོ་ནས། ཆོས་ཀྱི་དབྱིངས་ནས་སྐུར་བཞེངས་སོགས་ཚིག་བརྗོད་ཅིང་། ཡིད་གུས་པའི་སྒོ་ནས་ཡན་ལག་ལྔ་ས་ལ་བཏུད་པས་གུས་པའི་ཚུལ་གྱིས་ཕྱག་འཚལ་ཏེ་ཨ་ཏི་པུ་ཧོཿ མཆོད་པ་ལ་ཤིན་ཏུ་དགྱེས་སམ་ཞེས་བྱས་ཏེ། ལྷ་ཚོགས་རྣམས་ཀྱིས་པྲ་ཏི་ཙྪ་ཧོཿ ས་དེ་ལ་རབ་ཏུ་མཉེས་སོ་ཞེས་པའི་ལན་གནང་བར་བསམ་མོ། །གཉིས་པ་ཉེར་སྤྱོད་ཀྱི་མཆོད་པ་ནི། རུ་ཏྲ་བསྒྲལ་བ་ལས་བྱུང་བའི་དབང་པོའི་མེ་ཏོག་སོགས་མཆོད་རྫས་རྣམས་ཐོགས་པའི་ལྷ་མོ་མང་པོ་བདག་གི་ཐུགས་ཀ་ནས་སྤྲོས་ཏེ་མེ་ཏོག་དབུ་ལ་ཕུལ་བ་སོགས་གནས་སོ་སོར་སྟོབས་པས་མཉེས་པར་བསམ་མོ། །གསུམ་པ་དུག་གསུམ་གྱི་མཆོད་པ་ནི། འདོད་ཆགས་ཞེ་སྡང་གཏི་མུག་གི་ངོ་བོ། ཤ་ཁྲག་རུས་གསུམ་དཔལ་ཆེན་པོའི་ཚོགས་ལ་ཕུལ་ཏེ། མ་ཧཱ་མཾ་སོགས་བརྗོད་པས། དུག་གསུམ་རང་གནས་སུ་དག་པར་བསམ་མོ། །བཞི་པ་བདུད་རྩིའི་མཆོད་པ་ལ་གཉིས། མཆོད་པ་དངོས་དང་། དངོས་གྲུབ་བླང་བའོ། །དང་པོ་ནི། གདོད་ནས་དག་པའི་དམ་ཚིག་གི་རྫས་རྩ་བརྒྱད་སྟོང་སྦྱར་གྱི་སྨན། ཡེ་ཤེས་ལྷ་རྫོགས་ཤིང་དཀྱིལ་འཁོར་པ་གྲུབ་པའི་རྫས་ཆེན་པོ་འདི་དཔལ་ཆེན་པོའི་ཚོགས་ལ་འབུལ་ལོ་ཞེས་ཚིག་དང་། སརྦ་པཉྩ་སོགས་བརྗོད་ཅིང་། དྲི་མེད་བདུད་རྩིའི་རྒྱ་མཚོ་ལས་ཐེབ་སྐྱིན་ཉི་ཟླའི་གཡུ་ཁ་སྦྱོར་གྱིས་བཅུས་ཏེ་ཕུལ་བས་ལྷ་ཐམས་ཅད་བདེ་བ་ཆེན་པོའི་རོས་མཉེས་པར་བསམ་མོ། །གཉིས་པ་ནི། དེ་ལྟར་ལྷ་ཚོགས་རྣམས་ལ་མཉེས་པའི་མཆོད་པ་ཕུལ་བས། ལྷ་ཚོགས་རྣམས་ཀྱིས་སྐྱེས་ལ་སྐྱེས་ལེན་གྱི་ཚུལ་དུ་སྐུ་གསུང་ཐུགས་ཀྱི་དངོས་གྲུབ་ཐམས་ཅད་ཡི་གེ་གསུམ་གྱི་རྣམ་པར་བདུད་རྩིའི་ནང་དུ་འཕྲོས་པ་ལས། རྣལ་འབྱོར་པའི་ལྕེ་རྡོ་རྗེ་ཧཱུྃ་གིས་མཚན་པར་བསྒོམས་ཤིང་། བདུད་རྩི་ཡིག་འབྲུ་གསུམ་གྱི་རྣམ་པར་གནས་པ་དེ་ལས་མཐེབ་སྐྱིན་གྱིས་བླངས་པ་ལྕེ་ཐོག་ཏུ་བཞག་སྟེ་ལྕེ་ལ་ཐིམ་པས་སྐུ་གསུང་ཐུགས་མཆོག་གི་དངོས་གྲུབ་ཐམས་ཅད་ཐོབ་པར་བསམ།

suppressed on top and so forth, by saying, "SAMAYA TIṢTHA LHAN." Think that thereby, like water dissolving into water, the samaya maṇḍala dissolves into the wisdom maṇḍala, the main deity into the main deity, the retinue into the retinue, the palace into the palace, and they become indivisible.

Third, making offerings has seven parts:

First is the offering of pleasing homage. From the heart center of the main deity one emerges in the form of Vajrakumāra of activity. At the eastern gate one recites the verse beginning, "To the gatherings of herukas, who manifest in form from the basic space of phenomena." Then, with a respectful attitude one devotedly performs prostrations by bowing the five parts of the body to the ground. Then one says, "ATI PŪ HOḤ" which means "are you thoroughly pleased with the offerings?" Imagine that the gatherings of deities respond saying, "PRATIŚĀ PŪ HOḤ" meaning "they are absolutely pleasing."

Second is offering enjoyments. From the heart center of the lord many goddesses stream forth holding up offering substances from the liberation of Rudra such as the flower of the senses. Think that they create delight by making offerings to each part of the deities, such as giving flowers to the head.

Third is the offering of the three poisons. The flesh, blood, and bones that are the essence of desire, anger, and ignorance are offered to the gathering of Great Glorious Ones. Think that, by saying MAHĀMĀṂSA and so forth, the three poisons become naturally purified.

Fourth is the offering of amṛta. This consists of performance of the actual offering and receiving the accomplishments respectively. As for the former, one says, "To the gathering of the Great Glorious Ones I offer the primordially pure samaya substance, a medicine made from eight primary and one thousand subsidiary ingredients, a great substance that perfects the wisdom deities and accomplishes the maṇḍala." Then say, "SARVA PANCA" and so forth. Imagine that from the immaculate ocean of amṛta the thumb and ring-finger scoop up nectar with the sphere of the united sun and moon and offer it, making all the deities pleased by the taste of great bliss. As for the latter, having made pleasing offerings in this way to the gatherings of deities they radiate all the accomplishments of enlightened body, speech, and mind into the amṛta in the form of the three syllables—like a present returned for a gift. Then, visualize the tongue of the yogin as a vajra marked with a HŪṂ and take the amṛta with the ring-finger in the form of the three syllables and place it on your tongue. Think that by dissolving into the tongue all the supreme accomplishments of body, speech, and mind are attained.

ལྔ་པ་རཀྟའི་མཆོད་པ་ནི། དུང་ཆེན་སྣོད་དུ་བདག་ཏུ་འཛིན་པ་རུ་དྲ་བསྒྲལ་བ་ལས་བྱུང་བའི་དམར་ཆེན་ཐ་རླབས་མཁའ་ལ་འཕྱོ་བའི་རཀྟ་འདི་འཁོར་བ་སྟོང་པའི་ཕྱིར། དཔལ་ཆེན་འཁོར་དང་བཅས་ལ་འབུལ་ཞེས། སྔགས་བཅས་བརྗོད་པས། འཁོར་བ་ཁྲག་ཞག་གི་རྒྱ་མཚོ་མཆོད་པར་ཕུལ་བས་ལྷག་མེད་དུ་བཞེས་ཏེ། འཁོར་བའི་གནས་རྣམས་སྟོང་པར་བསམ། དྲུག་པ་གཏོར་མའི་མཆོད་པ་ནི། སྣོད་ཀྱི་འཇིག་རྟེན་བྷནྡྷ་འབར་བའི་ནང་དུ། བཅུད་སྲིད་པ་གསུམ་བསྒྲལ་བའི་གཏོར་མ་འདི་ཁྲག་འཐུང་ལྷ་ཚོགས་རྣམས་ལ་འབུལ་ཞེས་སྔགས་བཅས་བརྗོད་པས། འདོད་ཡོན་ལྔའི་ལོངས་སྤྱོད་མཐོ་དགུ་ལྡན་པས་ཐུགས་དམ་བསྐང༌། ལྷག་མ་ཤ་ཁྲག་ཏུ་གྱུར་པ་དམ་ཅན་རྣམས་ཀྱིས་ལོངས་སྤྱོད་པར་བསམ། བདུན་པ་སྦྱོར་སྒྲོལ་གྱི་མཆོད་པ་ནི། ཆོས་དབྱིངས་ཡུམ་གྱི་སོགས་དང༌། ང་ལ་བར་ཆད་བྱེད་པའི་སོགས་འབུལ་སྔགས་བཅས་བརྗོད་པས། ཁྲོ་མོ་ཤེས་རབ་དབྱིངས་ཀྱི་མཁའ་ལ། ཐབས་བདེ་བ་ཆེན་པོའི་རིགས་པའི་ཡེ་ཤེས་རྡོ་རྗེ་སྦྱོར་བས། རྣམ་རྟོག་ཡེ་ཤེས་སུ་བསྒྲལ་བས་སྦྱོར་སྒྲོལ་ཏེ། བདེ་སྟོང་འདུ་འབྲལ་མེད་པའི་སྦྱོར་མཚམས་ནས། བྱང་ཆུབ་སེམས་ཀྱི་མཆོད་པའི་སྤྲིན་དཔག་མེད་ཀྱིས་མཆོད་པར་བསམ། དགྲ་བགེགས་རྣམ་རྟོག་བསྒྲལ་བས་བསྟན་པའི་དགྲ་མེད་ཅིང༌། ཡེ་ཤེས་སྐྱེ་བ་ལ་གནོད་པའི་རྐྱེན་མེད་པར་བསམ་མོ། །བཞི་པ་བསྟོད་པ་ལ་བཞི་ལས། དང་པོ་བདག་ཉིད་རྩ་བའི་དཀྱིལ་འཁོར་ལ་བསྟོད་པ་ནི། ཡེ་ཤེས་གྲུབ་པའི་སྐུ་མཚན་དཔེ་ཡོངས་སུ་རྫོགས་ཤིང་སྒེག་པ་སོགས་སྐུའི་གར་དང་ལྡན་པ་གཟི་བརྗིད་བསྐལ་པའི་མེ་ལྟར་འབར་བ་དང༌། རྒོད་པས་སོགས་གསུང་གི་གར་དང༌། གྲགས་སྟོང་ཚངས་དབྱངས་ཡན་ལག་དྲུག་ཅུ་དང་ལྡན་པའི་གསུང་གཅིག་གིས་འཇིག་རྟེན་ཀུན་གྱི་མོས་པ་དང་མཚམས་པར་ཁྱབ་པར་གཡོ་བར་མཛད་པ་དང༌། སྙིང་རྗེ་བ་སོགས་ཐུགས་ཀྱི་གར་དང༌། མཁྱེན་པ་གཉིས་ལྡན་གྱི་ཐུགས་དང་ལྡན་པས་སྟོང་གསུམ་རབ་འབྱམས་མ་ལུས་པ་གང་ལ་གང་འདུལ་གྱིས་སྒྲོལ་བའི་དཔལ་ཁྲག་འཐུང་ཆེན་པོ་ཡབ་ཡུམ་གཉིས་སུ་མེད་པ་ལ་བསྟོད་པའོ། །གཉིས་པ་ཕྱོགས་བཅུ་ཁྲོ་བོའི་དཀྱིལ་འཁོར་ལ་བསྟོད་པ་ནི། འདོད་ལོག་སྤྱོད་པའི་སྐྱོན་སྒྲོལ་བའི་ཁྲོ་ཆེན་ཧཱུྃ་ཀ་ར་དང༌། དེ་བཞིན་མི་དགེ་བཅུ་སྒྲོལ་བའི་ཁྲོ་བོ་བཅུ་དང༌། ཤེས་རབ་ཕ་རོལ་ཕྱིན་པས་སྐུ་བཞེངས་པའི་སྒྲ་འབྱིན་མ་སོགས།

Fifth is the offering of rakta. "From the vessel of the great skull bright red waves gush forth into space as a result of having liberated Rudra—ego-clinging. In order to empty saṃsāra I offer this rakta to the Great Glorious One together with his retinue." Say this together with the mantra. Think that by offering saṃsāra as an ocean of blood and fat it is thoroughly accepted and thereby all the worlds of saṃsāra are emptied.

Sixth is the offering of bali. "To the gatherings of blood drinking deities I offer this bali made of the beings of the threefold existence who are liberated inside the vessel-like world of the blazing bhañja." Say this together with the mantra. Think that thereby enjoyments of the five sense pleasures, complete with all good qualities, amend the samaya vows and that the leftovers of meat and blood are enjoyed by the vow-holders.

Seventh is the offering of joining and liberation. Say the offering verses beginning with, "The expanse of the bhaga of the dharmadhātu consort ..." and "The obstructing spirits who create obstacles for me ..." together with their mantras. Thereby the means of the awareness-wisdom vajra of great bliss is joined into the female wrathful one's wisdom sphere, and conceptual thoughts are liberated into wisdom. Thus join and liberate. Imagine that from the place of their union, which is inseparably united bliss and emptiness, infinite cloud-banks of bodhicitta offerings are presented. Then, having liberated enemies, obstructers, and conceptual thought, no enemy for the teaching remains and so there is nothing to prevent the birth of wisdom.

The praises are divided in four:

First is the praise to the beings of the root maṇḍala. Praise the great glorious blood drinking lord and his indivisible consort whose bodies have accomplished wisdom and are fully complete with signs and marks. These bodies are endowed with the physical dance modes, such as the playful mode, and their majestic brilliance blazes like the fire at the end of an aeon. Their single voice, which is endowed with the verbal dance modes, such as agitation, as well as the empty resonance of the 60 aspects of the melodious voice of Brahmā fully pervades all worlds influencing their inclinations. Their minds are endowed with the mental dance modes, such as compassion, and the two-fold knowledge. In this way they liberate all the one billion world systems without exception through taming in any possible manner.

Second is the praise to the maṇḍala of the wrathful ones in the ten directions. The ten wrathful ones liberate the ten unwholesome actions, such as the great wrathful Hūmkāra who liberates the fault of engaging in sexual misconduct. Like Resounding Vajra, who arises from the pāramitā of wisdom,

ཕར་ཕྱིན་བཅུ་ལས་བཞེངས་པའི་ཁྲོ་མོ་བཅུ་དང་། ཐབས་ཡབ་ཀྱི་ཆ་ལས་སྐུ་སྤྲུལ་པའི་ཟ་བྱེད་བཅུ་དང་། ཤེས་རབ་ཡུམ་གྱི་ཆ་ལས་སྤྲུལ་པའི་གསོད་བྱེད་བཅུ་དང་བཅས་པ་ཕྱོགས་བཅུ་ཁྲོ་བོའི་དཀྱིལ་འཁོར་ལ་བསྟོད་པའོ། །གསུམ་པ་ཕུར་པ་རྫས་ཀྱི་དཀྱིལ་འཁོར་ལ་བསྟོད་པ་ནི། ཡོག་པར་རྟོགས་པའི་ཕྱོགས་ཞི་སྟོང་རང་ཁ་མ་ལྟ་བུས་བསད་ཅིང་། གཏི་མུག་གིས་མནན་པ་མ་ཡིན་ཏེ། ཐུགས་རྗེ་ཐབས་ལྡན་གྱི་སྦྱོར་བས་འགྲོ་བ་རྣམས་བསྒྲལ་བའི་ཕྱིར་དུ། རྒྱལ་བ་རྣམས་ཀྱི་སྙིང་རྗེ་འདུས་པའི་བདག་ཉིད། ཕུར་བུ་སྲས་མཆོག་རྣམས་ལ་བསྟོད་པ་སྟེ། དེ་ལྟར་དཀྱིལ་འཁོར་གསུམ་ལ་བསྟོད་བྱ་བསྟོད་བྱེད་གཉིས་སུ་མེད་པའི་ཚུལ་གྱིས་བསྟོད་པའོ། །བཞི་པ་སྒོ་སྲུང་དམ་ཅན་རྣམས་ལ་བསྟོད་པ་ནི། དཔལ་ཆེན་པོའི་སྤྱན་སྔར་ཁས་བླངས་པའི་སྒོ་མ་བཞི་དང་། ཕྱི་ཁྲམས་འཁོར་ཡུག་སྐྱོང་བའི་ཕོ་ཉ་དམ་ཅན་གྱི་ཚོགས་རྣམས་ལ་ཅི་ལྟར་བཅོལ་བའི་ཕྲིན་ལས་སྒྲུབ་པའི་ཕྱིར་ཕྱག་འཚལ་ལོ། །བདག་ཉིད་ལས་ཀྱི་ཧེ་རུ་ཀའི་རྣམ་པར་ཡོད་པ་དེ་ཉིད་གཙོ་བོའི་ཐུགས་ཀར་གཉིས་མེད་དུ་ཐིམ་པར་བསམ། ཡང་བསྟོད་པའི་ཚིག་བརྗོད་པ་བདག་གིས་བརྗོད་ཀྱང་དྲག་པོའི་གཞལ་ཡས་ཁང་ནམ་མཁའ་ནས་རང་སྒྲ་གྲགས་པའི་སྒོ་ནས་བསྟོད་པས་ལྷ་ཚོགས་རྣམས་མཉེས་པར་བསམ་ཞེས་པའང་སྟེ་མ་དག་བཞེད། འདི་དག་ནི་ཐབས་བསྐྱེད་པའི་རིམ་པ་གཙོ་ཆེ་བས་བག་ཆགས་སྣ་ཚོགས་པ་ལས་གྲུབ་པའི་རྟེན་སྣོད་ཀྱི་འཇིག་རྟེན་གཞལ་ཡས་ཁང་དང་། བརྟེན་པ་ལུས་ཀྱི་མངོན་ཞེན་ལྷ་ཡི་རྣམ་པས་སྦྱོང་ཞིང་སེམས་ཉིད་ཡུལ་ལ་འཕྲོ་བ་དེ་བཞག་པའི་ཐབས་ཏིང་ངེ་འཛིན་ཟབ་མོའི་བརྟེན་ལ་བཟུང་ནས་དག་རྫོགས་སྨིན་གསུམ་གྱི་ངོ་བོར་སྦྱོར་བའང་། འཁོར་བ་དང་རྣམ་པ་མཐུན་པས་སྲིད་པ་སྦྱོང་ཞིང་དག མྱང་འདས་དང་བཞུགས་ཚུལ་མཐུན་པས་འབྲས་བུ་གཞི་ལ་རྫོགས། གཉིས་ཀ་རྫོགས་རིམ་གྱི་སྨིན་བྱེད་དུ་འགྲོ་བ་ནི་སྤྱིའི་དོན་སྦྱོངས་པ་ལ་གཅེས་པ་ཡིན་ནོ། །

གཉིས་པ་རྣམ་དག་དྲན་པ་ནི། ཤེས་བྱའི་ཆོས་ཀུན་གཞི་ལམ་འབྲས་བུ་གསུམ་དུ་ངེས་པ་ལས། ལམ་བསྐྱེད་པའི་རིམ་པ་བསྒོམ་པའི་སྐབས་སུ་སྟོང་ཉིད་སྙིང་རྗེའི་སྙིང་པོ་ཅན་གྱི་རྩིས་ཐེབ་པའི་གཞི་འབྲས་སྦྱོལ་བའི་དག་པ་དྲན་པར་བྱ་སྟེ། དེ་ལྟར་མ་ཡིན་པའི་བསྐྱེད་རིམ་རང་རྒྱུད་པར་བསྒོམ་པའི་ཤེས་རབ་ཆུང་བ་རྣམས་གོལ་སར་ལྷུང་བར་འགྱུར་བས། དེ་ཡང་རྒྱུའི་ཡི་གེ་ལྟ་བུ་རང་རྒྱུད་པར་

the ten female wrathful ones arise from the ten pāramitās. The ten devourers are emanated from the male aspect of means and the ten slayers are emanated from the female aspect of wisdom. Praise this maṇḍala of the wrathful ones in the ten directions.

Third is the praise to the material kīla maṇḍala. Here one praises the supreme kīla sons who are the embodiment of the conqueror's compassion in order to liberate all beings by the application of skillful compassion that kills those with wrong ideas by natural anger unimpeded by ignorance.

In this way you should praise the three maṇḍalas in a manner where those praised and the one praising are indivisible.

Fourth is the praise to the gatekeepers and vow-holders. This means to pay homage to the four female gatekeepers who took oaths in the presence of the Great Glorious One as well as the gatherings of vow-holding attendants who guard the perimeter of the outer compound in order that they fulfill the activities as they have been entrusted. Think that, in the form of Karma Heruka, you dissolve indivisibly into the heart center of the central deity. Furthermore, although one is offering these praises oneself, past masters have taught how one may imagine that the gatherings of deities are pleased, since the praise naturally resounds from the sky of the wrathful palace.

In this regard, in the essential method of the development stage, the palace purifies the support of the vessel-like world, created through various habitual tendencies. The divine form purifies the supported, the attachment to the body being real. Likewise, when embracing the basis of profound samādhi, which is the way to stop the nature of mind projecting towards objects, it leads to the essence of purity, perfection, and maturation. Since they have features similar to saṃsāra they cleanse and purify existence, and as they are similar to the nature of nirvāṇa they perfect fruition in the ground. Both of these then lead to the maturation of the completion stage. These are important and precious general perspectives.

Recollection of Purity

Within the classification of all possible phenomena into ground, path, and fruition, when training in the development stage in the context of the path one should apply the recollection of purity that joins ground and fruition by reflection on emptiness imbued with compassion. Otherwise, people of low intelligence who train independently in the development stage will fall into sidetracks. Thus, if for example, one meditates independently on the seed syl-

བསྒོམ་ན། དེའི་དབྱིབས་ཅན་གྱི་སྲོག་ཆགས་དམན་པར་སྐྱེ་བར་འགྱུར་བ་དང་། ཞི་བའི་ང་རྒྱལ་རྒྱུད་པར་བསྒོམ་ན་ལྷ་ཚེ་རིང་པོར་སྐྱེ། ཁྲོ་བོའི་རྣམ་པ་རང་རྒྱུད་པར་བསྒོམ་ན་ལས་ཀྱི་སྲིན་པོར་སྐྱེ། མགོ་བརྙན་རང་རྒྱུད་པས་དུར་ཁྲོད་ཀྱི་ཕྲ་སྲུང་སོགས་སུ་སྐྱེ། ཞི་སྡང་རང་རྒྱུད་པས་དམྱལ་བའི་གནས་སུ་སྐྱེ་བར་འགྱུར་བས། དེས་ན་རྣམ་དག་དྲན་པ་ཤིན་ཏུ་གལ་ཆེ་བས། དེ་ལ་གཉིས། དང་པོ་རྟེན་གྱི་དག་དྲན་ནི། ནམ་མཁའ་ཀུན་ཏུ་བཟང་མོའི་མཁའ་ཀློང་སོགས། འབྱུང་བ་ལྔ་ཡུམ་ལྔའི་མཁའ་ཀློང་རྣམ་པར་དག་པ། གཉིས་འཛིན་གྱི་རྣམ་པར་རྟོག་པ་ལས་བྱུང་བའི་གདོན་བགེགས་གང་གིས་ཀྱང་མི་ཚུགས་པའི་བརྟར་བསྲུང་བའི་གུར་ཁང་སྤྱི་དང་། ཁྱད་པར་གདུལ་བྱའི་རྒྱུད་ཀྱི་ཉོན་མོངས་པ་རྩད་གཅོད་པའི་ནང་མ་མཚོན་ཆའི་འཁོར་ལོ་རྩིབས་བཅུ་པའི་གུར་ཁང་། ཚོགས་བརྒྱད་རྣམ་པར་དག་པའི་དུར་ཁྲོད་ཆེན་པོ་བརྒྱད། ཆོས་ཀྱི་དབྱིངས་ལས་འཁོར་བའི་སྐྱོན་གྱིས་ནམ་ཡང་མ་གོས་པའི་བརྟར་པདྨ། ལས་བཞི་ལྷུན་གྱིས་གྲུབ་པ་སྣ་ཚོགས་རྡོ་རྗེ། གཉིས་སུ་མེད་པའི་ཡེ་ཤེས་ཀྱི་སྣང་བ་ཉིད་པས་གཞལ་ཡས་ཁང་ཕྱི་རིན་པོ་ཆེ་སྣ་ཚོགས་ལས་གྲུབ་པ་ཚད་དང་མཚན་ཉིད་ཡོངས་སུ་རྫོགས་པ་ཡེ་ཤེས་ལྔའི་བདག་ཉིད་དང་། དུས་གསུམ་གྱི་སངས་རྒྱས་མ་ལུས་པའི་བཞུགས་གནས་སུ་གྱུར་པ་སྐུ་གསུམ་ལྷུན་གྱིས་གྲུབ་པའི་བརྟར། ནང་དུར་ཁྲོད་ཀྱི་རྫས་ཐོད་པ་སྐམ་རྙིང་རློན་གསུམ་གྱི་རྩིགས་པ་མངོན་སྤྱོད་ལས་ཀྱིས་གདུག་པ་ཅན་ཚར་གཅོད་པའི་ཕྱིར་དབུས་གྲུ་གསུམ་མཐིང་ནག་རྡོ་རྗེའི་བྲག་ཆེན། འཇིགས་སུ་རུང་བ་ལ་ཁྲག་གི་མཚེ་རིས་ཀྱིས་མཚན་པ་རྗེས་སུ་འཛིན་པའི་ལས་ཀྱི་གདུལ་བྱ་ལ་ཆགས་པས་ཕྱི་རོལ་ཟླ་གམ་ཁྲག་མཚོ་ཐ་རླབས་འཁྲུགས་པ་གསུམ་གྱིས་བསྐོར་བ་དེ་ཡང་གཉིས་མེད་ཀྱི་ཡེ་ཤེས་ཆེན་པོ་གཅིག་གིས་བསྡུས་པས་ཐོད་ར་ཟླུམ་པོ་དང་བཅས་པ་ཆེ་བའི་ཡོན་ཏན་ལྷུན་གྱིས་གྲུབ་པས་རིན་ཆེན་ཟུར་བརྒྱད་པ། བདེན་བཞི་རྣམ་པར་དག་པའི་གྲུ་ཆད་བཞི། མཉམ་ཉིད་བླང་དོར་མེད་པའི་ཁྲམས་ཀྱིས་ཡོངས་སུ་བསྐོར་བ། རྣམ་ཐར་བཞིའི་སྒོ་ནས་འཇུག་ཅིང་འཁོར་བ་རྒྱུན་གཅོད་པའི་སྒོ་བཞི་ཞིང་གི་སྒོ་ལོགས་བཅད་པ། འབྱུང་པོ་ཕོ་མོའི་རང་བཞིན་རུ་སྦལ་གྱི་ཡ་ཐེམ་མ་ཐེམ་བྱས་པ་སེར་སྣ་དག་པ་སྦྲུལ་ནག་གི་སྐྱེས་བུ་ཞི་སྡང་དག་པ། ལྷ་བརྒྱད་ཀྱི་ཀ་བ། ང་རྒྱལ་དག་པ། ཀླུ་བརྒྱད་ཀྱི་ཀ་གདན་གཏི་མུག་དག་པ། བཟའ་བརྒྱད་ཀྱི་ཀ་གཞུ་ཕྲག་དོག་རྣམ་པར་དག་པ། སྒྲུ་སྐར་དྲལ་ཕྱམ་འདོད་ཆགས་རྣམ་པར་དག་པ།

lable one will be born as an inferior insect having that shape. If one meditates independently on the pride of a peaceful deity one will be born as a long-living god. By meditating independently on the form of a wrathful deity one will take birth as an activity rākṣasa. By meditating independently on the multi-headed ones one will take rebirth as a cemetery fox or jackal. By meditating independently on anger one will be born in a hell. Thus, the recollection of purity is extremely important.

There are two points to this:

First is the recollection of the purity of the support. In the same way that the sky is the expanse of Samantabhadrī, the five elements are the absolute purity of the expanse of the five female buddhas. In general, the protective dome signifies not being harmed by any demon or obstructing spirit arising from dualistic thought. In particular, the inner dome of the ten-spoked weapon wheel symbolizes cutting the root of disturbing emotions of those to be tamed. The eight totally pure charnel grounds symbolize the eight collections of consciousness. The lotus is a sign that the faults of saṃsāra never stain the basic space of phenomena. The vajra-cross symbolizes the spontaneous accomplishment of the four activities.

Because of the appearance of non-dual wisdom, the outside of the palace is made of various precious stones. All proportions and distinguishing features are the identity of the five wisdoms and the abode of all buddhas of the three times. As a sign of the spontaneous accomplishment of the three kāyas, the inner walls are made of the charnel ground substances of dry, rotten, and fresh skulls. Having totally annihilated evil ones with the activity of direct action, there is a deep blue, triangular, mighty vajra rock in the middle. It is surrounded on the outside by three crescent shaped stormy oceans, terrifying and marked with designs of bloody fangs as a sign of fondness for those who can be trained through being accepted as followers. Furthermore, because this is subsumed into one by great nondual wisdom, the maṇḍala has a round wall of skulls. The eight-sided jewel symbolizes the spontaneous accomplishment of superior qualities. The four noble truths are the purity of the square. It is encircled by the wall of equality free from acceptance and rejection. The falling bars[352] of corpses at the four gates symbolize the entrance into the dharma by means of the four liberations and cutting the continuity of saṃsāra. The upper and lower tortoise sills that have the nature of male and female bhuta spirits are purified miserliness. The black serpents are purified anger, the eight deva pillars are purified pride, the eight nāga pillar bases are purified ignorance, the eight planetary pillar capitals are fully purified jealousy, and the roof wood-

ཞིང་ཆེན་ལྤགས་པའི་ཐོག་ཕུབ། བདག་འཛིན་རྣམ་པར་དག་པ། ཉི་ཟླའི་མཐོང་ཀར། འགྲོ་བ་རྣམས་མ་རིག་མུན་པ་སེལ་བའི་བརྡ། ལྕང་ལོར་བཅས་པའི་ཐོད་པའི་ཕ་གུ། ཡེ་ཤེས་སྣང་བས་ཀུན་ནས་མཛེས་པ་ཁ་བད་ཀྱི་འོག་ནས་ཙིཏྟ་སྣ་ཚོགས་པའི་ཕྲེང་བ་དང་། རུས་པའི་དྲ་བ་དང་དྲ་བ་ཕྱེད་པས་མཚན་པ། ཟག་པ་མེད་པའི་བདེ་བ་རྒྱུན་མི་ཆད་པའི་བརྡ། ཐ་མལ་གྱི་རྣམ་རྟོག་སྣ་ཚོགས་པ་ཡེ་ཤེས་ཀྱི་གཟི་བྱིན་གྱིས་རྣམ་པར་གནོན་པའི་བརྡར། ཞིང་ཆེན་དང་ཀེང་རུས་ཀྱི་འཕན་དང་རྒྱལ་མཚན་སྒྲེང་བ། ཕྱོགས་བཞིར་ཁྲག་གི་ཞམ་ཆུ་ཆེན་པོ་འབབ་པ་ལས་དང་རྟུལ་གྱི་ཚང་ཚིང་མི་གནས་པར་སྟོན་པ། ཐོ་བརྩེགས་གནམ་ལྕགས་ཀྱི་གཟེར་ཐལ་ལེ་བར་བཏབ་པ། ཐམས་ཅད་ཆོས་ཉིད་དུ་མི་འགྱུར་བ། ཙིཏྟའི་ཏོག་ཆེན་པོ་གཅིག་ཏུ་གྱུར་པ་ཀུན་ཀྱང་རང་བྱུང་ཡེ་ཤེས་ཆེན་པོ་གཅིག་ཏུ་ཡོངས་སུ་རྫོགས་པའི་བརྡ་རྟགས་དང་། ཡེ་ཤེས་ཀྱི་སྤྱོད་ཡུལ་ཉིད་ལས་མི་གཞན་པའི་བརྡར། ཕྱི་ནས་བལྟས་ན་ནང་གསལ་ཞིང་ནང་ནས་བལྟས་ན་ཕྱི་གསལ་བའོ། །དེའི་དབུས་སུ་གདན་ཉི་ཟླ་ཐབས་དང་ཤེས་རབ། མ་ཆགས་པ་པདྨ་གཙོ་བོ་ལ་ལྷ་ཆེན་ཕོ་མོ་རྒྱལ་བྱེད་དཔའ་རྟགས་ཀྱི་གདན་ཏེ། གཞན་རྣམས་ལའང་དེ་བཞིན་ཤེས་པར་བྱའོ། །གཉིས་པ་བརྟེན་པ་ལྷའི་དག་པ་དྲན་པ་ནི། དཔལ་ཆེན་པོའི་སྐུ་མདོག་མཐིང་ནག་ཆོས་ཉིད་འགྱུར་བ་མེད་པ། སྐུ་གསུང་མཆོན་པའི་ཞལ་གསུམ། ཐེག་པ་རིམ་དགུའི་དོན་ཇི་ལྟ་བར་གཟིགས་པའི་སྤྱན་དགུ། རལ་པ་གྱེན་དུ་བསྒྲེང་པ་བྱང་སེམས་འཕོ་བ་སྤངས་པ། བདུད་བཞི་ལས་རྒྱལ་བའི་དཔའ་རྟགས་རྡོ་རྗེ་ཕྱེད་པ། ཡེ་ཤེས་དྲུག་གི་ཕྱག་དྲུག བསྡུ་བ་བཞིའི་ཞབས་བཞི། གཡས་ཕྱག་དང་པོའི་རྩེ་དགུ་ས་དགུའི་རྟོག་པ་འཇོམས་པ། བར་པས་རྩེ་ལྔ་དུག་ལྔ་དབྱིངས་སུ་སྒྲོལ་བ། གཡོན་དང་པོ་མེ་ཕུང་མ་རིག་པའི་བུད་ཤིང་བསྲེགས་པ། བར་པས་ཁ་ཊྭཱཾ་དུག་གསུམ་རྩད་ནས་གཅོད་པ། འོག་མ་གཉིས་རི་རབ་ཕུར་བུས་གདུག་ཅན་ཐལ་བར་རློག་པ། སྒྲོ་གཤོག་ཐབས་ཤེས་ཟུང་འཇུག་གིས་འགྲོ་བ་སྒྲོལ་བ། སྤྱི་བོར་རུས་པའི་འཁོར་ལོ་བསམ་གཏན་ཕར་ཕྱིན་སོགས་རྒྱན་དྲུག་ཕ་རོལ་ཕྱིན་པ་དྲུག་རྫོགས་པ། སྦྲུལ་ཆུན་ཞི་སྡང་རྣམ་པར་དག་པ། གླང་ཆེན་ཀོ་རློན་གཏི་སྨུག་དག་པ། གཡང་གཞི་འདོད་ཆགས་རྣམ་དག སྟག་ཤམ་ང་རྒྱལ་རྣམ་པར་དག་པ། བྱུག་པའི་རྫི་གསུམ་རྟག་ཆད་དང་། གཉིས་ཀྱི་མཐའ་ལ་མི་གནས་པ། རྡོ་རྗེ་གོ་ཁྲབ་ཕྱི་ནང་གི་གནོད་བྱེད་གང་གིས་ཀྱང་མི་ཚུགས་པ། མ་རིག་མུན་པ་སེལ་བའི་ཡེ་

work of stars is fully purified desire. The ceiling of human skin is fully purified ego-clinging. The windows of the sun and moon are a sign of dispelling the darkness of ignorance. The skull border with braids of hair symbolizes utter beautification with the light of wisdom. Below the beams of the roof the garlands of several hearts and the bone lattice ornamented with tassels are signs of ceaseless untainted bliss. As a sign that the magnificent splendor of wisdom overcomes the various ordinary thoughts, streamers and victory banners of human skin and bones are hoisted. The descent of the mighty blood gutters at the four sides symbolizes that the denseness of karma and imperfections is obliterated without remainder. The meteoric nails that unimpededly pierce the tiers symbolize that everything remains unchanging in the natural state. The single great citta top ornament is a symbol that everything is perfectly contained within the single great self-existing wisdom. As a sign that there is no other experience apart from wisdom itself, the inside of the palace is seen when observed from the outside and when looking out from the inside the outside can be seen. In the middle is the main throne where the sun and moon seats constitute means and knowledge and the lotus unattachment. Thereupon are the seats of Mahādeva and Mahādevī, symbolizing victorious bravery. The other seats should be understood similarly.

Second is the recollection of the purity of the supported deities. The dark blue body color of the Great Glorious One symbolizes the unchanging intrinsic nature. Three faces illustrate the three kāyas. Nine eyes see the meaning of the nine gradual vehicles as they are. The upward streaming mane shows abandonment of bodhicitta transfer. The half vajra is a heroic symbol for having overcome the four māras. The six arms are the six wisdoms. The four feet are the four means of magnetizing. The nine-pronged vajra in the top right hand conquers the concepts of the first nine bhūmis. The five-pronged vajra in the middle right hand symbolizes the liberation of the five poisons into basic space. The mass of fire in the top left hand burns the firewood of ignorance. The skull staff in the middle left hand cuts the three poisons at the root. The kīla of the central mountain in the lower two hands destroys evildoers to dust. The feathered wings of united means and knowledge liberate beings. The six bone ornaments symbolize the perfection of the six pāramitās, like the bone wheel at the top of the head symbolizing meditative concentration. The bundle of snakes is fully purified anger. The elephant hide is purified ignorance. The antelope skin is fully purified desire. The tiger skirt is fully purified pride. The three essences symbolize not dwelling in the extremes of either permanence, disruption, or both. The vajra armor symbolizes not being harmed by

ཤེས་ཀྱི་མེ་ཕུང་རབ་ཏུ་འབར་བའོ། །བདེ་སྟོང་གཉིས་སུ་མེད་པའི་ཡེ་ཤེས་ཀྱི་ཡུལ་ཅན་དུ་གྱུར་པས། འཁོར་བ་ལ་སྟོང་ཉིད་ཀྱི་རྒྱས་འདེབས་པས་འཁོར་ལོ་རྒྱས་འདེབས། ཆོས་ཉིད་འགྱུར་མེད་གཅིག་ཏུ་རྟོགས་པར་བྱེད་པས་ཞལ་གཅིག ཐབས་ཤེས་ཟུང་འཇུག་གི་ཕྱག་གཉིས། ཆོས་དབྱིངས་ཀྱིས་རིག་པའི་ཡེ་ཤེས་ཐམས་ཅད་དུ་མི་གཏོང་བ་ཉིད་ཀྱིས་ཕྱག་ཞབས་གཡས་ཡབ་ལ་འཁྱུད་པ། ཤེས་རབ་ཀྱི་ཐབས་ལ་ཆགས་པས་གཡོན་དུང་དམར་ཞལ་དུ་སྟོབ་པ། གཞན་རྒྱན་ཆས་ཡབ་དང་མཐུན་པ་ལ། ཁྱད་པར་དུ་གཟིག་ཤམ་དགའ་བ་བཅུ་དྲུག་གི་རྟེན་ཐིག་ལེ་རྣམས་མ་འདྲེས་ཡོངས་སུ་རྫོགས་པ་ཉིད་དོ། །གཞན་ཡང་ཁྲོ་བཅུ་ཡབ་ཡུམ་རྣམས་སྐུ་མདོག་ཕྱག་མཚན་རྒྱན་ཆས་སོགས་འདྲ་བར་གོང་བཞིན་དག་དྲན་སྦྱར་ཏེ། ཁྱད་པར་མཚན་གྱི་དོན་ཙམ་ལ་ཁྲོ་བོ་ནི་ངམ་ངམ་ཞུགས་ཀྱིས་གདུལ་བྱ་འདུལ་བའི་ཕྱིར་རུ་ཏྲ་ཁྲོས་པ་ཡིན་ཀྱང་། འདིར་ཐབས་ཀྱིས་ཟིན་པས་ན་ཆེན་པོ། དེ་ཡང་ཚངས་པ་ལྷ་བུ་གཞན་གྱི་དབང་དུ་མ་གྱུར་པ་རྣམས་ཉིད་ཀྱི་གདུལ་བྱར་སྤྱོད་པར་མཛད་པས་ན་ཧཱུྃ་མཛད་དང་། ཐམས་ཅད་བསྐྱེད་པའི་ཕྱིར་རམ་སྲས་ཀྱི་དལ་འབྱུང་བས་ན་ཡུམ། གཉིས་སུ་མེད་ཅིང་མི་ཕྱེད་པས་ན་རྡོ་རྗེ། ཆོས་དབྱིངས་སྐྱེ་བ་མེད་པའི་སྒྲ་འབྱིན་པས་ན་སྒྲ་འབྱིན་མ་གཞི་ངེས་པ་ལ་སྣ་ཚོགས་སུ་སྤྲུལ་པས་སམ། ཡབ་ཡུམ་གྱི་ཐུགས་ལས་སྤྲུལ་ཞིང་བྱུང་བས་ན་སྤྲུལ་པ། བྱད་གཟུགས་མི་འདྲ་བ་གཅིག་ལ་གཅིག་གིས་སྲུས་པས་ན་ཕྲ་མན། ཕྱག་བརྙན་ནི་རྒྱལ་པོའི་བཀའ་ཉན་པའི་ཕྱག་བརྙན་པ་ལྟར། དཔལ་ཆེན་པོ་ཡབ་ཡུམ་དང་། ཁྲོ་བོ་ཁྲོ་མོའི་ལས་བྱེད་པ་སྟེ། དེ་ཡང་ཕག་གི་མགོ་ཅན། དཔེར་ན་ཕག་རྣན་ལ་གནས་ཤིང་གཙང་རྩོག་མེད་པ་བཞིན་དུ་སྙིང་རྗེས་སེམས་ཅན་གྱི་དོན་བྱེད་ཅིང་ཕྱོགས་རིས་སུ་མི་འབྱེད་པ། ཟྱིགས་བུ་གཉིད་ཆེ་ཞིང་རྙམ་ལ་གནས་པ་བཞིན་དུ་ཆོས་ཉིད་མི་རྟོག་པའི་ངང་ལ་གནས་ཤིང་འཁོར་བའི་འདམ་དང་བྲལ་བ། རྟག་ཆད་ཀྱི་མཐའ་ལས་རྒྱལ་བས་ན་རྣམ་པར་རྒྱལ་བ། ཆོས་ཉིད་ཀྱི་དོན་ལ་མངའ་སྙེམས་པས་ན་རྡོ་རྗེ་སྙེམ་མ། སྟག་ལ་རི་མོ་བཀྲ་ལ། ཟས་སུ་ཤ་ཟ་བ་བཞིན་དུ། ཕྱི་ནང་གི་ཆོས་ཐམས་ཅད་མ་འདྲེས་པར་གསལ་ལ་གཉིས་མེད་ཀྱི་ཡེ་ཤེས་ཐུགས་སུ་ཆུད་པ།

any outer or inner harm doer whatsoever. The completely blazing fire is made of the wisdom that lights up the darkness of ignorance.

Dīptacakra is so called since, as the one who experiences empty bliss, non-dual wisdom, she marks cyclic existence with the seal of emptiness.[353] Having realized the innate nature to be unchanging and single, she has one face. Her two hands are the unity of means and knowledge. Because the basic space of phenomena never lets go of awareness wisdom, she embraces the lord with her right arm and leg.[354] Because of her fondness for the wisdom method, her left hand offers a blood-filled skull to the mouth of the lord. The other ornaments and attributes are similar to the lord. However, the leopard skirt in particular signifies the completion of the distinctive spheres that constitute the support for the 16 joys. The body color, hand implements, ornaments, and attributes of the other ten pairs of wrathful males and females are similar, so apply the recollection of purity as mentioned above.

Stated in brief, the meaning of their names is the following: *wrathful* is used because Rudra is wrathful in order to tame spontaneously those who need taming. However, at this point the wrath is embraced by skillful means and so it is *great*. Furthermore, *Hūṃkāra* receives his name since he gathers disciples that, like Brahmā, are not under the power of others. *Consort* is used because of giving birth to all or because of being the womb of the offspring. Because she creates the sound of the unborn basic space of phenomena she is called *Resounding*, and *Vajra* because of being non-dual and undivided. The *emanations* are so called because they emanate into many beings from a single ground and because they are emanated and appear from the mind of the lord and consort. The *hybrids* receive their name because their different appearances adorn each other[355] while the *attendants* are so called as they carry out the work of the great wrathful lord and consort and the male and female wrathful ones like an attendant who obeys the king's command. The *Pig-headed One* is so called because it compassionately carries out the welfare of sentient beings without partiality in the same way that a pig lives in soggy filth and has no concept of clean and dirty. As for the *Lizard-headed One*, it is given its name because it dwells in a state free from conceptualizing the natural state and since it is free from the mud of saṃsāra just like a lizard sleeps a lot and lives in dry places.

Likewise, *Vijaya* receives his name because of having conquered the extremes of permanence and disruption and *Haughty Vajra* because she has mastered the meaning of the innate nature. The *Tiger-Headed One* is so called because it understands the non-dual wisdom that cognizes all outer and inner phenomena without mixing them up just like the tiger has a clear pattern and

བྱ་རྒོད་ཤ་ཟན་ཡིན་ཡང་སྲོག་མི་གཅོད་ཅིང་རོ་གང་དུ་འདུག་པ་མཐོང་བ་ལྟར། གདུལ་བྱའི་དོན་བྱེད་པར་རང་རྒྱུད་དུ་ཞེན་པ་མེད་ཀྱང་། དེ་དང་དེའི་བསམ་པ་མཁྱེན་པའོ། །ཆོས་ཉིད་འགྱུར་བ་མེད་པ་ཐུགས་སུ་ཆུད་པས། མཐར་འཛིན་པའི་ལྟ་བ་ངན་པ་བརླག་པར་བྱེད་པས་ཁྲོ་བོ་ཆེན་པོ་དབྱུག་པ་སྔོན་པོ་དང་། རིག་པའི་ཡེ་ཤེས་སྤྲེར་མོ་དང་འདྲ་བས་ཆོས་ཉིད་ཀྱི་དོན་འཛིན་པས་རྡོ་རྗེ་སྤྲེར་མོ། གཡག་ཉི་ཧམ་ལ་མི་འགྱུར་བ་བཞིན་དུ། རྣམ་པར་རྟོག་པའི་མངོན་སྤྱོད་ཀྱིས་གདུག་ཅན་ཚར་གཅོད་པ་དང་། བྱ་རོག་གི་མིག་གིས་སྟེང་འོག་གཉིས་ཀར་དུས་གཅིག་ལ་མཐོང་བ་དང་འདྲ་བར། འཁོར་འདས་གཉིས་ཀར་མི་རྟོག་པར་གཟིགས་པའོ། །ལྷོ་ཕྱོགས་ཀྱི་བགེགས་ཀྱི་གཉེན་པོ་ཡིན་པས་གཤིན་རྗེ་གཤེད་དང་། རྣམ་པར་མི་རྟོག་པའི་ཡེ་ཤེས་ལ་མངའ་བརྙེས་པས་ན་དུར་ཁྲོད་བདག་མོ། ཤ་བ་རྫི་རྣོ་ཞིང་འབྲོས་ལ་བརྟོན་པ་ལྟར་རྣམ་རྟོག་ཆོས་ཉིད་དུ་ངེས་ཟིན་ཅིང་འཁོར་བའི་གནས་ན་མི་གནས་པ་དང་འུག་པ་ཉིན་མོ་མི་མཐོང་ཞིང་། མཚན་མོ་མཐོང་བ་ལྟར། འཁྲུལ་རྟོག་ནུབ་ཅིང་ཡང་དག་པའི་དོན་གསལ་བའོ། །ཉོན་མོངས་པ་དང་རྣམ་པར་རྟོག་པས་མི་སྤྱོད་ཅིང་འགྲོ་བའི་དོན་ལ་བརྩོན་པས་མི་གཡོ་བ་དང་། རང་བཞིན་མི་རྟོག་ཀྱི་ཤེས་རབ་ཀྱིས་ཉོན་མོངས་པ་ཡེ་ཤེས་སུ་རྟུང་བས་ན་ཡུམ་རྡོ་རྗེ་གདུན་ཁྱུང་མ་དང་། གཟིག་ཐིག་ལེ་བཀྲ་མཆོང་རྩལ་ཆེ་བ། ཤེས་བྱ་མ་འགགས་པར་མཁྱེན་ལ་འགྲོ་བ་སྒྲོལ་བའི་སྟོབས་དང་ལྡན་པ་དང་། ཁྭ་ཏ་ལ་སྒྲིབ་ཤིང་ཡོད་པས་གཞན་གྱི་མི་མཐོང་བ་བཞིན་གནས་ལུགས་ཀྱི་དོན་ཆུད་པ་གཞན་གྱིས་མི་རྟོགས་པའོ། །བརྩོན་འགྲུས་སྒྱུར་བའི་ཤུགས་ཀྱིས་རྟའི་དབུ་བྱུང་བས་ན་རྟ་མགྲིན་དང་། མཚན་མའི་རྣམ་རྟོག་ལ་ཧམས་ནས་ན་ཡུམ་རྡོ་རྗེ་གཏུམ་མོ། བྱི་ལ་ཡང་རྩལ་ཆེ་ཞིང་རྒྱུད་ཞི་བའི་ཚུལ་དང་ལྡན་པ་ལྟར། འགྲོ་བ་སྒྲོལ་བའི་དོན་བརྩོན་ཅིང་ཐུགས་ཞི་བའི་ངང་ལས་མ་གཡོས་པ་དང་། སྤུ་ཤུད་ལ་མིག་རྩེ་ཡོད་ཅིང་གཤོག་པ་དྲག་པོར་གཡོབ་པ་ལྟར། མ་རིག་པའི་ལིང་ཏོག་སེལ་བར་བརྩོན་ཞིང་འགྲོ་བའི་དོན་བྱེད་པའོ། །

devours meat. The *Vulture-Headed One* gets its name because it remains aware of those to be tamed as well as their wishes and yet has no attachment to itself when benefiting them which is similar to a vulture that, although carnivorous, does not take life and notices corpses wherever they are.

The great wrathful *Nīladaṇḍa* is so called because of having taken the unchanging innate nature to heart and thereby having destroyed the evil view of clinging to extremes and *Vajra Claw* because awareness wisdom is like a claw and so can hold the meaning of the innate nature. The *Yak-headed One* gets its name since its non-conceptual subjugation thoroughly destroys evildoers, just like a Yak remains furious, while the *Crow-headed One* is so called because it non-conceptually perceives both saṃsāra and nirvāṇa in the same way that the eye of a crow sees both up and down at the same time.

Yamāntaka receives his name on account of opposing obstructing forces in the southern direction[356] and *Lady of the Charnel Ground* because she masters utterly non-conceptual wisdom. The *Deer-headed One* is so called since it identifies conceptual thought as the innate nature and does not abide in saṃsāra similar to a deer that has a keen sense of smell and tries hard to flee. The *Owl-headed One* gets its name as deluded thoughts have set and the utterly pure reality is shining in the same way that an owl cannot see in the day but at night.

As for *Acala*, he received his name as he does not indulge in disturbing emotions and conceptual thinking and perseveres in the welfare of beings while his consort *Vajra Mortar* got her name as she grinds disturbing emotions into wisdom by means of natural non-conceptual knowledge. The *Leopard-headed One* is so called as it unimpededly knows all there is to know and possesses the strength to liberate beings just like a leopard has bright spots and great skill in leaping. Likewise, the *Raven-headed One* is so called because it enters into the reality of the natural condition that others do not realize similar to a raven that is unseen by others because it possesses the wand of invisibility.

Hayagrīva is so called because a horse head appeared on top of his head through the power of swift diligence, and his consort *Fierce Vajra* because she rages at conceptual thought. The *Cat-headed One* receives its name because it endeavors in the purpose of liberating beings while remaining in a peaceful state of mind just like a cat has great dexterity and a calm state of mind. As for the *Hoopoe Bird-headed One*, it got its name since it endeavors in clearing away the pellicle of ignorance and carries out the benefit of beings similar to a hoopoe bird which possesses an eye elixir and flaps its wings violently.

ཆོས་ཉིད་ལ་རྣམ་པར་རྟོག་པས་མ་བསྐྱོད་ཅིང་། དྲེགས་པ་ཅན་འཇོམས་པས་གཞན་གྱིས་མི་ཐུབ་པ་དང་། རིག་པའི་ཡེ་ཤེས་མདའ་ལྷ་བུ་འཕངས་ནས་རྣམ་རྟོག་གི་ཡིད་གསོད་པས་ན། ཡུམ་རྡོ་རྗེ་མདའ་སྒྲིམ་མ། སྙིང་ཀི་སྲོག་གཅོད་པ་ལ་དགའ་ཞིང་སྙིང་རྗེ་ལ་ཕྱོགས་རིས་མེད་པ་བཞིན། དམ་ཉམས་སྒྲོལ་ཞིང་སྟོད་ལྡན་གྱི་དོན་བྱེད་པ་དང་། ཁྲ་ནི་སྤྱིར་མོ་རྟེ་ཞིང་སྤྲར་དམ་པ་བཞིན། ཐུགས་རྗེ་ཆེན་པོའི་གདུལ་བྱ་ཡལ་བར་མི་འདོར་བའོ། །རྣམ་རྟོག་གི་བདུད་ལ་ཡེ་ཤེས་ཀྱིས་རྩིས་འདེབས་པས་ན་བདུད་རྩི་འཁྱིལ་བ་དང་། གཉིས་མེད་ཡེ་ཤེས་རླུང་རྟ་བུས། རྣམ་རྟོག་སྤྲུར་མ་རྟར་གཏོར་བར་བྱེད་པས་ན་ཡུམ་རྡོ་རྗེ་རླུང་འཁྱིན་མ། སིདྡྷི་ནི་ཡང་རྩལ་ཆེ་ཞིང་གཅན་གཟན་གཞན་ཟིལ་གྱིས་གནོན་པ་ལྟར། རྟོགས་པའི་རྩལ་གྱིས་ཉོན་མོངས་པ་ཟིལ་གྱིས་གནོན་པ་དང་། ཕ་བོང་གིས་ཆོས་གསུམ་དྲན་པ་ལྟར། ཆོས་ཀུན་དུས་གཅིག་ཏུ་རྟོགས་པའོ། །འདོད་ཁམས་གཟུགས་ཁམས། གཟུགས་མེད་དེ་ཁམས་གསུམ་ལས་ཡང་ཐོག་གི་རྣམ་པར་རྒྱལ་བས་ན་ཁམས་གསུམ་རྣམ་རྒྱལ་དང་། མཚན་མའི་ཆོས་ཀུན་མཚན་མ་མེད་པའི་ངང་དུ་གསོད་པས་ན་ཡུམ་རྡོ་རྗེ་གསོད་བྱེད་མ། དོམ་ནི་ཁྲོ་གཏུམ་ཆེ་ལ་མདོག་གནག་ཀྱང་སྙིང་དཀར་བ་བཞིན། སེམས་ཅན་སྒྲོལ་བའི་ཐབས་ལ་བརྩོན་ཀྱང་ཐུགས་ཞི་བ་ཆོས་ཉིད་ལས་མ་གཡོས་པ་དང་། སྤྲེ་མོང་ཡང་རྩལ་ཆེ་ཞིང་ཕྱོགས་ཀུན་ཏུ་རྒྱུག་པ་ལྟར། ཕྲིན་ལས་མྱུར་མགྱོགས་ཀྱིས་གདུལ་བྱ་སྣ་ཚོགས་པའི་དོན་བྱེད་པའོ། །གདུལ་བྱའི་དོན་དབྱེ་བ་མེད་ཅིང་སྒྲོལ་ནུས་པས་སྟོབས་པོ་ཆེ་དང་། ཐུགས་རྗེ་འགྲོ་བ་དོན་ལ་ངེས་པར་སྐྱོད་པས་ན་ཡུམ་རྡོ་རྗེ་བསྐྱོད་མ། དྲེད་ནི་རོ་ངན་ལ་གཉིད་ཆེ་བ་ལྟར་ཐུགས་རྗེས་སེམས་ཅན་མི་གཏོང་ཞིང་རྣམ་རྟོག་གིས་མི་གཡོ་བ་དང་། བྱི་བ་ཚང་སྒོ་མང་ཡང་གཅིག་ཏུ་འགྲོ་བ་ལྟར། ཆོས་སྒོ་བརྒྱད་ཁྲི་བཞི་སྟོང་གི་དོན་བྱང་ཆུབ་ཀྱི་སེམས་སྐྱེ་བ་མེད་པ་གཅིག་ཏུ་སྡུད་པའོ། །དབྱིངས་དང་ཡེ་ཤེས་གཉིས་སུ་མེད་པ་སྣང་བ་ལས་བྱུང་བ་སྲས་མཆོག་རྡོ་རྗེ་གཞོན་ནུའི་ཕྱག་མཚན་དུ་གྱུར་པས་སོ། གཞན་ཡང་དུག་ཕུར་འདེབས་པའི་ཚེ་ན་སྲས་མཆོག་ཏུ་བྱིན་གྱིས་བརླབས་པ་དེ་བཏབ། དགྲ་བགེགས་ཀྱི་ལུས་རྟུལ་ཕྲན་བཞིན་དུ་བརླག་པར་བྱེད་པས་ཀྱང་ཕྱག་མཚན་དང་། འདེབས་ཤིང་སྒྲོལ་བའི་ཐབས་ཡོ་བྱད་དང་བཅས་པས་ན་ཕུར་པ་རྫས་ཀྱི་དཀྱིལ་འཁོར་ཞེས་བྱ་ལ།

Aparājita gets his name since he is unmoved by thoughts in the innate nature and is unbeatable by others having conquered the haughty spirits. His consort *Haughty Arrow Vajra* receives her name because she slays the thinking mind by releasing awareness wisdom like an arrow. The *Wolf-headed One* is so called because, just like a wolf enjoys taking life and has no compassionate preferences, it liberates samaya-breakers and benefits worthy recipients, and the *Hawk-headed One* because it never lets go of those to be tamed by great compassion just like a hawk has sharp nails and strong claws.

Amṛtakuṇḍalin is so called as he identifies the demons of conceptual thought with wisdom[357] and his consort *Wind Blowing Vajra* because her non-dual wisdom scatters the husk of conceptual thought like a wind. The *Lion-headed One* received its name because it overpowers disturbing emotions with the power of realization just like a lion which has great strength to overpower other predators. The *Bat-headed One* is so called because it realizes all phenomena in a single moment similar to a bat which remembers three days.

Furthermore, *Trailokyavijaya* has been named so because of being primordially victorious over the three realms—the desire realm, the form realm, and the formless realm and his consort *Vajra Slayer* because she slays all conceptual phenomena within a state devoid of concepts. The *Bear-headed One* gets its name since it persists in liberating sentient beings while keeping a peaceful state of mind that is unmoved from the innate nature just like a bear has enormous wrath and possesses a white heart although its fur is black. The *Weasel-headed One* is so called because it swiftly and speedily performs the benefit of various beings to be tamed similar to the way a weasel has great dexterity and runs in all directions.

Lastly, *Mahābala* is so called since he is unbiased regarding the welfare of those to be tamed and capable of liberating them and *Vajra Agitator*[358] as her compassion actualizes the welfare of others. The *Brown Bear-headed One* gets its name because it compassionately clings to sentient beings and is unmoved by thoughts similar to a brown bear which is rigid and sleeps a lot, while the *Rat-headed One* is so called because, just like a rat enters into only one hole although its nest has many entrances, it condenses the meaning of the 84,000 gateways to the dharma into the single unborn bodhicitta.

The supreme sons, as the display of indivisible space and wisdom, are the hand implements of Vajrakumāra. Furthermore, when striking with the poisonous kīla it should be blessed as the supreme sons and then planted. Since they crush the bodies of enemies and obstacle-makers into dust they are called hand implements. It is called the material kīla maṇḍala since it possesses the

དེའང་ཆོས་ཐམས་ཅད་དབྱིངས་དང་ཡེ་ཤེས་གཉིས་སུ་མེད་པའི་སྲས་བདེ་བ་ཆེན་པོར་ཡང་དག་པར་རྒྱས་གདབ་པས་རྒྱ་མདུད་ཀྱིས་མཚན་པ། དེ་ལྟར་མ་རྟོགས་པ་རྣམས་ཚད་མེད་པའི་སྙིང་རྗེ་ཆེན་པོའི་མི་གཏོང་བ་ཉིད་ཀྱིས་ཆུ་སྲིན་གྱི་ཁ་ནས་བྱུང་ཞིང་། དྲག་པོ་མངོན་སྤྱོད་ཀྱི་དོན་མཛད་པས་དཔལ་ཟུང་གསུམ་མགར་གྱི་སོལ་མལ་ནས་བཏོན་པ་དང་འདྲའོ། །བྱམས་པ་ཚད་མེད་པའི་རང་བཞིན་ཐུགས་རྗེས་མི་གཏོང་བའི་ལྕགས་ཀྱུ་ཅན་གྱི་པུ་ཤུད། སྙིང་རྗེ་ཚད་མེད་པའི་རང་བཞིན་འཆིང་བྱེད་ཞགས་པ་ཅན་གྱི་ཀང་ཀ དགའ་བ་ཚད་མེད་ཀྱི་རང་བཞིན་སྡོམ་བྱེད་ལྕགས་སྒྲོག་ཅན་གྱི་སྲིན་བྱ། བཏང་སྙོམས་ཚད་མེད་པའི་རང་བཞིན་བརྐྱག་མཛད་དྲིལ་བུ་ཅན་གྱི་ཁྲ་ཡི་མགོ་ཅན་དང་། ཕོ་ཉ་རྣམས་ཀྱང་། སྐུ་ལས་སྤྲུལ་པའི་ཤྭ་ན་སྨུ་ཁ། སྐུ་མདོག་མཐིང་ནག་ཆོས་ཉིད་འགྱུར་བ་མེད་པ། སྟོང་གསུམ་འཇིགས་པར་བྱེད་པས་སྐྱུང་གདོང་། སྒྲུབ་པ་དང་སྐུའི་ཕྲིན་ལས་མཛད་པས་ཕྱག་གཉིས་ཐོད་ཕྲེང་དང་། གནམ་ལྕགས་འཁོར་ལོ། སྐུ་ལས་ཕྱུང་པའི་ཤྭ་ཤྭ་འཕྲོ་བས་དགྲ་བགེགས་སྒྲོལ་བ་སོགས་ཕོ་ཉ་དམ་ཅན་ཀུན་ཀྱང་རྣམ་དག་དྲན་པ་དང་། དགོས་པའི་ཁྱད་པར་སོགས་ཤེས་པའི་ཏིང་ངེ་འཛིན་གྱིས་རང་རྒྱུད་དུ་འཛིན་པའི་མཚན་མའི་རྟོག་པ་ཀུན་ཡེ་ཤེས་ཀྱིས་རྒྱལ་འདེབས་པ་ནི་བླ་ན་མེད་པ་ཁྱད་པར་གྱི་ལམ་མོ། །

གསུམ་པ་ང་རྒྱལ་བརྟན་པ་ནི། རང་ཉིད་དཔལ་ཆེན་པོ་རྡོ་རྗེ་གཞོན་ནུ་དངོས་ཡིན་རང་གི་མིང་རུས་སོགས་ཀྱི་འཛིན་པ་ཁྱད་དུ་བསྐྱུངས་ཏེ། སྐྱོན་ཀུན་ཟད། ཡོན་ཏན་ཀུན་ལྡན་གྱི་དཔལ་ཆེན་རྡོ་རྗེ་གཞོན་ནུ་དེ་ཉིད་ང་ཡིན། དཔལ་ཆེན་པོའི་སྐུ་གསུང་ཐུགས་ཀྱི་ཡོན་ཏན་ཐམས་ཅད་ང་ལ་ཡོད། དེའི་ཕྱིར་ང་དཔལ་རྡོ་རྗེ་གཞོན་ནུ་དེ། ངའོ་སྙམ་པའི་ང་རྒྱལ་བརྟན་པོ་ལྷ་ཉིད་རྒྱུད་དུ་མ་གྱུར་པར་ཡུན་རིང་དུ་སྐྱོང་བའོ། །སྔར་ཡང་ང་རྒྱལ་དང་གསལ་སྣང་དེ་ཉིད་ཀྱི་སྟེང་དུ་རང་བཞིན་མ་བཅོས་པའི་ཚུལ་དུ་མཉམ་པར་འཇོག་པ་ནི་ཟབ་གསལ་གཉིས་སུ་མེད་པའི་ཚུལ་དུ་འགྱུར་རོ། །བསྐྱེད་རིམ་ལྷ་སྐུའི་ཉེ་བར་མཚོན་པའི་ཆོས་ཐམས་ཅད་གཅིག་དུ་བྲལ། རྟེན་འབྱུང་གི་རིག་པ་སོགས་ལ་བརྟེན་ནས་སྣང་བ་རང་བཞིན་མ་གྲུབ་པའི་ཚུལ་ལ་དམིགས་ནས་གསལ་སྟོང་དུ་བསྒོམ་པའོ། །

method and tools for striking and liberation. Furthermore, the kīla is marked with a knot since all phenomena are sealed as the Great-Bliss-Son of indivisible space and wisdom. Because of the commitment of limitless great compassion towards those without realization, it emerges from the mouth of Makara. Because of acting for the sake of fierce direct action the three-edged blade seems as if it is pulled straight from the blacksmith's furnace.

The hoopoe bird with an iron hook that holds onto sentient beings with compassion symbolizes the nature of limitless love. The heron with the constraining lasso symbolizes the nature of limitless compassion. The owl with the restraining chains symbolizes the nature of limitless joy. The one with the head of a hawk having the crushing bell symbolizes the nature of limitless equanimity.

Regarding the attendants, Śvanmukhā, who emanates from the body, has a dark blue body that symbolizes the unchanging innate nature. As she installs fear in the one billion universes she has a wolf head. By performing sādhana and the activities of body her two hands hold a skull garland and an iron wheel. The kīla sācchas issuing from her body symbolize that enemies and obstacle makers are liberated. Such is the recollection of purity for all attendants and vow-holders. When a meditative concentration that is aware of these special purposes in this way transfers wisdom to all conceptual thoughts that otherwise are apprehended as ordinary, it becomes a unique and unsurpassed path.

Stable Pride

"I am truly the great glorious Vajrakumāra! I have thoroughly abandoned clinging to my name and family! The great glorious Vajrakumāra who has exhausted all faults and is endowed with all qualities—that is me! I possess all the qualities of the body, speech, and mind of the Great Glorious One. Now I am the glorious Vajrakumāra!" Think like this for a long time and sustain this stable pride until the very deity is mastered. Furthermore, in addition to having developed pride and vivid appearance, if you are able to rest evenly in a natural and unfabricated manner, then that will bring about a state of nondual profundity and clarity. In fact, all phenomena that are here illustrated by the divine forms of the development stage do not truly exist as neither one nor many and so, once you have seen through reasonings, such as that of dependent origination, how appearances do not intrinsically exist you should train in aware emptiness.

གཉིས་པ་ཛ྄པ་བཟླ་བ་ལ་གསུང་གི་རྣལ་འབྱོར་ནི།

སྤྱིར་སྔགས་ལ་གསུམ་སྟེ། རྒྱུ་མ་ནོར་བ་རྩ་བའི་སྔགས་ནི་རྒྱུའི་ཡི་གེ་ཧཱུྃ་ལྟ་བུ་དང་། གཉིས་པ་བསྐྱེད་པ་རྐྱེན་གྱི་སྔགས་ནི། འབྱུང་རིམ་བསྐྱེད་པའི་ཨེ་སོགས་དང་། གཞལ་ཡས་ཁང་བསྐྱེད་པ་བྷྲཱུྃ། གཙོ་འཁོར་ཡོངས་རྫོགས་བསྐྱེད་པའི་བཛྲ་ཀཱི་ལ་ཡ་སོགས་སྔགས་རྣམས་སོ། །གསུམ་པ་བཟླ་བ་ལས་ཀྱི་སྔགས་ནི་ཛ྄པ་ཁང་དབྱེ་བ། ཛ྄པ་བསྐུལ་བྱ་བ་སོགས་གཞུང་དུ་གསལ་བ་ལྟར་སྐབས་དང་སྦྱར་ལ། ཛ྄པ་དགོངས། སྐུ་ཕྱག་རྒྱ་ལ་དམིགས་པའི་ཛ྄པ་ཀྱི་དགོངས་པ་ནི། གོང་དུ་ཇི་སྐད་བཤད་པ་བཞིན་ལྷ་ཡི་གསལ་སྣང་ཆེད་དུ་འདོན་པའོ། །གསུང་ཡི་གེ་ལ་དམིགས་པ་ནི། སྔར་བཞིན་དཀྱིལ་འཁོར་ལྷའི་གསལ་སྣང་བརྟན་པ་གཞིར་བྱས་ཏེ་སྒྲུབ་གཞུང་དུ་གསལ་བའི་དམིགས་པ་གསལ་བཏབ་སྟེ་བཟླས་པའོ། །ཐུགས་ཆོས་ཉིད་ལ་དམིགས་པ་ནི། འོག་ཏུ་འཆད་པ་ཐུགས་ཀྱི་རྣལ་འབྱོར་ལྟར་ཡིན་ལ། ཡོན་ཏན་དང་། ཕྲིན་ལས་བཟླས་དམིགས་ནི་སྒྲུབ་པའི་ཁོག་ཕུབ་ཏུ་འབྱུང་བ་ལྟར་ལ། གཙོ་འཁོར་རྣམས་ཀྱི་སྔགས་ལ་ཚེ་ཤམ་སྦྱར་བའི་ཚུལ་དང་། ལས་སྦྱོར་སྐབས་ཤམ་བུ་གདགས་པའི་ཟབ་གནད་མན་ངག་རྣམས་བླ་མའི་ཞལ་ལས་མཉན་པར་བྱ་བ་ཁོ་ནའོ། །གཞན་ཡང་ཀཱི་ལ་ཡ་ཆོས་ཉིད་དང་སྦྱར་ཏེ་བཟླས་པ་དང་། ལྷ་དང་སྦྱར་ཏེ་བཟླས་པ་དང་། ངན་སྔགས་དང་སྦྱར་ཏེ་བཟླས་པའོ། །དེ་ཡང་བུང་བ་ཚང་བཤིག་པའི་ཚུལ་དང་། མགལ་མེ་ཀླད་ལ་བསྐོར་བའི་ཚུལ་དང་། མགར་གྱི་ཚྭ་ཚྭ་འཕྲོ་བའི་ཚུལ་དུ་བཟླས་པའོ། །བཟླ་བྱའི་སྔགས་ནི། ཨོཾ་བཛྲ་ཀཱི་ལི་ཀཱི་ལ་ཡ་ཧཱུྃ་ཕཊ། ནི་བསྙེན་པའི་སྲོག་སྔགས་འབྲུ་དགུ་དང་སརྦ་བིགྷྣཱན་བཾ་ལས་སྔགས་འབྲུ་ལྔ་བཅས་པ་ལ། སྙིང་པོ་སྔགས་ཀྱི་འཁོར་ལོ་འབྲུ་བཅུ་བཞི་པ་སྟེ། ཡིག་འབྲུ་ལྷ་དང་ངོ་སྤྲོད་ན། ཨོཾ་ནི་རིགས་ལྔ་ཁྲག་འཐུང་ཡེ་ཤེས་ལྔ། བཛྲ་དོ་རྗེ་གཞོན་ནུ་ཡབ་ཡུམ་གཉིས་མེད། ཀཱི་གོང་མ་ཡབ་སྤྲུལ་ཁྲོ་བོ་བཅུ། ལི་ཡུམ་སྤྲུལ་ཁྲོ་མོ་བཅུ། ཀཱི་འོག་མ་ཁྲོ་བོའི་ཡང་སྤྲུལ་ཟ་བྱེད་བཅུ། ལ་ཁྲོ་མོའི་ཡང་སྤྲུལ་གསོད་བྱེད་བཅུ། ཡ་སྐུ་གསུང་ཐུགས་སྤྲུལ། སྲས་མཆོག་ཉེར་གཅིག སཏྲ་སུམ་སྤྲུལ་ཕུར་སྲུང་ཐམས་ཅད་འདུས། ཞིག་ཤྭན་བཞི་དང་སྒྲོག་བདག

The Verbal Yoga of Mantra Recitation

Generally there are three kinds of mantra. First is the unmistaken cause of the root mantra, such as the HŪṂ seed syllable. Second is the circumstantial mantra of the development, which consists of various mantras such as E and so forth that give rise to the gradual elements, the BHRUṂ that gives rise to the palace, and the Vajrakīlaya mantra that gives rise to the central deities and their retinue. Third is the mantra of activity recitation, such as dividing the recitation palace, the petitioning recitation, etc., which is to be appropriately applied as elucidated in the scriptures.

As for the intent of recitation, the intent of recitation that focuses on the bodily form of the deity is, as was explained above, to chant until the clear appearance of the deity is perfected. The intent of recitation that focuses the speech on the syllables is to create, as before, a basis of the stable clear appearance of the maṇḍala deities and to recite while giving rise to the visualization that is elucidated in the practice text. The intent of recitation that focuses the mind on the innate nature is what will be explained below during the yoga of mind in samādhi. The intent of recitation that focuses recitation on the qualities and activities is the way it appears in the framework of the sādhana practice. The instructions for the profound key-points of connecting the life-appendix to the mantras of the central deities and the retinue as well as attaching the appendix when enacting the activities should only be received orally from a master. Furthermore, at times Kīlaya is applied to the innate nature and recited, applied to the deity and recited, and applied to a subjugating mantra and recited. There are also recitations that are like breaking a bee hive, like a fire-brand spinning above, and like the flying sparks of a blacksmith.

The mantra to be recited is the 14 syllables of the essential mantra wheel consisting of the nine syllables OṂ VAJRA KĪLI KĪLAYA HŪṂ PHAṬ that are the life mantra of the recitation together with SARVAVIGHNĀN BAṂ that are the five syllables of activity mantra. When identifying the syllables as deities OṂ is the five families, the five wisdoms, and the blood drinkers. VAJRA is the indivisible Vajrakumāra and consort. The first KĪ is the ten male wrathful ones emanated from the lord. LI is the ten female wrathful ones emanated from the consort. The second KĪ is the ten devourers re-emanated from the male wrathful ones. LA is the ten slayers re-emanated from the female wrathful ones. YA is the 21 supreme sons that are emanations of body, speech, and mind. SARVA embodies all the thrice-emanated Kīlaya protectors. VIGH is the four Śvans and the

ནྣན་རེ་ཧྲི་བཞི་དང་མགོ་ཡག ཐཾ་ས་བདག་བསྟེ་ཡི་སྐྱེས་བུ། ཧཱུཾ་ནི་ཁྲོ་འདུས་དཔལ་གྱི་ཡེ་ཤེས་ཐུགས། ཕཊ། དགྲ་བགེགས་དམ་སྲི་འབྱུང་པོ་ཚར་གཅོད་པའི་སྔགས་སོ། །འཁོར་གྱི་བཟླས་པ་བྱེད་ན། ཁྲོ་བཅུ་ཡབ་ཡུམ། སྲས་མཆོག་ཕུར་སྲུང་བཅས་པའི་ཛཔ་བཟླས་ཏེ། མཐར་སྟོང་ཚིག་འབུལ་བ་དང་བཅས་པའོ། །ཁྱད་པར་གྱི་མིང་དོན་ནི། ལྷག་པར་ཐུགས་བསྐུལ་བར་བྱེད་ལས་སྙིང་པོ་ཞེས་བྱ། དེ་ཡང་ནན་ཏན་གྱི་ཚུལ་གྱིས་བསྐུར་ཞིང་བརྗོད་པས་ན་བཟླས་པ་ཞེས་བྱ། དེ་ཉིད་ཀྱི་ལྷག་པའི་ལྷ་དང་ཐུགས་ཉེ་ཞིང་འཛའ་བར་བྱེད་པས་ཛཔ་ཅེས་ཀྱང་བྱའོ། །བཟླ་བའི་ཚུལ་གྱི་བཟླས་པའི་སྐྱོན་དྲུག་སྤང་ལ་བཟླས་ཏེ། སྔ་སྨྱུར་ན་འབྲུ་འདྲིས་པའི་སྐྱོན། སྔ་བུལ་ན་བྱེར་བའི་སྐྱོན། སྔ་ཆེས་པའམ་དྲག་ན་ཕོག་ཐུག་འོང་ཞིང་བྱིན་རླབས་འགྲངས་པའི་སྐྱོན། སྔ་ཞན་པའམ་ཆུང་ན་ནུས་པ་མི་ཐོན་པའི་སྐྱོན། བྱིང་རྨུགས་སུ་སོང་ན་སྔ་མི་དག་པའི་སྐྱོན། རྒོད་ནས་གཡེངས་ཤིང་སེམས་འཕྲོས་པས་ཏིང་ངེ་འཛིན་མི་གསལ་བའི་སྐྱོན་ནོ། །གཞན་ཡང་མི་ཚིག་གི་བར་མ་ཆོད་པ་དང་། ཡིག་འབྲུ་ཆད་ལྷག་ཅན་སྤང་ངོ་། །ཇི་ལྟར་བཟླ་ན། གསལ་བར་བཟླ་སྟེ། མ་འདྲེས། མ་འབྲེལ་བ་སྔ་བར་མ་ཆད་པར་བཟླས། དག་པར་བཟླ་སྟེ། སྔགས་ཆད་ལྷག་མེད་པར་ཟུར་ཕྱིན་པར་བཟླས། བརྩོན་པར་བཟླས་ཏེ། རྒྱུན་མི་འཆད་པ་ཆུ་བོའི་རྒྱུན་ལྟར་བཟླའོ། །བསྙེན་པའི་བསྒྲུབ་བྱ་ནི། བསྙེན་པ་མ་རྫོགས་བར་དུ་གནས་སྤྱོས་ན་དངོས་གྲུབ་བོ་ཟག་དོན་མེད་དུ་འགྱུར་བས་གནས་མི་སྤོ། ཡང་བི་ཧོ་ལས། མི་བསྒོལ་མི་བཤད་གཞན་མི་བསམ། །ཞེས་པས་བསྙེན་པའི་མཚན་རྟགས་མ་ཐོན་བར་དུ་ལྷ་ཉིད་མི་བསྒོལ་ཏེ། གཞན་གྱི་ནད་པ་གདོན་ཅན་ཀུན་ལ་ལྷ་དེའི་སྒོ་ནས་བྱིན་རླབས་མི་བྱ། བྱས་ན་པོ་ཟག་མཚན་མ་འགྲིབ་པའོ། །ཟས་གོས་ཀྱང་རང་དབང་རྫས་ལ་བརྟེན་པས་འགྲུབ་སྟེ། སྙིང་པོའང་སྒྲུབ་པའི་དུས་མ་ཡིན་པ་གཞན་ལ་མི་བཤད་དོ། །མི་བསམ་ཞེས་པས་སེམས་རྩེ་གཅིག་ཏུ་ཡི་དམ་གྱི་ལྷ་ལ་དམིགས་པ་མ་གཏོགས་པ་རྟོག་ཚོགས་གང་ཡང་ཡིད་ལ་མི་བྱ། ཐ་ན་ལྷ་རྟོག་ཡི་གེའི་རིམ་ལ་སོགས་པ་གཡེང་བ་སྤངས་ཏེ་བསྒྲུབ་པར་བྱའོ། །དེ་ལྟར་བཟླ་བའང་། དུས་གྲངས་རྟགས་ཀྱི་བསྙེན་པ་གསུམ་གང་རུང་བྱ་སྟེ། དེ་ལ་དུས་ནི། དགོངས་རྒྱུད་ལས་ཡུན་ནི་ལོ་ཟླ་ཙམ་དུ་བསྙེངས།

Lord of the Life-force. NĀN is the four Retīs and The Yak-Headed One. BAṂ is the local lords, the Se-beings.[359] HŪṂ is the glorious wisdom mind of the assemblage of wrathful ones. PHAṬ is the mantra that completely annihilates enemies, obstacle makers, samaya breakers, and bhuta spirits. When performing the recitation of the retinue one should recite the mantra repetition for the male and female wrathful ones as well as the supreme sons and the Kīla protectors and offer the "Thousand Verse" at the end.[360]

The particular meaning of *essential* is that this recitation primarily invokes the mind of the deity. Furthermore, since it is diligently said again and again it is termed *recitation*. Since it approaches and assimilates its particular supreme deity it is also termed *jāpa*.

One should recite while avoiding the six faults of mantra repetition. If the speech is hasty there will be the fault of merging the syllables. If the speech is slow there will be the fault of disconnecting the syllables. If the voice is loud and intense there will be the faults of irritation and deferral of blessings. If the voice is weak or small there will be the fault of inability. If one gets drowsy there will be the fault of a blurred speech. If one is agitated, becomes distracted, and the mind wanders there will be the fault of unclear concentration. Furthermore, do not interrupt the recitation with ordinary talk and do not shorten or prolong the syllables. So how should one recite? Recite clearly, distinctly, calmly, with a continuous voice. Recite accurately and complete the recitation without shortening and prolonging the mantra. Recite diligently and uninterruptedly like the flow of a river.

The trainings of the recitation are the following. One should not change residence until the recitation has been completed since the accomplishments will get lost and become futile should one do so. The *Vidyottamatantra* says, "do not use the mantra, do not talk, and do not think of anything else." So one should not employ the deity until the marks and signs of recitation have appeared. Do not use the deity to bless all those who are sick or possessed because if you do, you will become defiled and the signs will become obscured. Use your own possessions to obtain food and clothes. Do not talk to others, even when you are not practicing the essential mantra. "Do not think" means do not engage in any thought whatsoever except from focusing the mind one-pointedly on the meditational deity. Give up even distracting concepts of the deity such as the shape of the syllables.

When reciting in this way one should also perform whichever recitation of time, number, or sign is suitable. Regarding that of time, the *Tantra of Realization* says, "The duration should be around a month." So one should

ཞེས་པས་རང་གི་ནུས་པ་དང་སྦྱར་བ་དང་གྲངས་ཀྱི་བསྙེན་པ་ནི། དེ་སྐད་དུ། བསྙེན་སྒྲུབ་ཚོ་ག་ཚང་བྱས་ནས། །འཇབ་གྲངས་བདུན་འབུམ་ཉི་ཁྲི་འདོན། ཞེས་པས། གྲངས་ཚད་བདུན་འབུམ་ཉི་ཁྲི་ཡན་ཆོད། མཚན་མའི་བསྙེན་པ་ནི། རབ་དངོས་སུ་ཞལ་སྟོན་པ། འབྲིང་ཕུར་པ་འཕུར་འཁྲབ་བྱེད་པ་དང་། ཐམ་སྒྲ་དང་། འོད་དང་རྨི་ལམ་དུ་ཛ་ཆེན་བཟུང་བ། དུང་འབུད་པ། ཉི་ཟླ་ལུས་ལ་ཤར་བ་དང་། མཆོན་རྣོན་པོ་ཐོག་པ་རྨིས་པ་སོགས་བློ་དང་སྦྱར་ཏེ་ཉམས་སུ་བླང་བར་བྱའོ། །

གསུམ་པ་ཐུགས་ཀྱི་རྣལ་འབྱོར་ནི།

རང་སེམས་སྤྲོས་པ་ཐམས་ཅད་དང་བྲལ་བ་རྡོ་རྗེ་གཞོན་ནུའི་ངང་དུ་རྫོགས་ཤིང་། ངོ་བོ་སྟོང་ལ་རང་བཞིན་གསལ་བའི་སྣང་ཆ་རྣམས་དངོས་མེད་སྒྱུ་མ་ལྟ་བུར། རྟོག་བྲལ་ཤར་གྲོལ་དུས་མཉམ་འོད་གསལ་གྱི་ངང་དུ་མཉམ་པར་བཞག་པའོ། །དེ་ལྟར་བསྐྱེད་པའི་རིམ་པ་སོགས་ཇི་ལྟར་བསྒོམ་པའི་སྐབས་མེད་དུ་མི་རུང་བའི་གདམས་པ་ལྟ་དོན་ལ་སྦྱར་བའི་ཕྱིར། རང་གི་སེམས་རྣམ་པར་ཤེས་པ་ཚོགས་བརྒྱད་དང་བཅས་པ། ལྷ་ཡི་སྐུ་དང་ཡེ་ཤེས་སུ་ཤར་བ་ལ། དེ་ཡང་རིག་པ་བྱང་ཆུབ་ཀྱི་སེམས། ལྷ་སྐུའི་འབྲས་བུར་གདོད་ནས་དུ་མ་རོ་གཅིག་ཏུ་སྨིན་པའི་བསྐྱེད་རྫོགས་དབྱེར་མེད་ཡེ་ཤེས་ཆེན་པོའི་སྐུར་ལ་མ་ཀློམས་ན། བསྐྱེད་རིམ་རང་རྒྱུད་པ་སྤྱད་པའི་བག་ཆགས་བརྟས་པ་ཙམ་ནི། རྣམ་པར་གྲོལ་བའི་ལམ་ལས་རིང་བའི་ཕྱིར་སྲོག་སྡོམ་གཟེར་བཞིའི་མན་ངག་གཅེས་པར་བསྟན་ཏེ། རྒྱུད་གསང་རྫོགས་ལས།

ཡེ་ཤེས་འཇིག་རྟེན་གང་ལ་ཡང་། །སྲོག་སྡོམ་གཟེར་བཞི་མ་ཐེབ་ན། །
ནམ་ཡང་དོན་མེད་ཡུག་པ་རྒྱང་། །ཡོངས་རྫོགས་དཔལ་གྱི་སྲོག་འཕྲོག་ཐབས། །
གཅིག་ཤེས་པ་ནི་ཀུན་སྲོག་ཐོབ། །དཔེར་ན་སྒྲ་གཅན་འཛིན་གྱི་ཁས། །
ནམ་མཁའི་ཉི་མ་གཅིག་ཟིན་པར། །ཆུ་བྲན་སྟོང་གི་ཉི་མ་ཀུན། །
མ་བཟུང་པར་ཡང་སྟོང་སྲོག་ཐོབ། །དེ་ཕྱིར་སྲོག་སྡོམ་གཟེར་བཞི་གཅེས། །

proceed according to one's own capacity. Concerning the number of recitations it is said that "having completed the approach and accomplishment, 720,000 mantras should have been recited." Therefore, the number to reach is at least 720,000. Concerning the signs of recitation the best is when the deity reveals itself in actuality. The medium sign is that the kīla begins to fly and jump about, and the lowest signs are sounds and lights appearing, having dreams such as beating a drum, blowing a conch, the sun and moon shining within one's body, and holding up sharp weapons. Please understand this and put it into practice.

The Mental Yoga of Samādhi

Rest evenly in the luminous state where your own mind, free from all complexities, is perfected into the state of Vajrakumāra and the appearances of the empty essence and cognizant nature manifest like unreal illusions, free from concepts and liberated the moment they arise. Through this indispensable instruction, which applies the deity to reality, your mind and the eight collections of consciousness will arise as the divine body and wisdom when the development stage practice is applied. Furthermore, without meditating on awareness bodhicitta in the form of great wisdom—the indivisible development and completion stages that primordially ripen the manifold into a single taste as the fruition of divine form—you merely create a habit of meditating independently on the development stage. Therefore, since you thereby will be far from the fully liberating path, the instructions of the four nails that bind the life force are taught to be essential.

The *Tantra of Secret Perfection* says:

> Whether the deities are worldly or of wisdom,
> Unless one plants the four nails that bind the life force,
> One will never be successful, like an outstretched leg.[361]
> The way to steal the life force of all Glorious Ones
> Is to know one and attain the life force of all,
> Just like Rahula's mouth,
> By taking the single sun in the sky,
> Attains a thousand life forces
> Without having to catch the suns in a thousand puddles.
> Therefore the four nails that bind the life force are essential.

ཞེས་པ་ལྟར་ལས། ཉིང་ངེ་འཛིན་གྱི་གཟེར་ནི། དམིགས་རྟེན་སོགས་ལྷའི་རྣམ་པ་ལ་སེམས་རྩེ་གཅིག་ཏུ་གཏད་ནས་བསྒོམ་པས་ལུས་ཐ་མལ་དུ་འཛིན་པའི་མངོན་ཞེན་ལྷའི་སྐུར་རྫོགས་པ་སྟེ། རྒྱུད་ལས་

ཏིང་འཛིན་གཟེར་ནི་ཐོད་སྐུ་ལ། རྩེ་གཅིག་སེམས་བཟུང་ཡེངས་མི་བྱ། །
ཡུལ་གསུམ་གྲུད་དུ་གྱུར་པ་དང་། །དཔལ་ཆེན་ཧེ་རུ་ཀ་དངོས་མཇལ། །
ལྡོག་པ་ཧེ་རུ་ཀས་མི་སྤྱོད། །ཏིང་འཛིན་མི་འགྱུར་གཟེར་མེད་ན། །
སྐུ་ནི་ནམ་ཡང་མཐོང་མི་འགྱུར། །

ཞེས་སོ། །དེ་ལ་ཡུལ་གསུམ་གྲུད་དུ་གྱུར་ཚུལ་ནི། །དང་པོ་བསམ་པའི་ཡུལ་དུ་གསལ། །དེ་ནས་མཐོང་བའི་ཡུལ་ལ་གསལ། །དེ་ནས་རེག་པའི་ཡུལ་ལ་གསལ་བས་སེམས་ལྷ་སྐུར་སྨིན་པའི་ལྷ་དང་ལྷ་ཕྲད་པ་ལ་གསལ་བ་གྲུད་དུ་གྱུར་པ་ཞེས་བྱའོ། །དེ་བཞིན་དུ་སྙིང་པོ་སྔགས་ཀྱི་གཟེར་ནི། ཐུགས་སྲོག་ལ་རྩ་སྔགས་འཕོར་བ་དང་། ནོ་ལི་ལ་འདུན་པ་རྩེ་གཅིག་ཏུ་གཞུར་ཏེ་རིགས་པ་བགྲངས་པས་འབྱུང་འཇུག་གནས་གསུམ་གསུང་གི་ངོ་བོར་དག་པ་སྟེ། རྒྱུད་ལས།

སྙིང་པོ་སྔགས་གཟེར་ཡོངས་རྫོགས་ཀྱི། གཙོ་བོའི་སྔགས་དག་སེལ་མེད་བཟླས། །
ཐུགས་སྲོག་ཧཱུྃ་ལ་རྩ་སྔགས་འཕོར། །གསལ་བའི་འཕྲོ་འདུ་སྲོག་སྔགས་བགྲངས། །
དེ་ཆེ་དཔལ་འགྱུར་ལུང་ཡང་སྟོན། །ནུས་པའི་རྩལ་རྫོགས་ལྷ་རྣམས་འཕོར། །
སྲོག་སྙིང་བསྙེན་རྫོགས་གཟེར་མེད་ན། །ལྷ་དང་དམ་ཙན་ཁྲུག་མི་སྲིད། །

ཅེས་སོ། །དགོངས་པ་མི་འགྱུར་བའི་གཟེར་ནི། དཔལ་ཆེན་པོ་ལ་སོགས་པ་ཞི་ཁྲོའི་ལྷ་ཅི་ལྟར་སྣང་ཀྱང་དེ་ཉིད་རང་སེམས་ལས་གྱུད་ན་མེད་པར་རྟོགས་པས་ལྷ་དང་ཆོས་ཉིད་རོ་མཉམ་ཆེན་པོར་བཅུད་དུ་སྨིན་པ་སྟེ། རྒྱུད་ལས།

Among these, the nail of concentration is to turn one's attention one-pointedly to the divine features in, for example, the support for the visualization. Thereby attachment to reality and the belief that the body is ordinary are perfected into divine form by the use of meditation. The tantra says:

> The nail of concentration is to be undistracted
> In focusing the mind one-pointedly on the skull form,[362]
> Perfecting the three fields,
> And actually meeting the Great Glorious Heruka.
> Anything but that will fail to please the Heruka.
> Without the nail of unchanging concentration
> The body will never be seen.

The way to perfect the three fields is to first develop clarity in the field of contemplation. Then follows clarity in the field of vision. Then clarity in the field of touch. Thereby one meets the deity which is mind ripened into divine form. This is called increasing clarity.

Likewise, the nail of the essential mantra is to engage one-pointedly in spinning the root mantra around the spiritual life force and focusing on the heart center. As you count the mantra, the exhalation, inhalation, and resting of the breath become purified into the essence of speech. The tantra says:

> The nail of the essential mantra is to correctly recite
> The mantras of the main deities in the entire maṇḍala,
> To spin the root mantra around HŪṂ, the spiritual life force,
> To clearly radiate and gather, and to count the life mantra.
> At that time the magnificent one will grant a prophesy,
> The capacity is perfected, and deities gather.
> Without the nail of approach and completion of the essential life
> force,
> It is impossible to subjugate gods and vow-holders.

The nail of unchanging intent is to fully ripen the deity and reality into great equal taste because of having realized that whichever peaceful or wrathful deity one practices, such as the Great Glorious One, it has no existence other than one's own mind. The tantra says:

དགོངས་པའི་གཟེར་ནི་ཞི་ཁྲོའི་ལྷ། །ཡོངས་རྫོགས་དཔལ་ཆེན་རང་སེམས་ལས། །
གུད་ན་མེད་ཅིང་རུ་ཏྲ་ཡང་། །ལོག་ན་མེད་དོ་རང་གི་སེམས། །
སེམས་ཉིད་སྟོང་པ་ཆོས་ཀྱི་སྐུ། །གསལ་ལ་མ་འདྲེས་ལོངས་སྤྱོད་རྫོགས། །
སྣ་ཚོགས་རང་ཤར་སྤྲུལ་པའི་སྐུ། །སྣང་བ་ཡབ་ལ་སྟོང་པ་ཡུམ། །
སྣང་སྟོང་དབྱེར་མེད་ཡེ་ཤེས་སྐུ། །འགྱུ་དྲན་རྣམ་རྟོག་བསམ་ཡས་ཀྱང་། །
ཡོངས་སུ་རྫོགས་པ་དཔལ་གྱི་འཁོར། །བསམ་གྱིས་མི་ཁྱབ་ཡེ་སངས་རྒྱས། །
རང་བཞིན་ཉིད་ལས་གཡོས་པ་མེད། །དགོངས་པ་མི་འགྱུར་གཟེར་མེད་ན། །
དཔལ་ཆེན་སྒྲུབ་ཀྱང་ཐུན་མོང་ལས། །མཆོག་མི་འགྲུབ་ཅིང་རུ་ཏྲར་གོལ། །

ཞེས་སོ། །འཕྲོ་འདུའི་གཟེར་ནི། རྣམ་བཞིའི་ཕྲིན་ལས་ཐམས་ཅད་ལ་རང་དབང་དུ་བྱེད་པའི་ཆོ་འཕྲུལ་ཆེན་པོ། བཞུ་བཏུལ་གྱི་ལས་ལ་ཆར་དཀར་གཅེས་པ་ལྟ་བུ་ཡིན་ཏེ། རྒྱུད་ལས།

འཕྲོ་འདུའི་གཟེར་ནི་དམིགས་པ་ཡི། །བསྒྱུར་ཁ་ཤེས་ན་འདོད་དགུར་འགྱུར། །
ཏིང་ངེ་འཛིན་གྱི་འཕྲོ་འདུ་ཡིས། །སེམས་ཀྱི་ནུས་པ་རྩལ་རྫོགས་ཏེ། །
གང་ལྟར་བསམ་པ་དེ་ལྟར་སྣང་། །སྔགས་དང་ཕྱག་རྒྱའི་བྱིན་རླབས་མཐུས། །
ཞི་རྒྱས་དབང་དང་མངོན་སྤྱོད་སོགས། །ཕན་གནོད་ལས་ཀ་གང་ཡང་འགྲུབ། །
དཔེར་ན་ནོར་བུ་གཅིག་ཉིད་ལ། །གསོལ་མཆོད་རྐྱེན་གྱི་བྱེ་བྲག་ཏུ། །
ཇི་ལྟར་འདོད་པ་སོ་སོར་བསྐྱངས། །འཕྲོ་འདུ་སྣ་ཚོགས་གཟེར་མེད་ན། །
དམིགས་གཏད་གཅིག་ལས་དོན་མི་འགྲུབ། །འཕྲོ་འདུས་ལས་ཁ་བསྒྱུར་ཤེས་ན། །
ཐེ་བྲང་ཐ་ཆུང་གཅིག་གིས་ཀྱང་། །ཕྲིན་ལས་ཐོགས་མེད་ལས་ཀུན་འགྲུབ། །
ཐམས་ཅད་སེམས་ཀྱི་ཆོ་འཕྲུལ་ཡིན། །

> The nail of unchanging intent is to understand that
> All the peaceful and wrathful deities and the Great Glorious One
> Have no existence apart from your own mind.
> Neither is there a Rudra anywhere else—they are your own mind!
> Mind essence is empty—dharmakāya;
> Cognizant and clear—sambhogakāya;
> Self-arising in multiplicity—nirmāṇakāya.
> Appearance is the lord and emptiness the consort.
> Indivisible appearance and emptiness is Jñānakāya.
> Even though discursive thoughts are incalculable,
> They are all the retinue of the Glorious One.
> The inconceivable primordial Buddha
> Never parts from the very nature of mind.
> Without the nail of unchanging intent,
> Even if you practice the Great Glorious One, apart from the ordinary,
> You will not attain the supreme and will go astray like Rudra.

The nail of radiating and absorbing is the great miracle of gaining mastery over all the four types of activities and is as important as white borax is for the task of refining. The tantra says:

> Knowing how to change one's visualization, every wish is fulfilled.
> That is the nail of radiating and absorbing.
> The radiation and absorption of concentration
> Perfects the capacity of mind,
> And whatever you wish for occurs.
> By the power of the blessings of mantra and mudrā,
> Any beneficial work is accomplished,
> Whether peaceful, enriching, magnetizing, or wrathful.
> Just as, for instance, the circumstance
> Of prayers and offerings made to a single jewel
> Can fulfill every single wish.
> If the nail of various radiations and absorptions is lacking
> The visualization will not accomplish goals beyond a single focus.
> But if one knows how to alternate between radiation and absorption,
> Then even the lowest of the Tedrang spirits
> Will have unhindered activity and accomplish all deeds.
> Everything is the miracle of mind.

ཞེས་གསུངས་པ་ལྟར་གཟེར་བཞིའི་མན་ངག་གནད་དུ་ཆུད་པས་སྐུ་དངོས་སུ་མཐོང་སྟེ་སྐུའི་སྒྲོག་འགྲོལ། །ངག་ལ་བདེན་པ་འགྲུབ་པས་གསུང་གི་སྒྲོག་འགྲོལ། །ཆོས་ཉིད་ལ་རང་དབང་ཐོབ་པས་ཐུགས་ཀྱི་སྒྲོག་འགྲོལ། །བདེ་གཤེགས་ཞི་ཁྲོའི་སྐུ་གསུང་ཐུགས་དང་རང་གི་སྒོ་གསུམ་དུ་མ་རོ་གཅིག་ཏུ་འདྲེས་པས་འཁོར་འདས་ཀུན་ལ་སྟོང་སྒྲོག་ཐོབ། ཡེ་ཤེས་ཀྱི་རྩལ་འབྱོངས་ཤིང་ཕྲིན་ལས་སྣ་ཚོགས་ལ་རང་དབང་འབྱོར་བ་ཡིན་ནོ། །

ཨེ་མ་ཚེ་འདིར་བྱང་ཆུབ་སྒྲུབ་པ་ལ། །མེད་ཐབས་མེད་པའི་ཁྱད་ཆོས་ཟབ་མོའི་ལམ། །
འབད་པས་གྲུབ་པ་དངོས་པོའི་ཆོས་ཉིད་སྟེ། །འབད་མེད་ལྷུན་གྲུབ་ཐབས་ཀྱི་ཆེ་བ་ཡིན། །

ཨ་ཧྲི་ཙཀྲས་བདུད་དགྲ་འདུལ་བས་ན། །གྲུབ་གཉིས་འདོད་པ་འཛེ་ཞེས་གྲགས་པའི་གཏམ། །
ཁྱབ་འཇུག་ཁྲོས་པའི་སྒྲ་སྐད་ཀྱང་འགོགས་ནུས་པ། བི་ཧོ་ཏ་མའི་དགོངས་པ་མ་ལགས་སམ། །

དེ་ལྟར་ནའང་རྫོང་འཕྲང་སྒྲོག་གསུམ་གྱི། །གནད་དང་ལྡན་ལས་ཐ་མལ་སྣང་ཞེན་གྱིས། །
བཅིངས་པས་བྱང་ཆུབ་ལམ་ལ་འཇུག་དཀའ་བས། །དེ་ཕྱིར་མན་ངག་གནད་དང་ལྡན་པར་གཅེས། །

འདི་ན་དཀྱིལ་འཁོར་གསུམ་གྱི་བསྒོམ་བྱའི་གནད། །རིག་འཛིན་བླ་མའི་ཞལ་ལུང་གང་གའི་རྒྱུན། །
ཐལ་འབྱིན་དགོངས་པའི་ཆུ་གཏེར་ལ་འཇུག་པ། །ཐར་འདོད་སྐལ་བཟང་སྒྲོག་གི་བདུད་རྩི་ཡིན། །

སྙིང་རྗེ་ཁྲོས་པའི་དཔའ་བོ་ཧེ་རུ་ཀ །ལོག་རྟོག་བདུད་དགྲ་འཇོམས་ལ་ཆས་པའི་ཚེ། །

As is said here, by condensing the instructions of the four nails into their key points, one will behold the divine form in actuality and seize the vital essence of that form. When accomplishing truth in speech one will seize the vital essence of speech, and when attaining mastery of the innate nature one will seize the vital essence of mind. When the body, speech, and mind of the peaceful and wrathful sugatas merge with your own body, speech, and mind as the manifold becoming one taste, one will seize the vital essence of all of saṃsāra and nirvāṇa, develop the strength of wisdom, and obtain mastery over all activities.

> Amazing! The profound path of the special teaching,
> Which is indispensable to attain enlightenment in this life,
> Can be accomplished through effort—that is the nature of things.
> Though being spontaneously accomplished without effort is a
> superior skill.
>
> When you tame demons and enemies with ABHICĀRYA,
> It is an utterance known as the two accomplishments fulfilling
> passions.
> It even has the capacity to silence the wrathful voice of Viṣṇu.
> Is that not the intent of the *Vidyottamatantra*?
>
> Likewise, if you do not the key points of the fortress, precipice,
> and life-force[363]
> You will be bound by clinging to ordinary appearances.
> Thus it will be hard to enter the path to enlightenment,
> So possessing the key points of oral instruction is essential.
>
> These key points for the meditation of the three maṇḍalas,
> The instructions of the knowledge-holder gurus,
> Are the stream of Ganges entering the ocean of effortless
> realization
> And become the nectar of life for the fortunate ones who wish for
> liberation.
>
> When the heroic Heruka of wrathful compassion
> Sets out to conquer demons and enemies who possess wrong view,

མཆོད་ཆའི་འཁོར་ལོ་བསྐོར་བས་དམ་ཉམས་སྲོག །
ཕྱི་མར་འཐག་པའི་མཐུ་སྟོབས་དང་ལྡན་ཞིང་། །

སྲིད་གསུམ་ཐལ་འབྱིན་སྲིད་པ་ཕུར་བུ་ཉིད། །དགོངས་པ་བཞི་ལྡན་ཡུལ་ལ་རབ་ཐེབ་ནས། །
འགྲོ་ཀུན་བྱང་ཆུབ་མཆོག་གི་ལམ་བགྲོད་དེ། །ཁྱབ་བདག་རྡོ་རྗེ་སེམས་དང་དབྱེར་མེད་ཤོག །

ཅེས་ཕུར་པའི་ལྷ་ཁྲིད་རང་བློ་དང་མཚམས་པར་བལྟ་བདེར་བཀོད་པ་འདི། །རིགས་ཀུན་ཁྱབ་བདག་གཏེར་ཆེན་ཆོས་ཀྱི་རྒྱལ་པོའི་ཐུགས་བརྩེ་བས་ཉེ་བར་གདམས་པའི་ཞལ་ཁྲིད་ལེགས་པར་ཐོས་པ་རྣམས་བསྒྲིལ་བར་དགོས་ནས་ལྷག་བསམ་དང་དད་འདུན་རྣམ་པར་དག་པས་མཚམས་སྦྱར་ཏེ། བླ་མའི་ཞལ་ལུང་མན་ངག་གི་རིམ་པ་རྣམས་གཞིར་བཞག རིག་འཛིན་དམ་པ་གོང་མ་རྣམས་ཀྱི་བཞེད་སྲོལ་གྱིས་ཉུང་ཟད་ཟུར་བརྒྱན་ཏེ་འོག་མིན་ཀརྨ་རི། གྲུབ་པ་མཆོག་གི་བསྟི་གནས་གསང་སྔགས་ཕོ་བྲང་རྡོ་རྗེ་བཀོད་པར། གཏེར་ཆེན་བླ་མའི་སློབ་འབངས་ཀུན་ལས། སྐྱེས་སྦྱངས་ཡོན་ཏན་གྱི་གྲལ་མཐར་གནས་པ། ཚ་བ་བཛྲེ་ཀརྨ་རིན་ཆེན་རྣམ་རྒྱལ་གྱིས་བྲིས་པའི་རྣམ་དཀར་ཇི་སྙེད་པའི་མཐུས། སྐྱབས་མཆོག་རིག་འཛིན་པ་རྣམས་ཞབས་པད་བསྐལ་པ་རྒྱ་མཚོར་བརྟན་ཅིང་། འགྲོ་ཀུན་བདུད་བཞིའི་གཡུལ་ལས་རྣམ་པར་རྒྱལ་བའི་རྒྱུར་གྱུར་ཅིག །སུ་ཛ་ཡ། །།

He is endowed with the power and force that grinds the life force
of samaya breakers
Into dust with the spinning of the wheel of weapons.

When the kīla of existence that cuts through the three existences,
Endowed with four intentions, has pierced its object fully,
May all beings traverse the path to supreme enlightenment
And become indivisible from Vajrasattva—the pervasive lord.

This Kīlaya deity instruction, which is arranged in a manner that is easy to read and apply to one's own being, was written with altruistic mind along with pure faith and good wishes having attentively received, while fearing forgetfulness, the oral instructions given out of the loving kindness of the pervasive lord of all buddha families, the Great Treasure Revealer and Dharma King. The sequence of the master's advice and oral instructions was then taken as the foundation and slightly elaborated upon according to the teaching traditions of the sacred knowledge-holders of the past.

This was written at the Akaniṣṭha Karma Mountain in the Vajra Arrayed Palace of Secret Mantra, the abode of the supreme siddha, by the monk from Tsawa—Karma Rinchen Namgyal—who, in terms of both natural and acquired qualities, ranks lowest among all students and servants of the Great Treasure Revealer Guru. By the power of whatever goodness may be in this, may the lotus feet of the knowledge-holders, the supreme refuge, be firm for an ocean of aeons and may it be a cause for all beings to fully conquer the army of the four demons. Sujaya!

Appendix A

Topical Outline for Instructions of the Knowledge-holders

1. **The Physical Yoga of Creation**
    - 1.1 Clear Appearance
        - 1.1.1 The three samādhis
            - 1.1.1.1 The Samādhi of Suchness
            - 1.1.1.2 The All-Illuminating Samādhi
            - 1.1.1.3 The Seed Samādhi
                - 1.1.1.3.1 The elements, palace and seat
                - 1.1.1.3.2 The deities
                - 1.1.1.3.3 Substance maṇḍala
        - 1.1.2 Blessing, empowerment, etc.
            - 1.1.2.1 Descent of blessing and conferring empowerment
            - 1.1.2.2 Invitation
                - 1.1.2.2.1 The request
                - 1.1.2.2.2 The actual invitation
                - 1.1.2.2.3 The request to remain
            - 1.1.2.3 Offerings
                - 1.1.2.3.1 Offering prostration to please
                - 1.1.2.3.2 Offering enjoyments
                - 1.1.2.3.3 Offering the three poisons
                - 1.1.2.3.4 Offering amṛta
                    - 1.1.2.3.4.1 The actual offering
                    - 1.1.2.3.4.2 Receiving the accomplishments
                - 1.1.2.3.5 Offering rakta
                - 1.1.2.3.6 Offering the bali
                - 1.1.2.3.7 Offering of joining and liberation
            - 1.1.2.4 Praises
                - 1.1.2.4.1 Praising the root maṇḍala of the lord
                - 1.1.2.4.2 Praising the maṇḍala of the wrathful ones in the ten directions
                - 1.1.2.4.3 Praising the material kīla maṇḍala
                - 1.1.2.4.4 Praising the gate keepers and vow holders
    - 1.2 Recollection of purity
        - 1.2.1 Remembrance of the purity of the support
        - 1.2.2 Recollecting the purity of the supported deities
    - 1.3 Stable Pride
2. **The Verbal Yoga of Recitation**
3. **The Mental Yoga of Samādhi**

Appendix B

Texts for Vajrakilaya of the Seven Profound Cycles in the New Treasures[364]

Volume TSA – 17

Text no:	PT TSA 4
Tibetan title:	*Yang gsang thugs kyi phur gcig gi rgyud kyi rtsa dum phur bzhi don chen dam pa'i rgyun sogs nas cog brdung glo bur sgrub pa'i bar bcas*
Pages:	71-204
Author(s):	Mchog gyur gling pa
Date:	-
Site:	Karma'i dam can brag
Description:	Zab bdun phur pa Treasure text

Text no:	PT TSA 5
Tibetan title:	*Yang gsang thugs kyi phur gcig gi brgyud 'debs byang chub lam bzang*
Pages:	205-208
Author(s):	Zla bzang sprul ming pa kar ma nges don bstan pa rab rgyas
Date:	-
Site:	Sa spyod gsung gi 'khor lo
Description:	Zab bdun phur pa lineage prayer

Text no:	PT TSA 6
Tibetan title:	*Sngon gtor*
Pages:	209-210
Author(s):	-
Date:	-
Site:	-
Description:	Local deity bali offering

Text no:	PT TSA 7
Tibetan title:	*Skyabs sems*
Pages:	211-212
Author(s):	-
Date:	-
Site:	-
Description:	Zab bdun phur pa refuge and bodhicitta verses

Text no: PT TSA 8
Tibetan title: *Yang gsang thugs kyi phur gcig las las byang phrin las 'dus pa*
Pages: 213-221
Author(s): a) Sprul pa'i gter chen mchog gyur gling pa
b) Prajñā Jñāna
Date: -
Site: Karma'i dam can brag
Description: Zab bdun phur pa practice manual

Text no: PT TSA 9
Tibetan title: *Rdzas phur byin rlabs*
Pages: 223-224
Author(s): O rgyan chen po'i phrin las mchog gyur gling pa
Date: -
Site: -
Description: Blessing of the material substance kīla

Text no: PT TSA 10
Tibetan title: *Sman mchod*
Pages: 225-226
Author(s): Zla ming pa
Date: -
Site: -
Description: Amṛta offering

Text no: PT TSA 11
Tibetan title: *Zab bdun mngon spyod phur pa las bstod bskul rdo rje'i thog 'bebs*
Pages: 227-235
Author(s): Mchog gyur gling pa
Date: -
Site: Revealed: Nam mkha' mdzod
Written: Dil yag dgon theg chen rdo rje gling
Description: Praise and exhortation of the Zab bdun phur pa deities

Text no: PT TSA 12
Tibetan title: *Japa khang dbye ba*
Pages: 237-238
Author(s): -
Date: -
Site: -
Description: Division of the recitation palace

Text no: PT TSA 13
Tibetan title: *Sngags byang*

Pages:	239-241
Author(s):	-
Date:	-
Site:	-
Description:	Mantras

Text no:	PT TSA 14
Tibetan title:	*Yang gsang thugs kyi phur gcig las tshe 'gugs*
Pages:	243-244
Author(s):	Mchog gyur gling pa
Date:	-
Site:	Karma'i dam can brag
Description:	Phur pa life hook ritual

Text no:	PT TSA 15
Tibetan title:	*Zab bdun mchog zab yang dag gi bka' srung sgrub pa'i phrin las*
Pages:	245-255
Author(s):	Mchog gyur gling pa
Date:	-
Site:	Revealed: Mdo khams nam mkha' mdzod Written: Tsa 'dra rin chen brag dpal spungs
Description:	Protector ritual

Text no:	PT TSA 16
Tibetan title:	*Zab bdun mchog zab yang dag gi bka' srung shwa na chen mo sgrub pa'i phrin las*
Pages:	257-273
Author(s):	Mchog gyur bde chen gling pa
Date:	-
Site:	Revealed: Mdo khams nam mkha' mdzod Written: Tsa 'dra rin chen brag gi g.yas phyogs dpal spungs thub stan chos 'khor gling
Description:	Shwa na chen mo sādhana

Text no:	PT TSA 17
Tibetan title:	*Zab bdun mchog zab yang dag gi phur srung shwa na chen po'i gtor mchog*
Pages:	275-301
Author(s):	Mchog gyur gling pa
Date:	-
Site:	Nam mkha' mdzod
Description:	Shwa na chen mo bali ritual

Text no:	PT TSA 18

Tibetan title: *Dpal chen rdo rje phur pa'i skong ba bdud 'dul sngags gling ma*
Pages: 303-307
Author(s): Padma gar dbang blo gros mtha' yas
Date: -
Site: -
Description: Mending ritual

Text no: PT TSA 19
Tibetan title: *Zab bdun mchog zab yang dag gi bka' srung shwa na chen po'i bskang ba'i las rim*
Pages: 309-320
Author(s): Mchog gyur gling pa
Date: -
Site: Nam mkha' mdzod
Description: Shwa na chen po protector mending ritual

Text no: PT TSA 20
Tibetan title: *Yang gsang thugs kyi phur gcig gi bdag 'jug bde chen rab 'bar*
Pages: 321-332
Author(s): Mchog gyur gling pa
Date: -
Site: Kar ma'i ri khrod bde chen gling
Description: Self-empowerment ritual

Text no: PT TSA 21
Tibetan title: *Zab pa skor bdun las yang gsang thugs kyi phur gcig go khog dbub dngos grub gter mdzod*
Pages: 333-482
Author(s): Mchog gyur gling pa
Date: -
Site: Sa spyod gsung gi gnas mchog 'og min kar ma'i gtsug lag khang chen po'i nye char gsang sngags pho brang rdo rje
Description: Sādhana framework

Text no: PT TSA 22
Tibetan title: *Dpal yang gsang thugs kyi phur gcig gi smad las e khrom gyi phrin las gtor zlog dang 'brel ba'i gdab kha bdud dpung 'joms pa'i mtshon cha*
Pages: 483-558
Author(s): Guṇah
Date: -
Site: -
Description: Ritual for the lower activity

Text no: PT TSA 23

Tibetan title: *Zab bdun mchog zab yang dag gi shwa na chen po'i zlog pa'i phrin las bcol ba*
Pages: 559-569
Author(s): Mchog gyur gling pa
Date: -
Site: Nam mkha' mdzod
Description: Shwa na chen po reversal ritual

Volume TSHA – 18

Text no: PT TSHA 1
Tibetan title: *Zab pa skor bdun gyi las bzhi'i sbyin sreg gi cho ga grub pa'i zhal lung las phur pa'i zhi ba'i sbyin sreg zhur phyungs nur 'gros su bkod pa*
Pages: 1-25
Author(s): -
Date: -
Site: -
Description: Peaceful fire offering

Text no: PT TSHA 2
Tibetan title: *Yang gsang thugs kyi phur gcig gi rgyas pa'i sbyin sreg grub gnyis rab 'bar*
Pages: 27-47
Author(s): -
Date: -
Site: -
Description: Increasing fire offering

Text no: PT TSHA 3
Tibetan title: *Yang gsang thugs kyi phur gcig gi dbang gi sbyin sreg nor bu'i lcags kyu*
Pages: 49-67
Author(s): -
Date: -
Site: -
Description: Magnetizing fire offering

Text no: PT TSHA 4
Tibetan title: *Yang gsang thugs kyi phur gcig gi drag po me'i las sbyor bskal pa'i me chen rab 'bar*
Pages: 69-87
Author(s): Mkhan po ratna
Date: -

Site:	-
Description:	Subjugating fire activity

Text no:	PT TSHA 5
Tibetan title:	*Zab bdun mngon spyod phur pa las gri 'dul gyi cho ga*
Pages:	89-110
Author(s):	Mchog gyur gling pa
Date:	Revealed: 12/07/ 1856 Written: 30/12/1857
Site:	Revealed: Mdo khams yel brag nam mkha' mdzod Written: 'Og min kar ma'i ri khrod
Description:	Knife taming ritual

Text no:	PT TSHA 6
Tibetan title:	*Zab pa skor bdun las yang gsang thugs kyi phur gcig gi smin byed khyer bde rnam gsal du bkod pa rig mchog gsang ba'i bcud 'bebs*
Pages:	111-158
Author(s):	Padma gar gyi dbang phyug blo gros mtha' yas pa'i sde
Date:	-
Site:	Rdzong shod bde gshegs 'dus pa'i pho brang
Description:	Empowerment ritual

Text no:	PT TSHA 7
Tibetan title:	*Zab bdun thugs kyi phur gcig las tshe gyang dpal gyi be'u*
Pages:	159-174
Author(s):	Mchog gling gnyis pa padma dbang chen las rab rdo rje
Date:	-
Site:	Rgyam gangs mgul g.yu mtsho'i sgrub gnas
Description:	Life luck ritual

Text no:	PT TSHA 8
Tibetan title:	*Zab bdun mngon spyod phur pa las bstan srung shwa na chen po'i yongs rdzogs gtor ma'i dbang mchog mthu rtsal nus pa'i bcud 'bebs*
Pages:	175-186
Author(s):	'Chi med bstan gnyis gyung drung gling pa
Date:	-
Site:	Rdzong shod bde gshegs 'dus pa'i pho brang
Description:	Shwa na chen po empowerment ritual

Text no:	PT TSHA 9
Tibetan title:	*Yang gsang thugs kyi phur gcig gi lha khrid gsal bar bkod pa rig pa 'dzin pa'i shal lung*
Pages:	187-232
Author(s):	Tsha ba bhan dhe karma rin chen rnam rgyal

Date:	-
Site:	-
Description:	Deity instructions

Text no:	PT TSHA 10
Tibetan title:	*Guru'i thugs dam zab pa skor bdun las mngon spyod drag po'i las kyi zab pa yang gsang thugs kyi phur gcig gi spyi don rnam bshad rig 'dzin rtsal 'chang rnam gnyis kyi zhal lung zab don bang mdzod*
Pages:	233-411
Author(s):	'Dul 'dzin mkhan po karma rin chen dar rgyas dpal bzang po
Date:	24/05/1876 – 21/06/1876
Site:	Og min stod lung mtshur phu
Description:	Commentary on the general meaning of Zab bdun phur pa

Titles, Personal Names, and Place Names

English Titles of Texts and Cycles	**Tibetan Titles of Texts and Cycles**
A Clarification of the Branches of the Auspicious Tune: the Life of the Great Treasure Revealer Chokgyur Dechen Lingpa	*Gter chen mchog gyur bde chen gling pa'i rnam thar bkra shis dbyangs kyi yan lag gsal byed*
Auspiciously Curling Tune: a Supplication to the Life of the Emanated Great Treasure Revealer Chokgyur Lingpa	*Sprul pa'i gter chen mchog gyur gling pa'i rnam thar gsol 'debs bkra shis 'khyil pa'i dbyangs snyan*
Basic Account of the Emanated Great Treasure Revealer's Biography Combined with a Few Treasure Chronicles	*Sprul pa'i gter ston chen mo'i rnam thar gyi sa bon zhal gsung ma dang gter 'byung 'ga' zhig 'bel gtam sna tshogs bcas*
Black Kīla Commentary in One Hundred Thousand Words	*Phur 'grel 'bum nag*
Breeze of Requesting the Auspicious Tune: Replies to Questions Arising from the Hagiography of the Great Treasure Revealer	*Gter chen rnam thar las 'phros pa'i dris lan bkra shis dbyangs snyan bskul ba'i dri bzhon*
Chronicle of Padmasambhava	*Padma bka' thang*
Congregation of Mamos	*Ma mo spyi bsdus*
Copper Temple Life Story	*Rnam thar zangs gling ma*
Differentiation of the Three Precepts	*Sdom gsum rab dbye*
Dispeller of All Obstacles	*Bar chad kun sel*
Divisions of The Auspicious Tune: The Condensed Meaning of the Supplication to the Great Treasure Revealer Chokgyur Lingpa	*Gter chen mchog gyur gling pa'i rnam thar gsol 'debs kyi bsdus don bkra shis dbyangs kyi yan lag*
Eight Examinations	*Brtag pa brgyad*
Embodiment of Realization	*Dgongs 'dus*
Embodiment of the Realization of the Dharma Protectors	*Chos skyong dgongs 'dus*

Embodiment of the Realization of the Master	*Bla ma dgongs ‘dus*
Embodiment of the Sugatas of the Eight Pronouncements	*Bka’ brgyad bde gshegs kun ‘dus*
Quintessential Inscription of Oral Instructions	*Zhal gdams snying byang*
Five Chronicles	*Bka’ thang sde lnga*
Five Cycles of the Essential Sacred Dharma	*Dam chos snying po skor lnga*
Four Dharma Protector Cycles of Ten Qualities That Bring Happiness to Tibet and Kham	*Bod khams bde thabs chos bcu yi bstan pa srung ba’i skor bzhi*
Full Intent of the Guru’s Heart Practice	*Thugs sgrub dgongs pa kun ‘dus*
Galpo Tantra	*Gal po rgyud*
Gem that Clears the Waters: an Investigation of Treasure Revealers	*Gter ston brtag ba chu dwangs nor bu*
Great Compassionate One Who Embodies All Sugatas	*Thugs rje chen po bde gshegs kun ‘dus*
Great Compassionate One Who Stirs the Depth of Saṃsāra	*Thugs rje chen po ‘khor ba dong sprugs*
Great Treasure Chronicle	*Gter ‘byung chen mo*
Great Treasure Chronicle: The Illuminating Lamp	*Gter ‘byung chen mo gsal ba’i sgron me*
Great Treasury of Detailed Exposition	*Bye brag bshad mdzod chen mo*
Great Ultimate Instruction of Dharmakāya	*Chos sku’i don khrid chen mo*
Guhyagarbha Tantra	*Gsang ba snying po*
Guru’s Heart Practice: Dispeller of All Obstacles	*Bla ma’i thugs sgrub bar chad kun sel*
Guru’s Heart Practice: Wish-fulfilling Jewel Spontaneously Accomplishing Intentions	*Bla ma’i thugs sgrub yid bzhin nor bu bsam pa lhun grub*
Guru’s Ocean of Accomplishments	*Bla ma dngos grub rgya mtsho*
Heart Essence of All Knowledge-holders	*Rig ‘dzin yongs rdzogs snying thig*
Heart Essence of Garab Dorje	*Dga’ rab rdo rje’i snying thig*
Heart Essence of Guru Drakpo: The Red Hūṃ	*Gur drag hūṃ dmar snying thig*
Heart Essence of Mañjuśrīmitra	*‘Jam dpal bshes gnyen snying thig*
Heart Essence of Pema Garwang	*Padma gar dbang snying thig*
Heart Essence of Samantabhadra	*Kun bzang thugs thig*
Heart Essence of the Gathering of Herukas	*Heruka ‘dus pa’i thugs tig*
Heart Essence of the Ḍākinī	*Mkha ‘gro snying thig*

Heart Essence of the Profound Meaning of Ati	*A ti zab don snying thig*
Heart Essence of the Three Families	*Rigs gsum snying thig*
Heart Essence of Tsogyal	*Mtsho rgyal snying thig*
Heart Essence of Vairocana	*Vairocana'i snying thig*
Hevajra Tantra in Five Hundred Thousand Verses	*Kye rdo rgyud 'bum lnga*
Inner Heart Essence	*Thugs thig snying po*
Inner Secret Essence	*Gsang thig snying po*
Innermost Essence of the Ḍākinī	*Mkha 'gro yang thig*
Instruction Section	*Man ngag sde,*
Instructions of the Knowledge-holders – Clearly Arranged Deity Guidance for the Single Form of the Most Secret Kīla of Mind	*Yang gsang thugs kyi phur gcig gi lha khrid gsal bar bkod pa rig pa 'dzin pa'i shal lung*
Jewel Mound Sūtra	*Dkon brtseg*
Kālacakra Root Tantra	*Dus 'khor rtsa rgyud*
Lake-born Vajra	*Mtsho skyes rdo rje.*
Lapis Lazuli Drama: General Notes on the Rosary of Red Pearls Past Lives Supplication	*Skyes rabs gsol 'debs mu tig dmar po'i phreng ba'i zin thun vaiçárya'i mdo 'dzin*
Lotus Crowned	*Padma gtsug tor*
Lotus Crowned Great Compassionate One	*Thugs rje chen po padma gtsug tor*
Magical Net	*Sgyu 'phrul drwa ba*
Magical Net of Pema Garwang	*Padma gar dbang sgyu 'phrul drwa ba*
Magical Net of the Five Families of Limitless Life	*Tshe dpag med rigs lnga sgyu 'phrul drwa ba*
Maṇi Kabum	*Maṇi bka' 'bum*
Manual of the Single Intent	*Dgongs gcig yig cha*
Melody of the Fifth Auspicious Birth: A General Outer Biography of the Great Treasure Revealer Chokgyur Lingpa	*Gter chen mchog gyur gling pa'i thun mong phyi yi rnam thar bkra shis skye ba lnga pa'i dbyangs snyen*
Mind Section	*Sems sde*
Most Secret Blade Kīla	*Phur pa yang gsang spu kri*
Mother Tantra that Brings the Ḍākinīs' Secret Onto the Path	*Ma rgyud mkha' 'gro gsang ba lam khyer*
New Treasures of Chokgyur Lingpa	*Mchog gling gter gsar*
Peaceful and Wrathful Magical Net	*Sgyu 'phrul zhi khro*
Powerful Vajra Wrath	*Rdo rje drag rtsal*

Practice Manual of Combined Activity	*Yang gsang thugs kyi phur gcig las las byang phrin las 'dus pa*
Precious Lapis Lazuli Rosary that Briefly Presents the Emergence of the Profound Treasures and the Accomplished Treasure Revealers	*Zab mo'i gter dang gter ston grub thob ji ltar byon pa'i lo rgyus mdor bsdus bkod pa rin chen vaiçárya'i phreng ba*
Profound Essence of Tārā	*Sgrol ma'i zab tig*
Profound Essence that Embodies the Families of the Three Kāyas	*Sku gsum rigs 'dus zab tig*
Radiant Lamp	*Gsal ba'i sgron me*
Realization of Zurza	*Zur bza'i thugs dam*
Rosary of Red Pearls: a Supplication to the Past Lives of the Vidyādhara Master -- the Great Treasure Revealer Chokgyur Lingpa	*Rje rig pa 'dzin pa gter chen mchog gyur gling pa'i skyes rabs kyi gsol 'debs mu tig dmar po'i phreng ba*
Sacred Tantra of the Great Purpose of the Four Kīlas	*Phur bzhi don chen dam pa'i brgyud*
Sūtra that Gathers the Intention of All Buddhas	*'Dus pa'i mdo*
Seven Cycles of Pacifying Goddesses	*zhi byed skor bdun*
Seven Cycles of the Sacred Dharma	*Dam chos nor bu skor bdun*
Seven Profound Cycles	*Zab pa skor bdun*
Single Form of Vajrakumāra	*Rdo rje gzhon nu phyag rgya gcig pa*
Single Kīla of Mind of the Scriptural Tradition	*Lung lugs thugs kyi phur gcig*
Six Scrolls of the Sacred Teaching	*Dam chos shog sde drug*
Space Section	*Klong sde*
Statement of Nub	*Gnubs kyi kha po*
Store of Precious Treasures	*Rin chen gter mdzod*
Summary of Dependency	*Rten 'brel mdo chings*
Sūtra of Mañjuśrī's Play	*Rnam rol mdo*
Sūtra on the Application of Mindfulness	*Mdo dran pa nyer bzhag*
Tantra of Longevity: Confluence of Immortality Nectar	*Tshe rgyud 'chi med bdud rtsi 'khyil ba*
Tantra of Realization	*Dgongs rgyud*
Tantra of Secret Perfection	*Rgyud gsang rdzogs*
Three Sections of the Great Perfection	*Rdzogs chen sde gsum*
Union with Buddha Saṃvara	*Bde mchog sangs rgyas mnyam sbyor*

Vajra Arrayed Scripture	*Lung rdo rje bkod pa*
Vajra Bridge of Acala	*Mi g.yo ba rdo rje zam pa*
Vajra Garland Accomplishing Longevity	*Tshe sgrub rdo rje'i phreng ba*
Vajrakīlaya of the Secret Essence	*Gsang thig phur pa*
Vajrakīlaya of the Seven Profound Cycles	*Zab bdun phur pa*
Vimalamitra's Guru Practice	*Vima'i bla sgrub*
Vimalamitra's Profound Essence	*Vimala'i zab thig*
Wisdom Essence of Oral Instructions on the Stages of the Path	*Zhal gdams lam rim ye shes snying po*
Words of Emptiness	*Stong tshig*

Names of People and Deities	**Names of People and Deities Transcribed**
Bumcham	*'Bum lcam*
Bummo Cham	*'Bum mo lcam*
Butön Rinchen Drub	*Bu ston rin chen grub*
Chak Lotsāwa Chöje Pal	*Chag lo tsā ba chos rje dpal*
Chime Dorje	*'Chi med rdo rje*
Chöchok Rinpoche	*Chos mchog rin po che*
Chokgyur Dechen Shigpo Lingpa Thinley Drodul Tsal	*Mchog gyur bde chen zhig po gling pa phrin las 'gro 'dul rtsal*
Chokling	*Mchog gling*
Chöwang	*Chos dbang*
Dampa Könchog	*Dam pa dkon mchog*
Dazang Karma Ngedön Tenpa Rabgye	*Zla bzang karma nges don bstan pa rab rgyas*
Dechen Chödrön	*Bde chen chos sgron*
Dechen Gyalpo	*Bde chen rgyal po*
Dilgo Khyentse	*Dil mgo mkhyen brtse*
Do Drupchen Tenpe Nyima	*Rdo grub chen bstan pa'i nyi ma*
Dorje Danyem	*Rdo rje mda' snyems*
Dorje Dermo	*Rdo rje sder mo*
Dorje Drachin	*Rdo rje sgra 'byin*
Dorje Draktsal	*Rdo rje drag rtsal*
Dorje Kulche Ma	*Rdo rje bskul byed ma*

Dorje Lingpa	*Rdo rje gling pa*
Dorje Lungchin Ma	*Rdo rje rlung 'byin ma*
Dorje Nayön	*Rdo rje sna yon*
Dorje Nyema	*Rdo rje snyems ma*
Dorje Söche Ma	*Rdo rje gsod byed ma*
Dorje Tummo	*Rdo rje gtum mo*
Dorje Tunkhung	*Rdo rje gtun khung*
Drakpa	*Grags pa*
Drime Lingpa	*Dri med gling pa*
Drogmi Palgyi Yeshe	*'Brog mi dpal gyi ye shes*
Drowa Zangpo	*'Gro ba bzang po*
Drubthob	*Grub thob*
Drukpa Kunley	*'Brug pa kun legs*
Dudjom Yeshe Dorje	*Bdud 'joms ye shes rdo rje*
Dudkyi Shechen	*Bdud kyi gshed chen*
Dungtsho Repa	*Dung mtsho ras pa*
Durtrö Dakmo	*Dur khrod bdag mo*
Dzamling Gyenchog	*'Dzam gling rgyan mchog*
Dzutrul Thuchen	*Rdzu 'phrul mthu chen*
Gampopa Sönam Rinchen	*Sgam po pa bsod nams rin chen*
Garab Dorje	*Dga' rab rdo rje*
Garwa	*Mgar ba*
Genyen Senge Zang	*Dge bsnyen seng ge bzang*
Gesar	*Ge sar*
Gönpo	*Mgon po*
Guru Bardö Trulnang Jom	*Guru bar do'i 'khrul snang 'joms*
Guru Chemchok	*Guru che mchog*
Guru Chiwey Dugngal Sel	*Guru 'chi ba'i sdug bsngal sel*
Guru Chökyi Wangchuk	*Guru chos kyi dbang phyug*
Guru Chöwang	*Guru chos dbang*
Guru Dewa Chenpo	*Guru bde ba chen po*
Guru Dorje Gocha Chen	*Guru rdo rje'i go cha can*
Guru Drodrug Kungyi Kyab	*Guru 'gro drug kun gyi skyabs*
Guru Drubpey Kekong Gyal	*Guru sgrub pa'i ke skong rgyal*
Guru Jungshi Wanggyur Gyal	*Guru 'byung bzhi dbang sgyur rgyal*
Guru Kyewey Dugngal Chong	*Guru skye ba'i sdug bsngal sbyong*

Guru Marung Trödze Che	*Guru ma rungs skrod mdzad che*
Guru Norlha Wanggyi Gyal	*Guru nor lha dbang gyi rgyal*
Guru Pawo Ginggi Tso	*Guru dpa' bo ging gi gtso*
Guru Pema Mengyi Gyal	*Guru padma sman gyi rgyal*
Guru Senge Dradrok	*Guru seng ge sgra sgrogs*
Guru Yidam Wanggyi Gyal	*Guru yi dam dbang gyi rgyal*
Gyalgong	*Rgyal 'gong*
Gyalmo Tse	*Rgyal mo rtse*
Gyalpo	*Rgyal po*
Gyalwa Chokyang	*rGyal ba mchog dbyangs*
Gyalwey Dungzin	*Rgyal ba'i gdung 'dzin*
Gyurme Tsewang Chogdrub	*'Gyur med tshe dbang mchog grub*
Gyutrul	*Sgyu 'phrul*
Jamgön Kongtrul Lodrö Thaye	*'Jam mgon kong sprul blo gros mtha' yas*
Jamyang Khyentse Wangpo Kunga Tenpey Gyaltsen	*'Jam dbyangs mkhyen brtse'i dbang po kun dga' bstan pa'i rgyal mtshan*
Jigme Lingpa	*'Jigs med gling pa*
Jigten Gönpo	*'Jig rten mgon po*
Ju Mipham	*Ju mi pham*
Kakarudzin	*Ka ka ru 'dzin*
Kalden Drendze	*Skal ldan 'dren mdzad*
Karma Lingpa	*Karma gling pa*
Karma Rinchen Dargye	*Kar ma rin chen dar rgyas*
Karma Rinchen Namgyal	*Karma rin chen rnam rgyal*
Karma Sangngag	*Karma gsang sngags*
Karmapa	*Karma pa*
Karmey Khenpo Rinchen Dargye	*Karma'i mkhan po rin chen dar rgyas*
Khakyab Dorje	*Mkha' khyab rdo rje*
Khandroma Kunga Bum	*Mkha' 'gro ma kun dga' 'bum*
Khenchen Dazang	*Mkhan chen zla bzang*
Khenpo Rinchen Dargye	*Mkhan po rin chen dar rgyas*
Khorlo Gyen Depma	*'Khor lo rgyas 'debs ma*
Khyentse Wangpo	*Mkhyen brtse'i dbang po*
Könchog Paldrön	*Dkon mchog dpal sgron*
Könchog Gyurme Tenpey Gyaltsen	*Dkon mchog 'gyur med bstan pa'i rgyal mtshan*
Kongtrul	*Kong sprul*

Kunga Bum	*Kun dga' 'bum*
Kunkyil Chesum	*Kun 'khyil mched gsum*
Kunzang Gyurme Tsewang Drakpa	*Kun bzang 'gyur med tshe dbang grags pa*
Kunzang Jigme Tsewang Norbu	*Kun bzang 'jigs med tshe dbang nor bu*
Kunzang Palden	*Kun bzang dpal ldan*
Kyechok Tshulzang	*Skyes mchog tshul bzang*
Kyepar Phagpey Rigdzin	*Khyad par 'phags pa'i rig 'dzin*
Kyewu Yeshe Dorje	*Skyes bu ye shes rdo rje*
Lang Palseng	*Glang dpal seng*
Langdarma	*Glang dar ma*
Lhalung Palgyi Dorje	*Lha lung dpal gyi rdo rje*
Lhase Damdzin Drak	*Lha sras dam 'dzin grags*
Lhase Degön Kar	*Lha sras dge mgon dkar*
Lhatsun Depachen	*Lha btsun dad pa chan*
Lhatsun Ngönmo	*Lha btsun sngon mo*
Limitless Light	*'Od zer mtha' yas*
Lobzang Gyatso	*Blo bzang rgya mtsho*
Longchenpa Drime Özer	*Klong chen pa 'dri med 'od zer*
Longchen Rabjam	*Klong chen rab 'byams*
Mamo	*Ma mo*
Mawey Sengge	*Smra ba'i seng ge*
Mipham Gyatso	*Mi pham rgya mtsho*
Murub Tsenpo	*Mu rub btsan po*
Mutig Tsenpo	*Mu tig btsan po*
Nanam Dudjom	*Sna nam Bdud 'joms*
Neten Tenpa Dzin	*Gnas brtan bstan pa 'dzin*
Ngagchang Dorje	*Sngags 'chang rdo rje*
Ngagchang Phakpa	*Sngags 'chang 'phag pa*
Norbu	*Nor bu*
Norbu Tenzin	*Nor bu bstan 'dzin*
Nordak Chesum	*Nor bdag mched gsum*
Nub Khulungpa Yönten Gyatso	*Gnubs khu lung pa yon tan rgya mtsho*
Nub Namkhey Nyingpo	*Snubs nam mkha' snying po*
Nub Sangye Yeshe	*Gnubs sangs rgyas ye shes*
Nyak Jñānakumāra	*Snyags jñānakumāra*

Nyima Drakpa	*Nyi ma Grags pa*
Nyang Tingdzin Zangpo	*Nyang ting 'dzin bzang po*
Nyangral Nyima Özer	*Nyang ral nyi ma 'od zer*
Śākya Yeshe	*Śākya ye shes*
Paltsun	*Dpal btsun*
Pawo Tsugla Trengwa	*Dpa' bo gtsug lag 'phreng ba*
Pema Dönyö Tsal	*Padma don yod rtsal*
Pema Gyurme Thegchok Tenpel	*Padma 'gyur med theg mchog bstan 'phel*
Pekar	*Pe kar*
Pema Jungne	*Padma 'byung gnas*
Pema Lingpa	*Padma gling pa*
Pema Wangchuk	*Padma dbang phyug*
Pema Yeshe	*Padma ye shes*
Pemey Nyugu	*Padma'i myu gu*
Phurba	*Phur pa*
Purwo Chathul Go	*Spur bo bya thul mgo*
Radza	*Rā dza*
Rakṣa Thötreng	*Rakṣa thod phreng*
Ratna Lingpa	*Ratna gling pa*
Ratna Lingpa Pal Zangpo	*Ratna gling pa dpal bzang po*
Ratna Urgyen	*Ratna o rgyan*
Rigdzin Gödem	*Rig 'dzin rgod ldem*
Rinchen Namgyal	*rin chen rnam rgyal*
Rinchen Tsultrim Dorje	*Rin chen tshul khrims rdo rje*
Rongzom Chökyi Zangpo	*Rong zom chos kyi bzang po*
Sakya	*Sa skya*
Sakya Paṇḍita	*Sa skya Paṇḍita*
Samten Gyatso	*Bsam gtan rgya mtsho*
Sangye Lama	*Sangs rgyas bla ma*
Sangye Lingpa	*Sangs rgyas gling pa*
Se	*Bswe*
Semo	*Bsre mo*
Shenpa Sokdrubma	*Shan pa srog sgrub ma*
Shigpö Chökyong	*Zhig po'i spyod skyong*
Shigpo Gyalwa	*Zhig po rgyal ba*

Shigpo Lingpa Gargyi Wangchuk	*Zhig po gling pa gar gyi dbang phyug*
Shinje	*Gshin rje*
Shiwa	*Zhi ba*
Situpa	*Si tu pa*
Sok Dokpa Lodrö Gyaltsen	*Sog zlog pa blo gros rgyal mtshan*
Songtsen Gampo	*Srong btsan sgam po*
Stainless Renown	*Dris med grags pa*
Sumpa Khenpo	*Sum pa mkhan po*
Taklungma Ngawang Tenpey Nyima	*Stag lung ma ngag dbang bstan pa'i nyi ma*
Tai Situpa Pema Nyinche Wangpo	*Ta'i Si tu pa padma nyin byed dbang po*
Tedrang	*The brang*
Tenma	*Brtan ma*
Tenzin Kyewu Shönnu	*Bstan 'dzin skyes bu gzhon nu*
Tersey Tulku	*Gter sras sprul sku*
Thangtong Gyalpo	*Thang stong rgyal po*
Thegchok Dorje	*Theg mchog rdo rje*
Trisong Detsen	*Khri srong lde'u btsan*
Tsa Sum	*Rtsa gsum*
Tsawa Bhande Karma Rinchen Namgyal	*Tsha ba bhan dhe karma rin chen rnam rgyal*
Tsele Natsog Rangdrol	*Rtse le sna tshogs rang grol*
Tsering Chenga	*Tshe ring mched lnga*
Tsering Yangtsho	*Tshe ring g.yang mtsho*
Tsewang Drakpa	*Tshe dbang grags pa*
Tsewang Norbu	*Tshe dbang nor bu*
Urgyen Lingpa	*U rgyan gling pa*
Urgyen Padma	*O rgyan Padma*
Wangchen Buddha Heruka	*Dbang chen buddha heruka*
Wangchok Dorje	*Dbang mchog rdo rje*
Yangdak Heruka	*Yang dag Heruka*
Yeshe Tsogyal	*Ye shes mtsho rgyal*
Yudrönma	*G.yu sgron ma*
Zangpo	*Bzang po*
Zur	*Zur*
Zurza Metog Drön	*Zur bza' me tog sgron*

Place Names, Monasteries, Schools	**Place Names, Monasteries, Schools Transcribed**
Ārya Nang	*Ārya nang*
Bön	*Bon*
Bumdzong	*'Bum rdzong*
Bundzong	*Bun rdzong*
Changra Mugpo	*Lcang ra smug po*
Chime Karmo Taktsang	*'Chi med dkar mo stag tshang*
Chimpu	*Mchims phu*
Danyin Khala Ronggo	*Zla nyin kha la rong sgo*
Do Kham	*Mdo khams*
Drada	*Gra mda'*
Drak Rinchen Barwa	*Brag rin chen 'bar ba*
Drakkar Dzongchung	*Brag dkar rdzong chung*
Drakyang Dzong	*Sgrags yang rdzong*
Drinyen Dong	*'bri gnyan sdong*
Dungchu	*Mdung chu*
Dzi	*'Dzi*
Dzongshö Deshek Dupey Phodrang	*Rdzong shod bde gshegs 'dus pa'i pho brang*
Entse	*En rtse*
Evaṃ Chögar	*Evaṃ chos sgar*
Gatö	*Sga stod*
Gatö Meseng	*Sga stod me seng*
Gelugpa	*Dge lugs pa*
Gomde Dranang	*Sgom sde grwa nang*
Gotö	*Go stod*
Guge	*Gu ge*
Gyamgyal Yutsho	*Rgyam rgyal g.yu mtsho*
Kagyu	*Bka' brgyud*
Karag Phukpa	*Ka rag phug pa*
Karmey Bumdzong	*Karma'i 'bum rdzong*
Karmey Damchen Drak	*Karma'i dam chen brag*
Kela	*Ke la*

Kela Norbu Punsum Drak	*Ke la nor bu spun gsum brag*
Kerong	*Ke rong*
Kham	*Khams*
Kham Mig Yedrak	*Khams mig ye brag*
Lhado	*Lha mdo*
Magyal Pomra	*Rma rgyal spom ra*
Mangyul	*Mang yul*
Maṇikha	*Maṇi kha*
Mapham Senggö Yutsho	*Ma pham seng rgod g.yu mtsho*
Mengyal Drawey Drak	*Sman rgyal 'dra ba'i brag*
Meshö Dzam	*Smad shod dzam*
Mön	*Mon*
Namke	*Gnam skas*
Namkha Dzö	*Nam mkha' mdzod*
Nangchen	*Nang chen*
Neten	*Gnas brtan*
Nyal	*Mnyal*
Nyang	*Nyang*
Nyingma	*Rnying ma*
Ogmin Karmey Palgyi Deu	*'Og min karma'i dpal gyi de'u*
Pal Riwoche	*Dpal ri bo che*
Palpung	*Dpal spung*
Paog Burmo	*Dpa' 'og 'bur mo*
Pawo Wangchen Drak	*Dpa' bo dbang chen brag*
Pema Shelri	*Padma shel ri*
Powo	*Po bo*
Purang	*Pu rang*
Rasa	*Ra sa*
Rinchen Drak	*Rin chen brag*
Rinpung	*Rin dpung*
Riwo Wangphuk	*Ri bo dbang phug*
Riwo Wangzhu	*Ri bo dbang zhu*
Rongme Chime Karmo Taktsang	*Rong rme 'chi med dkar mo stag tshang*
Rudam Gang	*Ru dam gangs*
Rudam Ganggyi Rawa	*Ru dam gangs kyi ra ba*

Rudam Gangtrö Dewa Chenpo	*Ru dam gangs khrod bde ba chen po*
Samye	*Bsam yas*
Samye Chimpu	*Bsam yas mchims phu*
Sarma	*Gsar ma*
Sengchen Namdrak	*Seng chen gnam brag*
Tanag	*Rta nag*
Tsādra Rinchen Drak	*Tsā dra rin chen brag*
Tsang	*Gtsang*
Tsawa	*Tsha ba*
Tsawa Marshö	*Tsha ba dmar shod*
Tsāri	*Tsā ri*
Tshurpu	*Mtshur pu*
Urgyen Mindrol Ling	*O rgyan smin grol gling*
Urgyen Zangling	*O rgyan zangs gling*
Wangdrak Barwa	*Dbang drag 'bar ba*
Yamakha	*Ya ma kha*
Yarlung	*G.yar lung*
Yegyal Namkha Dzö	*Ye rgyal nam mkha' mdzod*
Yeldrak Namkha Dzö	*Yel brag nam mkha mdzod*
Yertö	*Yer stod*
Yorpo Dra	*G.yor po gra*
Zalmo	*Zal mo*
Ze	*Bzad*

Endnotes

1 Although previously the Treasure tradition attracted only marginal interest from Western scholars, significant work has been done in the last two decades. The first major study in English was by Dargyay (1979), who researched the rise and development of the Nyingma School based on late nineteenth and twentieth century Tibetan historical surveys. Gyatso has been the most prolific writer on this tradition and has published a series of books and articles on a wide range of historical and hermeneutical topics related to the Treasures (1981; 1986; 1992; 1993; 1994; 1996; 1998; 1999; 2000; n.d.). Thondup has translated a survey of the Treasures by Do Drupchen Tenpe Nyima (1865-1926) (1986), addressed the issue of transmission and authenticity (1990) and the spiritual tradition stemming from the master Jigme Lingpa (1729-1798) (1996). This tradition has also been studied by Goodman on several occasions (1983; 1992) and by Van Schaik (2004). Other recent works include Aris 1989 (a study of the Treasure revealer Pema Lingpa (1450-1521)); Schwieger 1990 (a study of the *Store of Precious Treasures*); Mayer 1996 (the Indian philosophical background for the Tibetan Treasure system); Germano 1998 (a study of contemporary Treasure revelation in Tibet); Kapstein 2000 (discussing the authenticity of the Treasures); and Martin 2001 (a study of Bön Treasures with much relevance for the Buddhist Treasure tradition). See also Doctor 2002 and 2003 for studies of the Treasures of Chokgyur Lingpa (1829-1870). In addition to these sources, several translations of Treasure literature have been published (e.g., Douglas 1978; Schmidt 1989; Tsogyal 1999). For lists of major Tibetan surveys on the Treasure tradition see Gyatso 1994: 284, no. 10; and 1996: 161, no. 2. It should be noted that the Tibetan Bön religion likewise contains a transmission of Treasures that in many ways is similar to the Treasure revelations of the Nyingma School. This study, however, focuses on the Buddhist Treasures. For an excellent survey of the Bön Treasure system see Martin 2001.

2 *Babs so chen po gsum:* (a) *ring brgyud bka' ma*, (b) *nye brgyud gter ma*, (c) *zab mo dag snang*. The borders between these three systems are fluid. For example, Jamgön Kongtrul (1976: 650) explains that several of Chokgyur Lingpa's Treasures are better considered Transmitted Precepts due to the nature of their content. See also Gyatso 1992: 98; Chokling 2001: 6, 9.

3 Although most Treasures consist of spiritual teachings, a wide variety of other kinds of Treasures exist, which will be discussed below. See also Gyatso 1994.

4 The richest source for biographical information on the Treasure revealers is Jamgön Kongtrul's hagiographical survey of the main actors in the Treasure tradition, which covers the majority of Treasure revealers from the tenth to the nineteenth centuries (1976b). The most comprehensive biographical study of Treasure revealers available in English is Dudjom 1991, which gives biographical data for several important Trea-

sure revealers. Other individual Treasure revealers discussed in English are: Thangtong Gyalpo (1361-1485) in Gyatso 1981; Pema Lingpa in Aris 1989 and Harding 2003; Jigme Lingpa in Goodman 1983, 1992, Gyatso 1998, and Van Schaik 2004; and, finally, Chokgyur Lingpa in Tobgyal 1988 and Doctor 2002, 2003.

5 Most traditional accounts date Sangye Lama (considered the first Treasure revealer) to the eleventh century. Prats (1979: 256) places him in the late tenth century but his dates remain uncertain (Schwieger 1990: XXIX, no. 14).

6 Commentaries on the Treasure tradition have often pointed to this fact in reply to criticism. See Gyatso 1994: 277; Mayer 1996: 75-82; and Kapstein 2000.

7 To this day the Treasure tradition continues to reveal religious matter. For accounts of contemporary Treasure revealers see Germano 1998 and Hanna 1994.

8 For a study of Indian Buddhist approaches to scriptural authenticity see Davidson 1990.

9 This argument is made by Davidson, who suggests that the Tibetan creation of a closed canon was in large part a product of Chinese influence (2002a).

10 In general this period of Tibetan history is obscure. Traditional Tibetan accounts of this period are in large part founded on later Treasure scriptures (e.g., Nyangral 1976; Urgyen Lingpa 1996; transl. Tsogyal 1999; Douglas 1978). However, these accounts are religious epics rather than historical annals, and their value as historical testimony is limited. Consequently, modern historians have challenged some of the claims made in these epics and subsequent works founded on them. Such challenges include the role of the Indian master Padmasambhava (Germano 2002; Kapstein 2000; Wangdu 2000), the influence of Chinese Buddhism during this period (Dargyay 1979; Kapstein 2000; Lai 1983), and the reign of the Tibetan king Langdarma (Martin 2001), to name a few.

11 For example, Pawo 1986 and Dudjom 1967.

12 The two primary Treasure hagiographies of Padmasambhava are the *Copper Temple Life Story* revealed by Nyangral Nyima Özer (1124-1192) (Nyangral 1976, transl. Tsogyal 1999) and the *Chronicle of Padmasambhava* (Urgyen Lingpa 1996, transl. Douglas 1978) revealed by Urgyen Lingpa (1323-?). Erik Schmidt has prepared a bibliography of Tibetan hagiographies of Padmasambhava in Tsogyal 1999. See also Blondeau 1980. Traditional literature speaks of the concealment of large numbers of hagiographies on Padmasambhava, such as 10,900 mentioned in the *Chronicle of Padmasambhava* (Blondeau 1980: 45), or 1900, mentioned by the fifteenth Karmapa Khakyab Dorje (1871-1922) (Khakyab 1981b: 330).

13 The lack of historical data from this period makes it difficult to determine the actual impact of Padmasambhava. As Dargyay (1979: 31-59) points out, no historical sources verify later Tibetan accounts of the all-important role of Padmasambhava in the conversion of Tibet, particularly regarding his role in the transmission of the Great Perfection teachings (*rdzogs chen*). However, since the discovery of a Dun Huang scripture mentioning Padmasambhava by name, his presence in Tibet is no longer doubted (Bischoff 1971; Mayer 1994). See also Germano 2002; Kapstein 2000; and especially Wangdu 2000 for alternative accounts of Padmasambhava's Tibetan sojourn.

14 He is, however, not the only master attributed with concealment of Treasures. Gyatso (1993: 98), citing Pawo Tsugla Trengwa, presents the following list: Yeshe Tsogyal,

Trisong Detsen, Mutig Tsenpo, Nub Namkhey Nyingpo, Nyak Jñānakumāra, Vairocana, Nanam Dudjom, and Nub Sangye Yeshe. Ratna Lingpa presents a list that additionally includes: Vimalamitra, Gyalwa Chokyang, Drogmi Palgyi Yeshe, Lang Palseng, and Nyang Tingdzin Zangpo (1977: 54). In addition, Jamgön Kongtrul (1976a: 515.6) describes the Kagyu master Gampopa Sönam Rinchen (1079-1153) and his student Kyewu Yeshe Dorje (twelfth century) concealing Treasures that later were revealed by Dungtsho Repa the elder (twelfth/thirteenth century). The *Maṇi Kabum* is said to have been concealed by King Songtsen Gampo (Kapstein 2000: 145)" .

15 For a discussion of this point see Gyatso 1986; 1993.

16 On these stages see Gyatso 1986; Thondup 1986: 101-111; Dudjom 1991: 447-457.

17 Tib.: 1) *rgyal ba'i dgongs brgyud*, 2) *rig 'dzin brda brgyud*, 3) *gang zag snyan khung du brgyud*. On these three lineages see Gyatso 1993: 113-115.

18 In Longchenpa's writings this transmission is termed "the lineage of compassionate blessing" (*thugs rje byin rlabs kyi brgyud pa*) (e.g. Undated: 447).

19 Tib.: 1) *smon lam dbang bskur*, 2) *bka' babs lung bstan*, 3) *mkha' 'gro gtad rgya*. On these see Thondup 1986: 63-66, 104-109.

20 Longchenpa 1992b: 16.5-121.2. Dudjom (1996) and Do Drubchen (1975) do not specify at what point these latter events unfold in relation to the three general transmissions. Gyatso places these three events within the hearing lineage of ordinary people while the sources for this placement are not clear (1986: 15-16; 1993: 114-115). See also Thondup 1986: 105-109 for alternative discussions of the transmissions of the Treasures.

21 Jamgön Kongtrul 1976b, Do Drupchen 1975, and Dudjom 1996.

22 Studies drawing on these sources are Dargyay 1979; Gyatso 1986; 1993; Thondup 1986.

23 E.g. Gyatso 1992: 97; 1996: 148.

24 For instance, the decision on what material to include in the recent surveys reflects the particular positions and religious affiliations of their authors. An example of such subjectivity is the exclusion of the well-known Treasure revealer Nyima Drakpa (1647-1710) from Jamgön Kongtrul's *Store of Precious Treasures*, which later led to much controversy (see Blondeau 1988; Martin 2001: 138-140).

25 On the ecumenical tradition see Smith 2001: 227-272.

26 Nyangral 1976. Translated by Erik Schmidt in Tsogyal 1999.

27 Nyangral 1976: 133.3-148.2

28 Ibid: 138.1.

29 For these categories see 134.6-135.3. For spiritual Treasure see also 136.5; 148.2.

30 Ibid: 135.3-136.5.

31 Guru Chöwang 1979. See especially 89.2-5; 98.2-99.1. See also Gyatso 1994.

32 This flesh is considered precious because of its ability to confer buddhahood upon consumption (Ratna Lingpa 1977: 68.3).

33 Guru Chöwang 1979: 81.5-82.6. See also Gyatso 1994 where several of these Treasure classifications are discussed.

34 Guru Chöwang 1979: 82.6-87.5. Gyatso has discussed Chöwang's categorization of Bön Treasure in detail (1994: 280-283).

35 Ibid: 87.5-96.5.

36 Ibid: 96.5-97.4.

37 "*'jam dpal 'byung ba bzhi ni nam mkha'i gter nas 'byung gi / de bzhin tu chos thams cad rgyal ba'i thugs gter las 'byung bas gter gi don la longs spyod pa zhes par byos zhig*" (Ibid: 82.5).

38 In particular, Ratna Lingpa and Jamgön Kongtrul. Ratna Lingpa (1977) mirrors many of the same broad categories found in Chöwang's treatise (see below) while Kongtrul twice echoes Guru Chöwang's claim that the entire buddhadharma is to be understood as Treasure (1976b: 300.1; 684.2).

39 Longchenpa 1992a.

40 Urgyen Lingpa 1996.

41 Ibid: 555-556.

42 Ibid: 548.

43 See further below. Cf. Longchenpa's use of the term in reference to the entire collection of religious Treasures concealed in Tibet by Padmasambhava (Longchenpa 1992b: 117.5). I believe the significance of the Tibetan term *yang* (here translated 'essential') is meant to distinguish the specific religious Treasures from other more mundane Treasures. Still, this topic deserves a more thorough investigation.

44 For examples of these different usages, see Longchenpa 1992c:14.1-5; 1992d: 633.1-3; 1992e: 4.2-5.

45 On this later usage see further below.

46 Dudjom 1991: 585-586.

47 Jamgön 1976b: 423.3-428.4; 690.4-6. Longchenpa appears, by the way, also to be the first author to use the term earth Treasure which later becomes such a prominent Treasure classification (e.g. 1992b: 103.2).

48 Jamgön 1976b: 426.5.

49 *"Dgongs gter bstan bcos kyi tshul du… gtan la phab"* (Jamgön 1976b: 426.6).

50 Identifying Longchenpa's position in the Treasure hierarchy is further complicated by his absence from a list, composed by Ratna Lingpa in the fifteenth century, naming the 24 most influential Treasure revealers up to Ratna Lingpa's time (1977: 55.2-58.4). Later, however, we find him included as one of the major Treasure revealers in Pawo Tsugla Trengwa's discussion of the Treasures in his sixteenth century history of Buddhism (1986: 628).

51 Longchenpa 1992b: 117.5-119.2.

52 Ratna Lingpa 1977. Kongtrul's reference is found in Jamgön 1976b: 302.3.

53 *"De ltar… rnam grangs phyi nang bye brag so sor phye ste bstan pa 'di rnam kyang/ don bka' gter zung 'jug dbyer med du bstan pa dang/ shes rab kyi spyan dang ldan pa dang/ blo tshad ma gzu bor gnas pa rnams yid ches shing dang ba 'dren pa dang / sngon nas smon lam dang las 'phro dkar ba'i 'brel pas deng sang gter la mos shing rjes su 'jug pa tshul bzhin nyams su len cing bsgrub par nus pa rnams dga' spro'i nyams 'phel zhing/ tshad med kyi mos gus skye ba*

dang/ nges shes kyis thag chod dang nges 'byung brtson 'grus la sogs skye ba'i phyir bkod pa yin cing/ yang rtog ge ba phyogs 'dzin can/ thos rgya dang go ba rik pa gsum gyis dbul ba/ nges 'byung dang/ dag snang shes rab gsum gyis bkren pa/ tha snyad kyi tshig 'ga' re shes kyang/ don gyi go ba rdug pa/ ma rig rmongs bzhin du mkhas par rlom pa/ bslabs shing bsgom pas rang la ma phan pa/ bshad cing bstan pas gzhan la ma phan pa rnams tshar bcad pa'i phyir rgyas par bstan pa yin" (1977: 73.6-74.6).

54 Ratna Lingpa 1977: (1) 3.1-42.6, (2) 42.6-53.2, (3) 53.2-75.1, (4) 75.1-203.3, (5) 203.3-238.5.

55 Ibid: 40.5-41.1. This system mirrors Chöwang's four categories although the sequence differs. Chöwang's categories correspond to Ratna Lingpa's system in the following order: 1) ordinary material Treasures; 2) supreme Treasures of body, speech, and mind; 3) definitive Treasures of suchness; and 4) especially purposeful Treasures. Ratna Lingpa also mentions "particular Treasures" (*bye brag gi gter*) but it is not clear if this is a separate category or one included within the indefinite variegated Treasures (40.5). However, as the term usually refers to such Treasures as those included within the indefinite variegated Treasures I have not listed it separately here.

56 Jamgön 1976b.

57 In this survey the Treasure revealers are divided into revealers of earth Treasure (358.4-682.5) and mind Treasure (682.5-759.2) respectively.

58 See Gyatso 1998: 58.

59 *"Bka' nas bkar brgyud bar ma cad / zab mo dngos dang dgongs pa'i gter / yang gter rjes su dran pa'i gter / dag snang snyen du brgyud pa yi / bka' babs bdun gyi chu bo ni / mnga' bdag yab sras skal bar babs / snyigs dus bstan pa'i btsas chen byed / zab rgyas nyi 'od lhag par brdal"* (Jamgön 1976b: 649.6-650.2).

60 For an example of Kongtrul's use of the categories mentioned here see his hagiography of Chokgyur Lingpa (Jamgön 1976b: 643-658).

61 E.g., Könchog 1982: 179-260; Dudjom 1991: 845-846.

62 Note that the categories of material Treasure and wealth Treasure are early developments that persist throughout the tradition. Furthermore, scriptural Earth Treasures only rarely consist of actual longer texts. Instead they are small scriptural fragments, so-called "yellow scrolls" (*shog gser*), containing symbols that provoke a memory of Padmasambhava's teaching which is then put into writing. This is especially true for later revelations where claims to discovery of actual ancient original manuscripts, besides the yellow scrolls, are practically nonexistent. Tulku Urgyen, a recent master within the Treasure tradition, comments, "In fact, each of the sign script characters expand in size to be as large as a whole valley and all the writings appear within that and can then be copied down. One simply copies it down as it is seen but if one makes a mistake, either omitting or duplicating a word, then the script remains in mid-air until one corrects the mistake" (Urgyen 1995: 39).

63 Jamgön 1976b. This list has been reproduced by Dargyay (1979) and Thondup (1986).

64 Summarized as *bla rdzogs thugs gsum*. Dargyay 1979: 69-70. See also Guru Chöwang 1979: 116.5.

65 *Gter ston rgyal po lnga.* They are Nyangral Nyima Özer, Guru Chökyi Wangchuk, Dorje Lingpa (1346-1405), Pema Lingpa, and Khyentse Wangpo (Dudjom 1991).

66 *Mchog gi sprul sku gsum.* Nyangral Nyima Özer, Guru Chökyi Wangchuk, and Rigdzin Gödem (1337-1408) (Dudjom 1991).

67 *Gling pa bcu gcig.* Khakyab 1981b: 343. I have not seen these eleven masters identified by name. In Jamgön 1976b the number of Treasure revealers named Lingpa goes far beyond eleven.

68 *Gter chen brgya rtsa.* E.g. Khakyab 1981b: 343. Compare this number of Treasure revealers to Guru Chöwang's list of concealed Treasures: ten million "minor" Treasures (*phran gter*), 1100 divine Treasures of the king (*rgyal po lha'i gter*), 125 profound Treasures (*zab gter*), five spiritual Treasures of Padmasambhava (*padma'i thugs gter*), and finally, one single spiritual Treasure that embodies the essence of all other rediscovered Treasures of Padmasambhava's mind (*o rgyan thugs kyi yang gter kun gyi bcud 'dus pa thugs kyi gter*). This last Treasure is, not surprisingly, a Treasure revealed by Chöwang himself (1979: 98.5-7). The practice of laying claim to the profoundest truth is of course a phenomenon encountered in almost any religious tradition, order, and school and the Treasure tradition is certainly no exception to this.

69 Two notable critics of the many new revelations were Tsele Natsog Rangdrol (Tsele 1979), and Ju Mipham (1846-1912) (Mipham 1984). They will be discussed further below.

70 Gyatso 1994. See esp. pp. 279-280.

71 Guru Chöwang himself makes that clear in the colophon (1979: 187.3).

72 Cf. Ratna Lingpa 1977: 39.6-42.6; Kongtrul 1976b: 300.1

73 Note also the lack of mention of the earth Treasure/mind Treasure distinction by Pawo Tsugla Trengwa in the sixteenth century (1986), which further indicates that the mind Treasure category only gradually gained importance, even subsequent to Longchenpa's works. A future study might investigate whether the significance of the mind Treasure category in fact only achieved its present importance as the popularity of Jigme Lingpa's mind Treasures in the eighteenth century would have warranted a rethinking of Treasure codification showing greater sensitivity to the mode of concealment and revelation rather than the nature of the Treasure itself.

74 Although traditionally Sangye Lama, who flourished approximately in the eleventh century, is said to have been the first Treasure revealer it is uncertain whether this attribution is factual or represents a later attempt to trace the tradition to more ancient roots.

75 As pointed out by Davidson, even a figure such as Sakya Paṇḍita (1182-1251), always eager to promote Indian sources as authoritative, would occasionally neglect these sources when they conflicted with his own textual heritage. Davidson also points out that some of the practices criticized by Sapaṇ and his polemicist colleagues as inauthentic Tibetan inventions are now known to have had genuine Indian backgrounds (2002a: 209).

76 Chak Lotsāwa 1979: 2-18.2. See also Martin 2001: 111-116.

77 *"yang bsam yas bzhengs dus rgya gar nas gu ru padma 'byung gnas byon nas chos log tshar bcad / rjes su bzung ba'i rten 'brel 'ga' brtsams nas slar rgya gar du gshegs so / de rjes su rgyal*

po pe kar bal po ka ka ru 'dzin bya ba'i spungs su zhugs nas mgo la sgom zhu byon / de la bya spu btsugs lus la za ber gyon nas / bsam yas su padma yin zhes bsgrags nas / chos log dpag med bshad / de'i rjes su chos log dpag med dar te gter yig yin zhes zer nas rā dza snying la zhugs nas byin gyi brlabs pa'i gu ru chos dbang bya cig gis / chos log dpag med brlams / des byas pa'i chos log la klu dang bdud dang rgyal 'gong 'khor nas / mdze dang smyo 'bogs la sogs pa 'ong ba yin te de la grub rtags su byed pa yin no / de la sogs pa'i gter nas byung ba rnams yang dag pa ma yin no" (Chak Lotsāwa 1979: 13.2-14.2). This passage is also translated in Martin 2001: 114. On the name Kakarudzin, see Martin 2001: 114, no. 16.

78 On the critique of the Treasures by Jigten Gönpo, see Martin 2001: 157. See also below.

79 A polemical work attributed to Butön is contained in Chak Lotsāwa 1979: 25.3-36.3. Kapstein has argued against this attribution (2000: 253, no. 35).

80 *"De yi bka' ltar bcos pa'i chos log rnams / chos dbang zhes bya bdud kyi 'phrin las bas / gter nas bton zhes chos log du ma sbyar / 'gro ba mang po log pa'i lam la 'khrid"* (Chag Lotsāwa 1979: 26.4-5).

81 *"De bzhin rang rang so so nas / lung pa re nas gter rdzun re / bton nas phyogs bcur rgyas par byas / 'di dra'i mngon sum rdzun tshig la'ang / kha ba can pa bden zhen byed"* (Chag Lotsāwa 1979: 27.1-2).

82 *"gter nas byung ba'i glegs bam dang / gzhan nas brkus pa'i chos lugs dang / brtsam chos dang ni rmi lam chos / blo bzung ma yi chos lugs la/ brgyud pa rdo rje 'chang la bsnyags / de la'ang gzhan dag lung len pa/ chos dang 'gal ba lta ci smos / rang lugs dang yang 'gal ba yin"* (Sakya Pandita 2002: 321). This passage is also translated in Sakya Pandita 2002: 162-163. For further discussion of the critiques by Sakya Paṇḍita and Jigten Gönpo see Martin 2001, esp. 111-116; 156-157. See also Karmey 1988: 152.

83 "*Gang zag gi rigs dregs pa can/ phyogs zhen can…gter ma la 'di skad du rtsod de/ gter bya ba mi bden sbas pa med/ gter bden na yang/ sa brag shing/ chu la sogs pa la sbas pas/ sa chos rdo chos shing chos yin zer/ yang 'ga na re/ gter o rgyan padma'i dus/ bstan pa snga dar dus sbas pa da rtsam song nas rdul song nas mi rul rang res sbas nas rang gis bton pa'i zog po yin zer/ yang gter chos rtsod pa can yin dar rgyas 'gro don chung zer ba dang/ yang gter ma bka' brgyud med pas bka chad yin/ snyan rgyud dang dbang bka' med rdol chos yin zer ba sogs*" (Ratna Lingpa 1977: 219.4-220.4).

84 Kapstein 2000: 131-132.

85 Ibid: 132.

86 Chöwang 1979; Ratna Lingpa 1977. Apart from these two compositions we also find several shorter apologetic remarks on Treasure revelation scattered in works concerned with the general defense of the texts and practices of the Nyingma School. See for example Sok Dokpa 1998.

87 Gyatso 1994.

88 *"Gab pas gter / sbas pas gter/ zad mi shes pas gter/ dgos 'dod 'byung bas gter ro"* (Ratna Lingpa 1977: 39.3).

89 Ratna Lingpa 1977: 220.4-232.1.

90 Ibid: 220.4-221.2.

91 Although this approach to textual validation indeed can be surprising given the otherwise sophisticated nature of Tibetan Buddhist literature, it is important to keep in mind

how the political realities underlying the polemical writings in large part would have prevented any significant softening of the overly assertive tone so characteristic of this genre.

92 Martin 1997: 157.

93 Ratna Lingpa 1977: 221.2-222.2.

94 First, towards the claim that the Treasures would have been unable to survive the long period since Padmasambhava's concealment without decay, Ratna Lingpa urges that the allegation be reconsidered in view of the way the Treasures were originally concealed. According to Ratna Lingpa, the Treasures were not hidden "the way that ordinary folk store radishes and turnips" but were placed in special containers made of rock, carefully sealed, and finally entrusted to well-suited storages, such as cliffs, caves, stūpas, and temples (222.2-223.2). Second, against the critique that the Treasures should be faulty simply because of being mistrusted in certain quarters, Ratna Lingpa points out that no Buddhist teaching has ever been fully beyond dispute as all vehicles and schools of Buddhism continuously criticize one another's views, texts, and practices. Even the Buddha, Ratna Lingpa says, was not beyond being challenged during his life (222.2-224.3). Third, the charge that the Treasures never benefited anyone is dismissed by arguing that a great number of masters in the Nyingma School indeed received full accomplishments through Treasure teachings and subsequently spread them to all parts of Tibet, granting both temporal and ultimate happiness to numerous beings in the process (224.3- 225.6).

95 Ibid: 225.6-231.2.

96 Ibid: 231.2-232.1.

97 Interestingly, skeptics never countered the Nyingma School's equation of the general Mahāyāna and Vajrayāna canons with its own Treasure revelations by pointing out the difference between the highly institutionalized form of revelation practiced by the Nyingma School and the much less formalized Indian revelations.

98 Kongtrul first quotes from scriptures (*lung*) in support of fresh revelation and then provides logical arguments (*gtan tshigs*) in favor of the authenticity of the Treasures. As these arguments closely mirror those of Chöwang and Ratna Lingpa he is brief on the subject and instead refers to these earlier works for detail. Kongtrul argues that first, all Buddhist teachings are Treasures since they pass through the three basic transmission lineages, and second, all the teachings of the Mahāyāna canon are Treasures as they were previously concealed in secret locations and realms. Thus, Kongtrul concludes, no real distinction between the Mahāyāna canon and the Treasure scriptures proves tenable (Jamgön 1976b: 297.3-302.4). Even though the Tibetan Treasure commentators on either side of the debate appear to have been largely content to follow the beaten track outlined by previous polemical writers, there are brief exceptions to this rule regarding specific topics. Consider, for example, the response by Sok Dokpa Lodrö Gyaltsen (1552-1624), one of the most diligent polemicists to defend the Nyingma School, to Sakya Paṇḍita's critique of the Treasures quoted above. Generally, in arguing the validity of the Treasures, Sok Dokpa adheres to traditional arguments (Sok Dokpa 1998: 149-152) but in discussing Sapaṇ's Treasure criticism he offers a new position. Because of Sapaṇ's exalted status in Tibetan scholarship, the many

traditions affected by his eager criticisms often seem to have dealt with his objections by quietly pretending that they simply did not exist and only a few scholars chose to meet his criticisms head on, regardless of how obnoxious they may otherwise have appeared. Therefore, in replying to Sapaṇ's critique of the Treasures, Sok Dokpa is not surprisingly hesitant to directly confront the great scholar. Instead he offers the following compromise:

"Although, according to some, this [critique by Sapaṇ] is of the Nyingma School, that is not the case as the followers of the Nyingma School do not trace their lineage to Vajradhara. Beyond him they trace their lineage to the five buddha families and to Samantabhadra. This [critique] is therefore meant for the well-known Treasures of the Kagyu School, such as the *Six Cycles of Equal Taste*."

"'di rnying ma la yin no zer kyang ma yin te/ rnying ma bas rdo rje 'chang la brgyud pa mi bsnyags de'i dgong na rigs lnga dang/ kun tu bzang po yod pa la bsnyag/ 'di ni ro snyoms skor drug la sogs pa bka' brgyud la grags pa'i gter chos rnam" (Sok Dokpa 1998: 237).

In this way, Sok Dokpa is able to deflect Sapaṇ's criticism without openly criticizing him. How this move was appreciated by the practitioners of the *Six Cycles of Equal Taste* is of course an altogether different story. A collection of Sok Dokpa's apologetical writings is found in Sok Dokpa 1998. This collection addresses, individually, the polemical attacks advanced against the Nyingma School up until the sixteenth century, thus providing a useful overview of the skeptical critique.

99 Tsele 1979. Parts of this text are translated by Erik Schmidt in Tsogyal 1999.

100 Tsogyal 1999: 14-15. Cf. Tsele 1979: 426.5-427.6.

101 Lamotte 1988: 124-140, 274-292; Davidson 1990.

102 See Williams 2001: 11-33. Davidson has argued that the concept of a closed Buddhist canon is a non-Indian notion adopted by the Tibetans based on Chinese influences (2002a: 207). Paradoxically, Davidson concludes, by closing the canon to preserve Indian Buddhism it was in effect only those minority communities that stood outside this decision who could "perpetuate the dynamics and values of Indian Buddhism that caused India to produce the world's most massive scriptural corpus" (221). See Kapstein 2000: 123-126 for a discussion of the historical approach to authenticity vs. the soteriological.

103 E.g. Gyatso 1993: 105-106.

104 In the early polemical writings arguing against Treasure revelation the historical claims of concealment are actually not directly questioned. Instead, the central critique of Chak Lotsāwa, Jigten Gönpo, and, Sakya Paṇḍita is centered on a perceived interruption of spiritual transmission (Martin 2001: 111-113; 156-157). The Treasures are therefore mockingly called stone teachings (*rdo chos*), wind teachings (*lung chos*), water teachings (*chu chos*), etc. (see Guru Chöwang 1979: 105.1-5). Still, this criticism by implication casts doubt on the historical legitimacy of the Treasures. In later centuries we find this criticism more fully developed (Kapstein 2000: 132).

105 There are, however, a few notable exceptions to this use of historical legend in the Treasure revelations; in particular regarding Treasures intended as accurate historical accounts of the past dynastic era such as Nyangral Nyima Özer's *Copper Temple Life Story* and Urgyen Lingpa's *Five Chronicles*. Still, these texts represent a small minority

within the Treasure literature, where they are significantly outnumbered by accounts told to engender confidence in specific visionary masters or revelations internal to that particular tradition.

[106] Had the Treasure revealers wished for a more general acceptance of their revelations they could have presented their visionary teachings as just that—meditative visions (*dag snang*) in which deities or past authoritative figures communicate enlightened messages. In that case, their revelations, unburdened by the historical claims specific to Treasure revelation, would have been less prone to skeptical critique.

[107] See Gyatso 1986. The role of the yellow scrolls is significant, as the Nyingma School claims that these scrolls must be physically dateable to the eighth or ninth centuries (Gyatso 1993: 106). Interestingly, although both skeptics and devotees would find a common platform for Treasure authentication in the yellow scrolls, to my knowledge, no study has yet attempted an actual dating of these objects. This, however, has not prevented a fair number of categorical statements on the subject. Lopez even suggests that the reluctance of some scholars to form definitive conclusions in spite of the absence of solid evidence would make for a "fascinating topic" of study (1998: 243, no. 32). See Martin 2001: 16-19 for arguments cautioning against such generalizing conclusions.

[108] Thondup 1986: 164-166.

[109] For example, even though the Treasure tradition commonly identifies Treasure revealers as the reincarnations of Padmasambhava's original Tibetan disciples in the eighth and ninth centuries, such associations do not imply acceptance of a linear historical consciousness as the identities of such past masters are conceived of in highly abstract ways. For example, Könchog Gyurme, a reincarnation of the Treasure revealer Chokgyur Lingpa, makes the claim that all important masters of the New Schools, including all the central figures of the Gelukpa School are emanations of Padmasambhava (1982: 150.5-151.6). Note also how the tantras of the Nyingma School originate within the realization lineage of the conquerors. See, for example, the *Sacred Tantra of the Great Purpose for the Four Kīlas,* discussed below in ch. 6, where the Buddha Vajrakumāra arises from the basic space of phenomena (*dharmadhātu*) and teaches a gathering of students inseparable from him in a reality that clearly defies historical and geographical pinpointing.

[110] See, for example, Gyatso 1998: 149.

[111] Dudjom 1991: 889.

[112] This has been pointed out by Kapstein (2000: 135), who remarks: "During the mid-1980s I expected that we would soon see new developments in traditional approaches to these matters, catalyzed by the encounter with contemporary methodologies of textual criticism. I could not have anticipated however, that European and American scholars of Tibetan Buddhism would find themselves defending or condemning the "Treasures" in a manner that closely recapitulates the polarities of the old Tibetan disputes."

[113] Aris 1989.

[114] Ibid: 97.

[115] Aris has indeed received much criticism for his study of Pema Lingpa (e.g., Martin 2001: 16-17; Harding 2003: 151, no. 53; Pemala: 1995) and as a representative of the skeptical position he is no doubt an extreme. Still, he is not the only scholar to employ

the traditional canonical/apocryphal textual framework for discussing the Treasure tradition. See Gyatso 1998: 295, no. 64 for a listing of other studies skeptical of Treasure revelation. Note also Schwieger's characterization of the Treasures as false and deceptive (1990: xxix-xxxi). On Drukpa Kunley see Dowman 1998.

116 Aris 1989: 96-97.

117 Note also Samuel's comments on Aris' study: "Pema Lingpa is perhaps a poor case on which to argue the authenticity of *terma* revelations, but Aris' judgment of fraud may go too far. Pema Lingpa probably used his skills as an artisan to dress up and stage-manage the production of his revealed texts, but his numerous trances and visions, with their traditional shamanic language seem to have been real enough" (1993: 298). Determining the validity of a shamanic vision is in itself not an easy matter but to validate a Treasure based on its 'shamanic language' would only seem to further complicate matters as the literary style of most Treasure texts is overwhelmingly uniform and hence easily reproducible (cf. Mipham's comments below). Still, Samuel's main point is not to establish whether the Treasures are verifiably authentic and he does in fact remark that, "In the last analysis, the question of how far particular *tertön* [i.e. Treasure revealers] are acting in good faith is less important than whether their revelations are accepted and what the implications are for the ongoing processes of Tibetan religious life of their acceptance and rejections" (299). There are also a number of scholars who have tried to avoid taking sides in the traditional debate. Most do so by staying clear of the discussion of authenticity altogether while a few actively search for alternative ways to engage with the traditional skeptic-devotee dichotomy. For example, Davidson calls attention to the "consensual authentication" of Indian Buddhism that helped shape the canonical openness characterizing Treasure revelation (2002a). See also Kapstein 2000: 121-137; Mayer 1996: 70-90.

118 Alternatively, if the continued application of historical criticism is to have relevance for Treasure analysis, the application of actual philological, historical, and art historical methodologies should be required. As mentioned above, although most Treasures are revealed independent of physical reality, certain texts and artifacts are claimed to have genuinely ancient origins and could potentially be subjected to historical analysis.

119 Cantwell Smith 1993, esp. 15-18.

120 Ibid: 18 (italics not mine).

121 Mipham 1984 (abbr. *Gem*). On Mipham see Pettit 1999; Schuh 1973b. For an introduction to his collected works see my "Introduction to the Tibetan Text" in Ju Mipham 2004. The complete translation, juxtaposed to the original Tibetan, appears as Chapter 3 of this volume. For technical notes on the Tibetan text, readers are referred to Doctor 2003.

122 Mipham was posthumously recognized as a revealer of mind Treasures (Dudjom 1991: 880). More importantly, he was one of the foremost students of Jamyang Khyentse Wangpo, who was intimately involved in Treasure revelation throughout his life.

123 Kunzang Palden: 67.

124 Mipham 1984: 487.

125 Ibid.: 476. 1. Mipham was not the first to acknowledge the merit of outside criticism of the Nyingma School. Note, for example, the comments of Tsele Natsog Rangdrol two centuries earlier, "The teachings of the Secret Mantra of the Early Translations

are profound, extensive, and marvelous. Unfortunately their followers fool themselves with pursuing the upkeep of livelihood and attainment of temporary aims, instead of endeavoring through practice to gain realization. Leading the life of a householder, they neither belong to the category of sūtra nor tantra. They are nothing but a dishonor to the Early Translations. This is exactly the reason why followers of the Sarma Schools, both learned and ignorant, not only expel the teachings and followers of the Nyingma School from the confines of Buddhism, but find them as loathsome as beholding a pool of vomit" (Tsogyal 1999: 14. Cf. Tsele 1979: 424.5-425.3).

126 See Khakyab Dorje 1981b; Blondeau 1988.

127 "*Kye gter ston pa dag gangs can pa dag guru padma la snying nas mi mos mi den zer phod mkhan su mi 'dug kyang gter ston yin zer ba tshos rdzun sogs kyis zol mthong nas yid sun te...rgyal dbang padma la sems can mos pa'i skal pa chung ngur ma byed cig*" (Mipham 1984: 476).

128 "*Gter nas khyi ro min pa gang yang byung*" (484). The original passage is found in Urgyen Lingpa 1996: 576.

129 A fact noted by the German philosopher Immanuel Kant (1724-1804), who comments, "That 'the world lieth in evil' is a plaint as old as history... All agree that the world began in a good estate, whether in a Golden Age, a life in Eden, or a yet more happy community with celestial beings. But they represent that this happiness vanished like a dream and that a fall into evil...presently hurried mankind from bad to worse with accelerated descent; so that now (this "now" is as old as history) we live in the final age, with the Last Day and the destruction of the world at hand" (1960: 15).

130 Note again Tsele Natsog Rangdrol's similar comments: "In this dark age it seems that no one engages in teaching, studying, or practicing the flawless older [Treasures]... The teachers waste their lives chasing after the novelty of so-called new [Treasures] or anything that resembles a [Treasure], which nowadays proliferate like mushrooms on a summer meadow. On seeing this sad state of affairs, an old ignorant monk like me can do nothing but shed tears" (Tsogyal 1999: 14. Cf. Tsele 1979: 425.6-426.3).

131 *"Legs par brtags na gter chos zer pa rnams / grags 'dod nor 'dod bud med 'dod pa'i phyir / gter la re zhing skam chags me ltar 'bar / rdzun dang zog po med pa dkon 'di ci"* (482).

132 485.2-3.

133 *"De la the tshom za ba'i dus byung na / mthu ldan yod na yid gnyis sel bar rigs"* (487.4).

134 Martin has noted the importance of strong aristocratic affiliations for the potential Treasure revealer and points out that some of the most successful visionaries, headed by Nyangral Nyima Özer and Rigdzin Gödem, were themselves of blue-blooded descent (2001: 26-27).

135 Here the encouragement of Søren Kierkegaard (1813-1855) to develop faith "on the strength of the absurd" may come to mind (e.g. 1985: 79). Kierkegaard's positions on faith and its relevance for the religious life and ethics contain a number of notable parallels in the Buddhist Mahāyāna tradition, such as the perceived legality in Mahāyāna Buddhism of a spiritual being discontinuing his or her outward ethical behavior for the sake of a greater and higher good that may not always be identified through reason alone. However, in this particular context of evaluating religious authorities Mipham, while possibly approving of the basic principles in Kierkegaaard's famous "teleological

suspension of the ethical" would no doubt have questioned his exhortation to abandon the universal ethics prescribed by tradition.

136 The saying goes: When a child has had its tongue burnt by milk it will blow even before drinking yogurt (*byis pa 'o mas kha 'tshigs nas / zho la phu yang 'debs bzhin 'thung*). See Cüppers 1998: 170 (6410). See also Pemba 1996: 134.

137 The proverb goes: Whatever heals the sore will be applied, even if it is dog fat (*rma kha la phan na / khyi tshil yin yang byugs*). See Cüppers 1998: 200 (7613).

138 "Pronouncements" refers to the cycles such as Embodiment of the Sugatas of the Eight Pronouncements and "Realizations" refers to cycles such as Embodiment of the Realization of the Master.

139 This refers to Rigdzin Gödem (1337-1408).

140 Thanks to Dan Martin and Per Kvaerne for helpful suggestions for the translation of these two lines. If my reading of this rather obscure passage is correct, the persecution of Bön Treasures mentioned here most likely refers to events during the reign of the Fifth Dalai Lama Lobzang Gyatso (1617 – 1682) during which time Bön Treasures in 1649 were attacked on the grounds that they were forgeries. (Karmay 1972: XXXI – VX). However, as both Martin and Kvaerne have let me know, the exact meaning of these two lines is hard to determine.

141 Abbr.: *New Treasures*.

142 Chokgyur 1982a. See also Doctor 2002.

143 Most prominently, Chokgyur Lingpa is the only Treasure revealer to have brought forth revelations on all three sections of the Great Perfection. See further below.

144 To date, the most detailed study of the ecumenical tradition is Smith 2001: 227-272. See also Barron 2003.

145 Previous studies of Chokgyur Lingpa and his tradition are scarce. Erik Schmidt has been the primary contributor by translating a number of practice rituals from the *New Treasures* (for a brief selection see Chokgyur 1990a-c) and several commentaries on the tradition by lineage masters (e.g. Kongtrul 1999). Likewise, from the oral tradition, Schmidt has translated several commentaries by contemporary masters addressing Chokgyur Lingpa's tradition (Chokling 2001, Tobgyal 1988, and Urgyen 2000, 2005). Smith also briefly mentions the tradition of Chokgyur Lingpa (2002: 235-272). Translations of Dudjom's hagiography of Chokgyur Lingpa are found in Dargyay 1979: 190-197 and Dudjom 1991: 840-848. Recently, I have studied the *New Treasures* on two occasions (Doctor 2002; 2003).

146 Chokgyur 1982b.

147 Ibid: 190-198.

148 See Smith 2001: 227-272.

149 Cf. Mipham's similar remarks above.

150 Jamgön 1982a.

151 Ibid: 9.3-4.

152 This can be assumed since the framework employed by Kongtrul forms the basis for all other hagiographical works on Chokgyur Lingpa.

153 Jamyang 1982a. This outline was later adopted to structure the longer hagiography by Könchog Gyurme (circa 1870-circa 1930) (Könchog 1982).

154 Dazang 1982a.

155 Jamyang 1982b.

156 This text is extensively quoted throughout the *New Treasures*. The entire relevant passage is quoted twice in the collection (Unknown 1982: 341.1-352.2; Jamyang 1982a: 65.1-78.4).

157 The connection between Chokgyur Lingpa and Shigpo Lingpa is made by Jamgön Kongtrul, who states that the rebirths of Murub Tsenpo, the middle son of King Trisong Detsen, included the following masters: Sangye Lingpa, Lhatsun Ngönmo, Shigpo Lingpa, and Chokgyur Lingpa (Jamgön 1976, vol. 1: 324.1).

158 Jamyang 1982b: 64.4.

159 Jamyang 1982c.

160 Jamgön 1976b: 643-658; Dudjom 1991: 840-848.

161 According to this text (and several other sources in the *New Treasures*), Chokgyur Lingpa's four primary teachers were: Taklungma Ngawang Tenpey Nyima (b. 1788) who granted the refuge vows, Dazang Karma Ngedön Tenpa Rabgye who conferred the bodhisattva vows, Jamgön Kongtrul who initiated Chokgyur Lingpa into the vehicle of secret mantra, and Khyentse Wangpo who introduced him to the nature of mind (Jamyang 1982c: 20.3-22.2).

162 As for the division of the Treasures revealed by Chokgyur Lingpa, Khyentse primarily focuses on the earth Treasure revelations. Other divisions of Chokgyur Lingpa's Treasures mention three sets of guru practice in which, according to Khyentse, the guru practice of dharmakāya is the *Great Ultimate Instruction of Dharmakāya* (Chokgyur Lingpa 1982a vol. 23: 391-412), the sambhogakāya practice is the *Magical Net of the Five Families of Limitless Life* (vol. 14: 313-391), and the nirmāṇakāya practice is contained in the various sādhanas of Padmasambhava. This last grouping is in turn divided into four divisions: the outer practice of *Dispeller of All Obstacles*, the inner practice of *Spontaneously Accomplishing Intentions*, the secret division being the *Lake-born Vajra* (this cycle is not included in the *New Treasures* since it is counted as a Treasure of Khyentse Wangpo's), the most secret division of *Powerful Vajra Wrath*, and the combined division of the *Guru's Ocean of Accomplishments* as well as the *Full Intent of the Guru's Heart Practice* (Jamyang 1982c: 25).

163 This topic will be covered below.

164 Ibid: 38.2-49.1.

165 Pema Yeshe 1982a.

166 Pema Yeshe 1982b.

167 Unknown 1982.

168 Könchog 1982.

169 Another possibility would be that Pema Yeshe's hagiography was not yet composed by the time Könchog Gyurme wrote his biography. Pema Yeshe's work is undated, and since I have not yet been able to determine his exact dates it is difficult to say conclusively what relationship, or lack thereof, exists between these two works.

[170] *Drang nges kyi rnam thar gyis mdor bstan.* Könchog 1982: 8.1.

[171] *Ngo mtshar ba'i gtam bcus rgyas par bshad.* Ibid: 11.4.

[172] *Gsol 'debs smon lam don bsdu ba.* Ibid: 621.2.

[173] *Nges don snying po'i rnam thar.* Ibid: 8.2.

[174] *Drang don brda yi rnam thar.* Ibid: 10.2.

[175] *"Nges pa'i don du gzod nas kun khyab nam mkha' lta bu'i rang bzhin bde ba chen po gzhi 'bras dbyer med 'od gsal lhag pa'i chos kyi skur bzhugs pa yin."* Ibid: 8.3.

[176] *Sku gsum gyi rnam thar spyir bstan pa.* Ibid: 11.5.

[177] *Ljongs 'dir sprul pa'i snang tshul khyad par du dbye ba.* Ibid: 18.3.

[178] Ibid: (1) 31.3, (2) 48.4, (3) 51.5, (4) 85.5, (5) 91.5, (6) 100.6, (7) 175.4, (8) 423.4, (9) 490.5, and (10) 583.2.

[179] The richness of these stories requires a detailed study beyond the present work. In the future these chapters will surely come to prove a valuable source for a better understanding of the ecumenical tradition. Although Könchog Gyurme's writing does contain a limited number of oral accounts, it was apparently criticized at the time of its publication for drawing too heavily on the early written sources at the expense of the oral tradition. According to Erik Schmidt, Tulku Urgyen, a late lineage holder in the tradition of Chokgyur Lingpa, spoke of his uncle Samten Gyatso (also an important lineage holder; see Tobgyal 1988: 39-40) criticizing Könchog Gyurme for not having included the oral accounts of Chokgyur Lingpa's daughter Könchog Paldrön into his writings (Oral communication, Boudhanath, February, 2003).

[180] Könchog 1982: 606.4.

[181] Jamgön 1976b: 643-658.

[182] Dudjom 1996: 515-524.

[183] Orgyen Tobgyal. Oral communication, Boudhanath, January 2003.

[184] *"Lus kyi sme ba dang sha mtshan 'di lta bu 'byung rtsam yang gzigs."* Ratna Lingpa 1977: 232.3.

[185] Cf. Mipham's earlier comments. Still, not all prophetic Treasure literature is concerned with events already transpired. An equal number of prophecies describe people and events yet to come. This type of prophecy, such as those found in the *Chronicle of Padmasambhava* (Urgyen Lingpa 1996), is often appropriated by subsequent revealers, at times through considerable hermeneutical gymnastics, to support the value of their revelations.

[186] For the connection between Shigpo Lingpa and Chokgyur Lingpa see note 157. This connection is also made clear in many references found in the *New Treasures* where Padmasambhava declares Murub Tsenpo and Sangye Lingpa as the past incarnations of Chokgyur Lingpa—for example in the *Lotus Crowned Great Compassionate One* (Chokgyur Lingpa 1982c: 255). Furthermore, in a prophecy by Sangye Lingpa (quoted in Pema Yeshe 1982a: 92.5) it is stated that Sangye Lingpa (in a future life) will be born in the region of Kham, in an ox year, as a Treasure revealer by the name of Chokgyur. Subsequent tradition understands this to be the life of Chokgyur Lingpa and so the link is made to Shigpo Lingpa who, according to his own prophetic scripture, is a reincarnation of Sangye Lingpa.

[187] *Bya rung kha shor.* Since the revelations of Urgyen Lingpa in the fourteenth century, the location of the stūpa has been identified by Tibetans as the village of Boudhanath just outside Kathmandu, Nepal. Prior to these revelations, however, the stūpa was said to have been constructed in the Indian kingdom of Magadha (Dowman 1973). Longchenpa also places the stūpa in Magadha (1992b: 54.4-56.1).

[188] Jamyang 1982b: 65.1-66.4.

[189] The rebirths listed are lives as the benefactor Bhadra from Maguta, a Brahmin temple keeper, a deer living in a forest grove, a poor girl from the Indian city of Śāntika, a wealthy and generous businessman from Kuśīnagarī called Ākshepaṇabhadra,* a buffalo in the city of Gandhamādana whose milk was offered to the arhats, the generous householder Sujātabhadra in the city of Bhedar, a child of Ākshepaṇa also from Gandhamādana, a Chinese scholar, a businessman from Bhoṭa who made offerings to the local King at Vaiśāli, an unnamed translator from the district of Guge, a Nepalese scholar from the kingdom of Pātan, the son of a wealthy family from Tsawa Marshö, a benefactor called Zangpo from Changra Mugpo, and a Chinese court chaplain. Ibid: 67.1-68.5.

[190] Ibid: 69.2-70.1.

[191] The other names of Murub Tsenpo listed in this account are: Lhase Damdzin Drak, Purwo Chathul Go, Lhase Degön Kar, Genyen Senge Zang, Wangchen Buddha Heruka, Pema Dönyö Tsal. Ibid: 69.1-70.4.

[192] Such as Lhalung Palgyi Dorje (ninth century), the well-known master who assassinated King Langdarma (r. 838-842). Ibid: 71.4-5.

[193] These births are as a certain Jñāna from the Zur clan who is said to clarify the intent of the *tantras*; then the monk Lhatsun Depachen from Purang; a hidden yogi from Mangyul called Shigpö Chökyong; a non-monastic temple keeper from Rinchen Drak named Paltsun; a mantrin from Karag Phugpa by the name of Siṃha Phāla; a female Treasure revealer called Gyalmo Tse who reveals Treasures from a site west of Samye; a madman (*smyon pa*) living under a bridge at Tanag; a mantrin named Śākya Yeshe from Ze; a person named Tenzin Kyewu Shönnu from Nyal; a yogi called Ngagchang Phakpa from Yorpo Dra; Neten Tenpa Dzin from Drada; a temple keeper from Samye called Drakpa; Ngagchang Dorje—a temple keeper of the Rasa temple who in secret will liberate the enemies of the dharma; a spiritual teacher named Dampa Könchog from Tsāri; a spiritual teacher called Shiwa from the Mön region; a mantrin who will rebuild the Dungchu temple in Powo; and a spiritual teacher known as Drubthob who will live at that very same temple. Then follows another existence as Treasure revealer (this time also a woman)—the master Lhatsun Ngönmo (eleventh century) from Samye (her biography is found in Jamgön 1976b: 409-410). Next we are told of his existences as the spiritual teacher called the Avalokiteśvara Yogi who constructs a temple in Rinpung, the yogin Shigpo Gyalwa from Tsāri and, Chokgyur Lingpa's last life as an animal, a monkey who tames demonic spirits to the north of Samye (Jamyang 1982b: 72.2-76.2).

[194] Perhaps this is the female Treasure revealer Kunga Bum (thirteenth century). In her hagiography it is mentioned that Chokgyur Lingpa later remembered his past existence as Kunga Bum and was able to revive the transmission of her revelations (Jamgön 1976b: 517.6).

195 Könchog 1982: 77.2-78.3.

196 The tenth day of the sixth month (*chu stod zla ba*) in the Earth Female Ox year (Jamgön 1976b: 644.2). This is the most common date given in the biographical sources but Kongtrul provides a different date in his praise of the life of Chokgyur Lingpa, where it is said that Chokgyur Lingpa was born in the eleventh month (*mgo zla ba*) of the Earth Female Ox year (Jamgön 1982a: 3.4). Although most sources subscribe to the former date, the latter date is noteworthy as it appears to be the earliest available. However, given the proliferation of other writings (including other works by Kongtrul) placing his birth in the sixth month, that date seems, after all, the most likely.

197 Misspelled as *Yor stod* in Jamgön 1976b: 644.1.

198 Könchog 1982: 38.1-4.

199 Pema Yeshe 1982a: 94.5. In the Buddhist tradition these signs commonly accompany the birth of saints.

200 Tobgyal 1988: 9. The prophecy of Drime Lingpa is quoted in Könchog 1982: 39.1. Könchog Gyurme establishes the connection between Ratna Urgyen and Chokgyur Lingpa by considering the name given by his parents—Norbu Tenzin (*Norbu* in Skt. *Ratna*) (43.2). He further explains that prophesies mentioning people named "Ratna" apply to Chokgyur Lingpa as *Chokgyur* (supreme) is an epithet for *Norbu* (jewel) and so also *Ratna*. For Drime Lingpa's biography, see Kongtrul 1976, vol. 1: 632.6-634.3.

201 Tibetan sources recount this story to have happened when Chokgyur Lingpa was thirteen years old but also mention that it occurred in the early months of the Iron Female Ox year, which would be 1841. The apparent discrepancy between this date and the age claimed for Chokgyur Lingpa is explained by the way that Tibetans count a person's age, starting at one when a child is born and reaching two on the first day of the following lunar year. Thus, a child born in January of a given year will be counted as two years old in February or March (i.e., on the first day of the Tibetan new year).

202 "*'O na sa la maṇi kha ming la nor bu bstan 'dzin ya ki lung pa la ārya nang zer bas khyod la 'jig rten na khyad par 'phags pa 'ong*" (Könchog 1982: 49.4). This prophecy connects the word 'maṇi' to Chokgyur Lingpa's name 'Norbu' as both mean 'jewel' in Sanskrit and Tibetan, respectively. Likewise, 'Ārya' is Sanskrit for 'noble'.

203 "*zab mo gter gi bang mdzod la rang dbang brnyes pa'i rjes su gnang ba stsal*" (Könchog 1982: 49.5).

204 The issue of the Treasure revealer's role in the manifestation of Treasures is complex. As Kapstein points out, although the Treasure revealer is not formally considered the author of his or her revelations, the Treasures are always classified according to their discoverer, indicating that the tradition considers the revealer's role as more than the mere conveying of the messages of others (2000: 259, no. 112).

205 See Germano 2002.

206 This prophecy was translated above in ch. 1. See also Könchog 1982: 177.3; Pema Yeshe 1982a: 134.4. The texts of *Three Sections of the Great Perfection* are found in Chokgyur 1982a vols. 21-23. Of the seven transmissions, section I represents the Transmitted Precepts, sections II-V the Treasure transmission, and VI-VII the Pure Vision transmission.

[207] Jamgön 1976b: 650.3-5. Kongtrul is the first to structure Chokgyur Lingpa's works in terms of the seven transmissions, but this method was adopted by all subsequent hagiographers. The three sections of the Transmitted Precepts are popularly known as "Sūtra, Magic, and Mind" (*mdo sgyu sems gsum*). "Sūtra" represents the Anuyoga teachings by referring to the Anuyoga scripture *Sūtra that Gathers the Intention of All Buddhas* (*'dus pa'i mdo*); "Magic" illustrates the Mahāyoga teachings by referring to the Mahāyoga cycle of *Magical Net* (*Sgyu 'phrul drwa ba*); and "Mind" represents the Atiyoga teachings by referring to the Atiyoga teachings of *Mind Section* (*Sems sde*) - here understood to include the other two sections of Atiyoga; the *Space Section* and *Instruction Section* as well. These three sections of the Transmitted Precepts are also equated to the development stage (*skyed rim*), completion stage (*rdzogs rim*), and Great Perfection (*rdzogs chen*) respectively (Könchog Gyurme 1982: 178).

[208] Pema Yeshe 1982a: 135.2-4.

[209] Jamgön 1976, vol.1: 650.4. Kongtrul does not identify what Treasures belong within this category.

[210] Tobgyal 1988: 9. In general there does not seem to be any consensus within the Nyingma School as to which of the two, earth Treasure and mind Treasure, is most efficacious or valuable. Uniformly, however, earth Treasures are said to be more complex to reveal, since they depend on outer circumstances, but the understanding of this varies. Not surprisingly, followers of earth Treasures claim superiority for their Treasures based on the verifiable yellow scrolls, whereas followers of mind Treasures argue that the independence of their revelations from the physical world leaves them immune to decay and therefore supreme. For examples of arguments in favor of these two positions, see Tobgyal 1988: 10 and Thondup 1986: 81-82.

[211] *"Snga phyir sa gter gyi gter kha sum chu rtsa bdun tsam phyung tshul ni spyir 'ga' zhig gsang rgya'i bab dang la la yang gter du'ang sbas pa sogs zhib par 'chad dka'"* (Jamyang 1982c: 25.5).

[212] Jamyang 1982c: 26.1-32.1. The following presentation of the 37 earth Treasures takes Khyentse's list as its basis. Alternatives suggested by other hagiographers are discussed throughout.

[213] Tobgyal mentions that these teachings were meant for Chokgyur Lingpa's personal practice (Tobgyal 1988: 8). According to Kongtrul, on that occasion Chokgyur Lingpa also revealed a skull and a seal for the cycle of *Embodiment of Realization* (Jamgön 1976b: 650.6).

[214] Jamyang 1982c: 26.2.

[215] Although Taklungma is counted as one of Chokgyur Lingpa's four main teachers, there are no descriptions of Chokgyur Lingpa's receiving spiritual instruction from this master, and it seems that his importance stems solely from his conferring the novice vows on Chokgyur Lingpa.

[216] Chokgyur: 1982b: 181.5.

[217] Sources provide no date for this event but mention that it occurred when Chokgyur Lingpa was 14 years old by the Tibetan system of counting. This would mean that the revelation occurred either in 1842 or 1843. Chokgyur Lingpa mentions in his autobi-

ography that shortly after meeting Padmasaṃbhava he discovered a Treasure inventory (*kha byang*) from the Crystal Rock (*shel brag*) at Yarlung, but he does not specify for which Treasure(s) it was meant (1982b: 181.5). This is most likely the same Treasure listed by Khyentse. It could, however, also be an alternative Treasure inventory, mentioned by Orgyen Tobgyal, prophesizing all Chokgyur Lingpa's earth Treasures (1988: 7-8). I have not been able to locate any mention of this inventory in the older sources.

218 Jamyang 1982c: 26.3.

219 Ibid.

220 The 12 emanations of Padmasambhava appear in the following order: Gyalwey Dungzin, Mawey Sengge, Kyechok Tshulzang, Dudkyi Shechen, Dzamling Gyenchog, Pema Jungne, Kyepar Phagpey Rigdzin, Dzutrul Thuchen, Dorje Draktsal, Kalden Drendze, Rakṣa Thötreng, and Dechen Gyalpo. The cycle of *Guru's Heart Practice: Dispeller of All Obstacles* together with its subsequent commentaries and ritual arrangements, composed by a number of influential masters (most notably Khyentse and Kongtrul), occupy the first nine and a half volumes of the *New Treasures*. The first volume contains the root *tantra* called *Quintessential Inscription of Oral Instructions,* and the remaining volumes consist of practices related to the above-mentioned deities in the order listed here. In addition to these major deities, the *Dispeller of All Obstacles* cycle also contains various practices directed to the four classes of ḍākas and ḍākinīs as well as the protectors of the cycle, such as Tsering Chenga and Kunkyil Chesum (Chokgyur 1982a, vol. 1-10). See also Schmidt 1989: I-VI.

221 See further Tobgyal 1988: 10.

222 This cycle is found in volumes 10 and 11 of the *New Treasures.*

223 According to Pema Yeshe this statue was made from a bone of Padmasambhava's consort Yeshe Tsogyal (1982a: 97.6). In a note to this revelation Khyentse mentions that some people incorrectly claim this revelation to have occurred in the following year (1850) (Jamyang 1982c: 26.5). The date given by Khyentse is confirmed in both Chokgyur Lingpa's autobiography (Chokgyur 1982b: 182.2) and the *Lotus Crowned* Treasure text itself (Chokgyur 1982d: 291).

224 *"nga yi gsung sprul padma nyin byed ces / rgyal ba'i gdung tshab sprul pa'i rgyal mtshan btsug / dus mtha'i mun rum nang du sgron me bzhin / lha sras nyid kyis nyer lnga'i dus su mjal / sba gsang med par blo gtad de ru skyol / de nas ma bsgrigs lhun grub rten 'brel mang"* (Pema Yeshe 1982a: 98.1).

225 Pema Yeshe 1982a: 99.5-100.2

226 Ibid: 100.2-100.6; 103.6. Here, Pema Yeshe further explains that on this occasion Khyentse and Chokling remembered seven past lives spent in each other's company. Several prophesies exist in the *New Treasures* mentioning the close relationship between Khyentse and Chokling, but the most famous is the prophecy of the *Summary of Dependency* (Chokgyur: 1982a vol. 22: 439-499). For a translation see Dudjom 1991: 843.

227 This cycle is found in volumes 11 and 12 of the *New Treasures.*

228 According to Khyentse, this Treasure was discovered when Chokgyur Lingpa was 27, which would mean sometime in 1855 or early 1856 (Jamyang 1982c: 26.5). Chokgyur

Lingpa, however, mentions that it occurred when he was 26 and says it was in the year of the tiger, which would be 1854 or early 1855 (Chokgyur 1982b: 182.3). Pema Yeshe places this revelation in a third year altogether when Chokgyur Lingpa first met Situpa (1853). This is the only source to mention a specific month for the revelation (the first two weeks of the 10th month = December 1- 15, 1853) (Pema Yeshe 1982a: 99.1). The most probable date for this revelation seems to be the one provided by Chokgyur Lingpa himself, but assuming that the month mentioned by Pema Yeshe is reliable (in spite of the incorrect year) the time of this revelation would be sometime between November 21 and December 6, 1854.

229 Chokgyur 1982b: 182.4.

230 In the *New Treasures* the texts of this revelation together with the auxiliary texts for *Seven Profound Cycles* (see earth Treasure no. 7) are found in volumes 12-19.

231 Jamyang 1982c: 27.1.

232 Jamyang 1982c: 27.3. These texts are found in volume 1 of the *New Treasures.*

233 Chokgyur 1982b: 183.1.

234 Jamyang 1982c: 32.1-4. It is not entirely clear on what basis this distinction is made and, in particular when comparing with Khyentse's classification of earth Treasures no. 32 and 35 (see below), the grounds for classification are unclear. This further illustrates that the enumeration of 37 earth Treasures merely is indicative—a fact also pointed out by Khyentse and most of his fellow subsequent hagiographers.

235 Ibid: 27.3. This cycle is found in volumes 21-23 of the *New Treasures.*

236 Urgyen 2000: 1. Prior to Chokgyur Lingpa's revelations several Treasure revealers had discovered teachings on the *Mind Section* and *Instruction Section,* but no one had revealed teachings on the *Space Section.*

237 The role of Kongtrul in this revelation seems unclear. According to Kongtrul's autobiography his involvement appears limited (Barron 2003: 110), but see also Tobgyal 1988: 14-15.

238 Pema Yeshe 1982a: 105.6. Kongtrul mentions that "since most of these were public Treasures they were perceived by everyone with their own senses and so they were beyond dispute" (*de dag phal cher khrom gter du mdzad pas kun gi dbang po'i spyod yul rtsod pa dang bral par gyur*) (Jamgön 1976b: 652.2).

239 The place of revelation was "the upper part of the Crystal Cave" *(padma shel phug gi dbu rtse)* (Könchog 1982: 229.6).

240 Khyentse states that this revelation was a *phral gter* (accidental Treasure?) (Jamyang 1982c: 27.5). In Chokling's own account this revelation is mentioned before the revelation of *Three Sections of the Great Perfection* and said to be revealed from Kham Mig Yedrak (Chokgyur 1982b: 183.1-5). This appears to be incorrect, as the colophon to the *Heart Essence of Garab Dorje* itself states that its revelation occurred at the Lotus Crystal Cave (*padma shel phug*) (Chokgyur 1982e: 14.1). Chokgyur Lingpa mentions only the revelation of a Garab Dorje statue, but also says that he revealed a minor Treasure (*phran gter*) from the vicinity (Chokgyur 1982b: 183.5). Could this be the *Heart Essence of Garab Dorje*? Note also the similarity between *phral gter* (mentioned by Khyentse) and *phran gter* (spoken of by Chokgyur Lingpa).

241 Jamyang 1982c: 27.5. This inventory became very influential in east Tibet and is extensively quoted throughout the *New Treasures* (found in vol. 24). See also Zangpo 2001: 97-100; 225-228.

242 Jamyang 1982c: 27.5. This Treasure is not mentioned by Pema Yeshe who, nevertheless, in describing the 13th Treasure, mentions the date for the *Heart Essence of Mañjuśrīmitra* revelation (Pema Yeshe 1982a: 106.4). This Treasure was not included in the *New Treasures* and might be lost.

243 Jamyang 1982c: 27.6. Chokgyur Lingpa mentions that on this occasion, while all present were watching, he revealed from the rock a stream of water supporting longevity (Chokgyur 1982b: 184.3). The texts revealed on this occasion are also not found in the *New Treasures* and, like the previous Treasure, were probably lost before Chokling's Treasures were compiled.

244 Jamyang 1982c: 28.1-2. Chokgyur Lingpa's autobiography has a longer list and mentions the revelation of the following artifacts: an undergarment, cloak, crown, and vajra belonging to Padmasambhava; a piece of cloth belonging to the Buddha (*ston pa*); gold earrings belonging to Yeshe Tsogyal ornamented with jewels such as sapphires and rubies; clothes belonging to Trisong Detsen, Yeshe Tsogyal, Mandharava, Vairocana; various ornaments belonging to Vajrasattva; a statue of Padmasambhava; various sacred substances; a container with blessed medicine; and a seal belonging to Padmasambhava (1982b: 184.3-6). The teachings of *Six Scrolls of the Sacred Teaching* are found in vol. 24-25 of the *New Treasures*.

245 Jamyang 1982c: 28.2.

246 Ibid: 28.3.

247 Chokgyur Lingpa names this cave the Lotus Crystal Cave (*padma shel phug*) (1982b: 185.2).

248 Jamyang 1982c: 28.4. Gyalwa Chokyang was one of the 25 disciples of Padmasambhava. The guide text is found in vol. 25 of the *New Treasures*.

249 Jamyang 1982c: 28.4. This revelation is undated. The inventories are not included in the *New Treasures*.

250 Chokgyur 1982b: 185.2.

251 Jamyang 1982c: 28.4. This cycle is found in vol. 25-26 of the *New Treasures*.

252 Könchog Gyurme has the longest description (1982: 235.3). All accounts are undated but the revelation must have occurred around the time of the previous one, if not on the same day.

253 Princess Zurza Metog Drön is counted among the disciples of Padmasambhava. This cycle is found in vol. 26 of the *New Treasures*.

254 Jamyang 1982c: 28.6. This account is likewise undated but must also have occurred together with the other discoveries at Bumdzong. The inventory is found in vol. 26 of the *New Treasures*, while the cycle of *Magical Net of Pema Garwang* occupies vols. 26-28.

255 Jamyang 1982c: 29.1. This cycle is found in vol. 28 of the *New Treasures*.

256 Ibid.: 29.2. I have not used the date given by Khyentse (October 17, 1858) since in his own colophon to the Treasure text (written only shortly after the revelation) he men-

tions that the revelation occurred at the above date (Chokgyur 1982f: 139.1). This cycle is found in vol. 28-29 of the *New Treasures*.

[257] The retinue consists of: Guru Dewa Chenpo, Guru Pema Mengyi Gyal, Guru Norlha Wanggyi Gyal, Guru Yidam Wanggyi Gyal, Guru Drubpey Kekong Gyal, Guru Pawo Ginggi Tso, Guru Jungshi Wanggyur Gyal, Guru Marung Trödze Che, Guru Dorje Gocha Chen, Guru Chiwey Dugngal Sel, Guru Bardö Trulnang Jom, Guru Kyewey Dugngal Chong, Guru Drodrug Kungyi Kyab.

[258] Khyentse mentions that this occurred in the 10th month (November 6 – December 5, 1858) (Jamyang 1982c: 29.3). However, given his incorrect dates for the previous revelation, this date might also be one month too early. These texts are all found in vol. 29 of the *New Treasures*.

[259] Jamyang 1982c: 29.4. These cycles are found in vols. 29-30 of the *New Treasures*.

[260] Könchog 1982: 244.2. Although the reasons for classifying this as merely an auxiliary discovery are not stated, one may assume that it would have been considered improper to include Bön teachings among Chokgyur Lingpa's major revelations. Khyentse's omission of these revelations would likewise support this thesis. These two texts are found in vol. 30 of the *New Treasures*.

[261] Jamyang 1982c: 29.5. The inventories are found in vol. 30 of the *New Treasures*.

[262] Ibid: 30.1.

[263] Chokgyur 1982a, vol. 30: 3. Pema Yeshe has the same list as Khyentse but his text is generally a verbatim copy of that text (Pema Yeshe 1982a: 110.2). Still, Pema Yeshe later speaks of the *Four Dharma Protector Cycles of Ten Qualities That Bring Happiness to Tibet and Kham* having been revealed just after the revelation of the two cycles of *Vajra Garland Accomplishing Longevity* and the *Tantra of Longevity: Confluence of Immortality Nectar* (here listed as revelation no. 29). Könchog Gyurme's list is in accordance with the table of contents (Könchog 1982: 251.6). The protective rituals are found in vol. 30 of the *New Treasures*. Neither revelation is dated.

[264] Jamyang 1982c: 30.2. This cycle is found in vol. 30 of the *New Treasures*.

[265] The latter two cycles are not mentioned by Khyentse but are listed by Könchog Gyurme (1982: 249.2-250.5). They are found in vol. 31 of the *New Treasures*. From Pema Yeshe we can gather that the revelations of Chokgyur Lingpa were not entirely paused in the years preceding these revelations. He mentions, for example, several occasions where Chokgyur Lingpa revealed statues and sacred pills in the period following his revelations at Gatö (Pema Yeshe 1982a: 110.3). Apparently these revelations were not considered sufficiently important to be listed by Khyentse in his enumeration of the major earth Treasures.

[266] Pema Yeshe 1982a: 115.5: south. Könchog Gyurme 1982: 250.5: southwest.

[267] Jamyang 1982c: 30.4. This cycle is found in vol. 31 of the *New Treasures*.

[268] Ibid: 30.5.

[269] Ibid.

[270] Found in Chokgyur 1982a, vol. 32: 67-519. Jamgön Kongtrul's commentary is partly translated by Erik Schmidt (Kongtrul 1999).

[271] Könchog 1982: 253.4.

[272] *"Zab chos mtshan tsam thos pas srid pa hrul por bgyid pa / thos bsam byas na zag med kyi ye shes skye ba / nyams su lang na sangs rgyas kyi 'bras bu ster ba 'grel ba 'di'ang dam pa ye shes kyi klong las brdol pa'i gter chos yin gyi gang zag ji ltar mkhas kyang 'di lta bu brtsams par mi nus so"* (Könchog 1982: 254.1-2). This Treasure, together with Kongtrul's commentary, is found in vol. 32 of the New Treasures. It is partially translated by Erik Schmidt in Kongtrul 1999.

[273] Jamyang 1982c: 30.6. Khyentse also mentions that Chokgyur Lingpa in the early morning had revealed a vajra belonging to Padmasambhava but he does not count this vajra as one of the thirty seven Treasures.

[274] Pema Yeshe 1982a: 117.2.

[275] Jamyang 1982c: 31.1. The inventory is found in vol. 32 of the *New Treasures.*

[276] Ibid.: 31.2. The inventory is found in vol. 32 of the *New Treasures.*

[277] Ibid: 31.3.

[278] Könchog 1982: 254.3. the *New Treasures* also contain no texts from this revelation.

[279] Khyentse gives the date as May 13, 1867 ("*sa ga zla ba'i sher phyogs gyi rgyal ba gnyis pa*") (Jamyang 1982c: 31.4). However, Chokgyur Lingpa's colophon to the Treasure mentions that it was revealed on the festival day of that month, which is the fifteenth day, thus, May 20, 1867 (Chokgyur 1982g: 145.5).

[280] Jamyang 1982c: 31.4. These texts are found in vol. 33 of the *New Treasures.*

[281] Könchog 1982: 254.3. Although I have not been able to find any reference to this Treasure in other sources, a future study might identify it in references to Treasures revealed between April 16 and May 13, 1867.

[282] Jamyang 1982c: 31.5. Kongtrul mentions that the statue was of Padmasambhava (Jamgön 1976, vol. 1: 651.1).

[283] Chokgyur 1982a, vol. 33: 2.

[284] The seven kinds of inventories were preliminary inventory (*snga kha byang*), general inventory (*phyir kha byang*), actual inventory (*kha byang dngos*), essential inventory (*gnad byang*), abridged inventory (*mdo byang*), further inventory (*yang byang*), and innermost inventory (*snying byang*) (Jamyang 1982c: 32.1). Khyentse speaks of seven inventories but omits the abridged inventory. The list is complete in Pema Yeshe 1982a: 120.3.

[285] Jamyang 1982c: 32.2-5.

[286] Ibid: 32.6–33.6.

[287] Dargyay 1979; Dudjom 1991.

[288] Jamyang 1982c: 35.1.

[289] Ibid.: 35.2. Sources do not mention a time and place for this discovery.

[290] Könchog 1982: 257.1.

[291] Könchog 1982: 256.3. On Lhatsun Ngönmo see Jamgön 1976b: 409.2-410.5.

[292] Jamgön 1976, vol. 1: 651.2.

[293] Chokgyur 1982h: 201.1. This cycle is found in vol. 33 of the *New Treasures.*

[294] Jamyang 1982c: 35.3. Neither Khyentse nor Kongtrul provide details of the time and place for this revelation.

[295] On Kunga Bum see Jamgön 1976b: 516.4-518.4. On Dungtsho Repa the younger see 518.4-519.4. *Mother Tantra that Brings the Ḍākinīs' Secret Onto the Path* is found in vol. 34 of the *New Treasures*.

[296] Jamgön 1976b: 517.5.

[297] Jamyang 1982c: 35.4.

[298] Jamgön 1982c: 368.3-369.2. Kongtrul provides no date for this revelation but a likely time seems January 1857 around the time of the revelation of *Three Sections of the Great Perfection* from the same cave (see earth Treasure no. 9). The texts of this cycle are found in vol. 33 of the *New Treasures*.

[299] Jamyang 1982c: 35.6. No date and place are mentioned. Nub Khulungpa was the foremost student of Nub Sangye Yeshe and the principal transmitter of his Anuyoga teachings (Dargyay 1979: 42).

[300] Jamyang 1982c: 36.1. No date and place are mentioned.

[301] Ibid: 36.2. No date and place are mentioned.

[302] Könchog 1982: 260.1. However, no other recollected revelations are identified by name.

[303] Kongtrul names it *Vimalamitra's Profound Essence* (Jamgön 1976b: 653: 4).

[304] Jamyang 1982c: 36.4-5. Although Khyentse gives no date for this event we may assume that it happened together with the Treasure revelations at Riwo Wangzhu, which would mean in 1854/1855 (see earth Treasure no. 5 above). This cycle is found in vol. 34 of the *New Treasures*.

[305] "*Mchog gyur bde chen gling pa'i dgongs pa'i klong nas brdol*" (Chokgyur 1982i: 380.2). This text is likewise found in vol. 34 of the *New Treasures*.

[306] Dilgo 1982: 410. Note that even though this teaching and *Vimalamitra's Guru Practice* are classified as pure vision they are both marked with the Treasure signs (*gter tsheg*) that usually are reserved for Treasure texts.

[307] Jamyang 1982a: 36.5-6.

[308] Ibid: 37.1-3. This teaching is found in vol. 34 of the *New Treasures*.

[309] Könchog 1982: 101.5-142.5. For an English summary of this and several other of Chokgyur Lingpa's visions see Tobgyal 1988: 27-31.

[310] Jamyang 1982c: 36.3-4.

[311] Jamgön 1976b: 655.6-658.1.

[312] See above note no. 161.

[313] The information of titles, authors, places of revelation and writing, as well as Tibetan and Western dates are listed in Doctor 2002.

[314] *"Lha sras rgyal po'i rnam par 'phrul pa gter chen mchog gyur gling pas dgung lo nyer brgyad pa me pho 'brug gi lo'i chu stod zla ba'i tshes bcu'i nyi shar la mdo khams lho zla zal mo sgang gi sa'i thig le dus gsum mkhyen pa o rgyan rin po che'i sgrub gnas yel brag nam mkha' mdzod kyi sgrub phug gong ma nas las ldan gyi grogs bdun gyis mthon bar spyan drangs*

pa'i zangs shog dmar po'i ngos las lo de nyid kyi mgo zla ba'i mar phyogs mkha' 'gro 'du ba'i dus chen nyin rdzogs par gtan la phabs pa'i yi ge pa ni rjes nyid kyi gsung gi bdud rtsis skal bzang du gyur pa 'jam dbyangs mkhyen brtse'i dbang po kun dga' bstan pa'i rgyal mtshan gyis bris pa bstan 'dzin mchog zhabs pad skal brgyar brtan cing zab gter gyi bstan pa phyogs dus gnas skabs thams cad du dar zhing rgyas la yun ring du gnas par gyur cig" (Chokgyur 1982j: 267.1-268.4).

315 Tobgyal 1988: 14-15. The catalogue of the *New Treasures* lists collaborations of these three master on five additional occasions: PT GA 23, PT GA 32, PT A 27, PT KHI 1, and PT KHI 4 (Doctor 2002).

316 Cf. Mipham's above comments on this matter.

317 Khyentse authored more than 40 individual texts for the *New Treasures* while Kongtrul composed more than 130 individual commentaries and ritual arrangements (Doctor 2002). These numbers do not include the collaborations with Chokgyur Lingpa listed above.

318 As Smith points out, the common Tibetan praxis of a single author writing under a plethora of names makes the task of reliably identifying authors a challenging enterprise (2001: 258). In the colophons to the *New Treasures*, for example, we find no less than 290 different names or name variations referring to no more than 40 authors (Doctor 2002).

319 E.g. the practices of *Vajrakīlaya of the Seven Profound Cycles* (see below) and *Vajrakīlaya of the Secret Essence* (Zangpo 1994: 117).

320 Tobgyal 1988: 37-60; Urgyen 2000. See also Urgyen 2005.

321 In addition to these two figures, the masters identified in this supplication as the primary holders of Chokgyur Lingpa's teachings are: Khakyab Dorje, Tsewang Drakpa (Chokgyur Lingpa's son), Tsewang Norbu (Chokgyur Lingpa's son), Khenpo Rinchen Dargye, Chöchok Rinpoche, Dechen Chödrön (Chokgyur Lingpa's consort), Könchog Paldrön, (Chokgyur Lingpa's daughter), Samten Gyatso, Chime Dorje, Karma Sangngag, Tersey Tulku (these four were the sons of Könchog Paldrön), Dilgo Khyentse, and Tulku Urgyen. Dates for these master are for the most part unavailable.

322 Not only do lineages differ in terms of the lineage holders subsequent to Chokgyur Lingpa; they also differ on the transmission *prior* to his lifetime. Some lineages originate with the dharmakāya buddha Samantabhadra, while others are traced to Amitābha or another buddha within the dharmakāya pantheon. I am grateful to Erik Schmidt for sharing with me three rare and unpublished catalogues of transmission compiled on the occasion of the *New Treasures* being transmitted from Tulku Urgyen to the sixteenth Karmapa.

323 Vajrakīla or Vajrakīlaya? Although several scholars today seem to favor the name Vajrakīla as the Sanskrit form of the Tibetan Dorje Phurba, this preference has, in my view, not been convincingly argued as yet. Although the name Vajrakīla exists in Indian Buddhist sources from the early tantric period (Boord 2002: 3-75), it is not clear whether this term actually refers to the deity found in the later Tibetan practices or instead to an earlier Indian prototype. In the Indian sources the term Vajrakīla refers to a ritual dagger used in wrathful practices or a wrathful deity manifesting in the form of such an implement, but lacks the fully developed iconography found in the later Ti-

betan sources. Therefore, considering the long Tibetan tradition of practicing this deity using the name Vajrakīlaya, and with a view to the grammatical arguments set forth by Mayer in support of that name (1996: 165, no. 1), I have opted for Vajrakīlaya as the proper title for this deity until further evidence emerges. Wherever reference is made to the ritual dagger itself, I use of course *kīla*.

324 Boord has argued in favor of Vajrakīlaya's Indian origin by pointing out the presence of the fully developed Vajrakīlaya mantra in the *Sarvatathāgatatattvasaṃgraha* and the *Guhyasamājatantra*'s inclusion of kīla rituals (1993: 57-60). Recently, Boord 2002 has published a translation of the *Black Kīla Commentary in One Hundred Thousand Words*, an influential Vajrakīlaya commentary belonging to the tradition of Transmitted Precepts. This publication includes further textual evidence supporting Vajrakīlaya's Indian genesis (note that Boord argues for Vajrakīla as the correct form of the deity's name). Mayer has also presented historical arguments indicating the deity's Indian roots (1991; 1996). See also Smith 2001: 238-239.

325 Although the early patrons of Vajrakīlaya practice were the Nyingma and Sakya schools, the Kagyu and Gelug schools over time likewise adopted this deity into their pantheon. As for the Gelug, it was the fifth Dalai Lama's interest (1617-1682) in the Treasures of Rigdzin Gödem that paved the way for Vajrakīlaya to enter the rituals of that school (see Boord 1993: 31-32). The Kagyu School has had a longer, though perhaps less official, affiliation with Vajrakīlaya practice through the frequent overlap of masters in the Kagyu and Nyingma traditions.

326 The Anuyoga cycle is the *Single Kīla of Mind of the Scriptural Tradition* (Chokgyur 1982a, vol. 20: 275-321) while the Atiyoga cycle is the *Single Form of Vajrakumāra* from the *Inner Secret Essence* (Chokgyur 1982a, vol. 30: 35-157).

327 See the above description of Chokgyur Lingpa's sixth earth Treasure.

328 Until the Chinese occupation of Tibet this Treasure was practiced as a "great accomplishment" (*grub chen*) at the Karmapa's seat in Tshurpu. Since then the practice has been continued by Tibetans in exile at the Rumtek Monastery in Sikkim. This monastery has even produced its own woodblock edition of the cycle (Chokgyur 1972). The ritual of *Vajrakīlaya of the Seven Profound Cycles* is also practiced as a yearly event at the Benchen and Ka-Nying Shedrup Ling Monasteries in the Kathmandu Valley where it is the final ritual event of the year aimed at expelling negativities before the beginning of the new year.

329 The whole collection of texts related to this cycle is found in Chokgyur 1982a, vol. 17: 71-569; vol. 18: 1-512. The Treasure text itself is contained in Chokgyur 1982a, vol. 17: 71-204.

330 See further in Appendix B.

331 Chokgyur 1982k: 71-76.

332 *Śrī vajrakumāra namo / yang dag pa' skad du rdo rje gzhon nu zhes bya ba / chos kyi dbyings nas snying rje kro bo'i skur bzhengs pa ni / zhal mi bzad pa mthing nag g.yas dkar g.yon dmar ba phyag mi bzad pa'i gar 'gyur ba'i rdo rje rtse dgu rtse lnga me dpung khaṭvāṅga phur pa gdengs pa / rngams pa'i sku la dur khrod chas brgyad kyis brgyan cing / gshog pa gdengs shing zhabs bzhi bgrad nas 'dod khams kyi gnas su thog bab pa ltar byon nas / 'dod khams kyi rudra bsgral phung po dur khrod kyi gzhal yas khang du byin gyis rlabs pa de'i*

nang g.yo ba med par bzhugs nas 'dis skad ces gsung so // hūṃ / rab tug sang ba thugs kyi snying / gtsang rtag bde ba'i rdo rje yis / kun gzhi ka dag dbyings su 'debs / nga ni dbyings rig dbyer med yin / oṃ vajrakīli kīlaya hūṃ phaṭ / ces gsungs pas blo che ba'i gang zag thams cad dbyings ye zung 'jug gin gang du bsgral lo / phur bzhi don chen dam pa'i rgyud las rig pa ka dag gi phur pa bstan pa'i le'u ste dang po'o // (71-73.3).

333 73.3-76.3. For details on these topics see Boord 2002.

334 *Samaya / rgya rgya rgya / 'di ltar vidyotta 'bum nas / rtsa dum phur bzhi'i rgyud 'di ni / padma bdag gis 'di phan du / sked pa'i srung ba mchog tu byas / da ni phyir bas don ched du / mi bzad gter du sbas te bzhag / skal ldan gcig dang 'phrad par shog / zab rgya / gnyan rgya / gter rgya / sbas rgya / gsang rgya / khataṃ gya / rgya rgya rgya //* (76.3-5).

335 Chokgyur 1982k: 86.6-93.5; 1982l. The translations in this part of the book are presented juxtaposed to their original Tibetan. For technical notes on the Tibetan texts readers are referred to Doctor 2003.

336 Tsawa 1982. Unfortunately little is known about Rinchen Namgyal. Although the *New Treasures* contain several texts authored by him I have not been able to find much personal data regarding his person. Apart from this commentary on *Vajrakīlaya of the Seven Profound Cycles,* his most famous works include a commentary on the deity Mawey Sengge (Chokgyur 1982a, vol. 39: 489-516) and a commentary on the *Guhyagarbha Tantra* (Tsawa 1984).

337 The practice of Vajrakīlaya is divided into "higher activities" (*stod las*) aimed at achieving enlightenment and "lower activities" (*smad las*) aimed at liberating enemies and demons (See Boord 1993; 2002). The scriptures repeatedly stress that the lower activities can only be performed by someone who has first achieved mastery of the higher activities. Therefore, the common meditator on Vajrakīlaya is likely to center the majority of practice within the rituals of the higher activity, leaving aside the wrathful rituals prescribed in the lower activities. This is illustrated well in Rinchen Namgyal's commentary, where the lower activities are hardly mentioned while the higher activities are explained in detail "in a manner that is easy to read and apply to one's own being" and therefore ideally suited to the needs and abilities of the common devotee.

338 Dorje Drachin (*Śābdavajra).

339 Dorje Nyema.

340 Dorje Dermo.

341 Durtrö Dakmo (*Śmaśānikā).

342 Dorje Tunkhung (*Vajramūśikā).

343 Dorje Tummo (*Vajracaṇḍāli).

344 Dorje Danyem.

345 Dorje Lungchin Ma (*Vāyuvegā).

346 Dorje Söche Ma.

347 Dorje Kulche Ma.

348 The editor of the text has placed a note of uncertainty after the sentence 'stating its measure'.

[349] The editor of the text places a note of uncertainty after the word '*sgros 'phyang*' (here translated as 'cluster ornament'). I have not been able to find a translation for this term and translate it as the common term '*chun 'phyang*'.

[350] The editor of the text places a note of uncertainty after the sentence 'at the top.' The following ornaments normally appear at the side of the gates.

[351] The shape is actually not a square but rather a square with small rectangles attached to each side.

[352] The bars that fall down at the gate of a castle.

[353] The Tibetan name for Dīptacakra is Khorlo Gyen Depma, which means "Wheel Sealer." It is this name that the author comments on. The Sanskrit name Dīptacakra means "Blazing Wheel."

[354] Normally, she is depicted embracing Vajrakīlaya with her right arm and left leg.

[355] The Tibetan term for hybrid is "*phra man*" which means "variegated." The term *phra can*, however, also means *jewel* - thus they adorn each other. The Sanskrit term *piśācī* might be derived from their fondness for flesh (*piśa*).

[356] This name means "slayer of Yama."

[357] The Tibetan name for Amṛtakuṇḍalin, is Dutsi Khyilwa, which means "Confluence of Nectar." However, playing on the word *rtsi* (nectar) the author makes use of the similarly spelled verb "*rtsis 'debs pa,*" which means "to measure."

[358] Above this deity was named Vajra Activity and Vajra Exhortation.

[359] Refers perhaps to the four Semo sisters.

[360] A "Thousand Verse," in a sādhana, is the repetition of offering and praise after each thousand mantras.

[361] Lying with ones legs outstretched, one does not accomplish anything.

[362] A drawing of the deity in a skull.

[363] The fortress of the view (*lta ba'i rdzong*), the precipice of meditation (*sgom pa'i 'phrang*), and the life-force of action (*spyod pa'i srog*).

[364] Chokgyur 1982a. Text numbers refer to Doctor 2002.

Bibliography

Tibetan Sources:

Chak Lotsāwa (Chag lo tsā ba) et al. 1979. *Snags log sun 'byin gyi skor.* Thim-phu : Kunsang Topgyel and Mani Dorji.

Chokgyur Lingpa (Mchog gyur gling pa) (et al.). 1972. *Yang gsang thugs kyi phur gcig sgrub skor.* Xylographic print from blocks preserved at Rum btegs (Rumtek) karma chos sgar in Sikkim. Rum btegs.

———. 1975. *The collected rediscovered teachings (gter ma) of gter chen mchog gyur gling pa / gter chen mchog gyur bde chen gling pa'i zab gter chos skor.* Vols. 1-32. Reproduced from a set of the rtsi rke block prints and unpublished manuscripts from the library of mchog glin sprul sku. New Delhi, Patshang Lama Sonam Gyaltsen, Dolanji, H.P.

———. 1982a. *The treasury of revelations and teachings of Gter chen mchog gyur bde chen gling pa.* Vols. 1-39. Expanded redaction of the Mchog gyur bde chen gling pa revelations. Reproduced from an enlarged collection of texts representing the tradition of gnas brtan dgon pa supplemented with texts from Tibet. Paro, Bhutan: Lama Pema Tashi.

———. 1982b. Sprul pa'i gter ston chen mo'i rnam thar gyi sa bon zhal gsung ma dang gter 'byung 'ga' zhig 'bel gtam sna tshogs bcas. In Chokgyur Lingpa 1982a, vol. chi: 175-230.

———. 1982c. Thugs rje chen po padma gtsug tor dri ma med pa'i sgrub thabs theg dgu dang 'brel ba gter gzhung. In Chokgyur Lingpa 1982a, vol. tha: 125-266.

———. 1982d. Thugs rje chen po padma gtsug tor gyi bka' srung rdo rje phyag drug pa'i phyi sgrub dang las byang bstan dgra tshar gcod bcas gter gzhung. In Chokgyur Lingpa 1982a, vol. tha: 267-291.

———. 1982e. Dga' rab rdo rje'i snying thig las yi dam zhi ba'i sgrub pa. In Chokgyur Lingpa 1982a, vol. ya: 3-14.

———. 1982f. Bla ma'i thugs sgrub yid bzhin nor bu las phrin las dgos 'dod kun 'byung. In Chokgyur Lingpa 1982a, vol. ha: 101-139.

———. 1982g. Yon tan gnas gtso ru dam gangs kyi ra ba'i sbas gnas chen po'i lo rgyus 'gro don mtha' yas. In Chokgyur Lingpa 1982a, vol. gi: 127-146.

———. 1982h. Zhi byed bdun gyi man ngag bdud rtsi bum pa gter gzhung. In Chokgyur Lingpa 1982a, vol. gi: 159-201.

———. 1982i. Ge sar skyes bu don 'grub kyi sgrub thabs grub gnyis dpyid ster las bzhi lhun grub. In Chokgyur Lingpa 1982a, vol. ngi: 379-399.

———. 1982j. Zab bdun rtsa gsum gdams skor las 'chi med tshe yi las byang padma'i phreng ba. In Chokgyur Lingpa 1982a, vol. pha: 231-269.

———. 1982k. Yang gsang thugs kyi phur gcig gi rgyud kyi rtsa dum phur bzhi don chen dam pa'i rgyud sogs nas cog brdung glo bur sgrub pa'i bar bcas. In Chokgyur Lingpa 1982a, vol. tsa: 71-204.

———. 1982l. Yang gsang thugs kyi phur gcig las las byang phrin las 'dus pa. In Chokgyur Lingpa 1982a, vol. tsa: 213-221.

———. No date. *Zab bdun phur pa cha tshang*. Rumtek Monastery, Gangtok.

Dazang Karma Ngedön Tenpa Rabgye (Zla bzang karma nges don bstan pa rab rgyas). 1982a. Rje rig pa 'dzin pa gter chen mchog gyur gling pa'i skyes rabs kyi gsol 'debs mu tig dmar po'i phreng ba. In Chokgyur Lingpa 1982a, vol. ti: 53-59.

Dilgo Khyentse (Dil mgo mkhyen brtse). 1982. Dag snang ge sar skyes bu don 'grub kyi dbang mchog phrin las kun khyab. In Chokgyur Lingpa 1982a, vol. ngi: 401-410.

Do Drupchen Tenpe Nyima (Rdo grub chen bstan pa'i nyi ma). 1975. Las 'phro gter kyi rnam bshad nyung gsal ngo mtshar rgya mtsho. In *The Collected Works of rDo Grub Chen 'Jigs Med Bstan Pa Nyima*, vol. 4: 177-447. Gangtok: Dodrup Chen Rinpoche.

Dudjom Yeshe Dorje (Bdud 'joms ye shes rdo rje). 1996. *Bdud 'joms chos 'byung*. Beijing: mi rigs dpe skrun khang.

Guru Chökyi Wangchuk (Guru chos kyi dbang phyug). 1979. "gTer 'byung chen mo." In *The Autobiography and Instructions of Gu-ru chos-kyi-dbang-phyug*. Paro, Bhutan: Ugyen Tempai Gyaltsen, vol. 2: 75-193.

Gyurme Tsewang Chogdrub ('Gyur med tshe dbang mchog grub). No date. *Bskyed pa'i rim pa cho ga dan sbyar ba'i gsal byed zung 'jug snye ma*. No publication data.

Jamgön Kongtrul ('Jam mgon kong sprul) (ed.). 1976a. *Rin chen gter mdzod*. Vols. 1-63. Paro, Bhutan: Lama Ngodrup and Sherab Drimey.

———. 1976b. Zab mo'i gter dang gter ston grub thob ji ltar byon pa'i lo rgyus mdor bsdus bkod pa rin chen vaiḍūrya'i phreng ba. In Jamgön 1976a, vol. 1: 291-759.

———. 1982a. Sprul pa'i gter chen mchog gyur gling pa'i rnam thar gsol 'debs bkra shis 'khyil pa'i dbyangs snyan. In Chokgyur Lingpa 1982a, vol. ti: 1-9.

———. 1982b. Rje gter chen bla ma dbus phebs skor gyi lam yig mdor bsdus bkra shis dpyid kyi rgyal mo'i dbyangs snyan. In Chokgyur Lingpa 1982a, vol. ti: 155-184.

———. 1982c. Dgongs gter sgrol ma'i zab tig las legs so gsum gyi don khrid gsal bar bkod pa grub gnyis thig le. In Chokgyur Lingpa 1982a, vol. gi: 365-459.

Jamyang Khyentse Wangpo ('Jam dbyangs mkhyen brtse'i dbang po). 1982a. Gter chen mchog gyur gling pa'i rnam thar gsol 'debs kyi bsdus don bkra shis dbyangs kyi yan lag. In Chokgyur Lingpa 1982a, vol. ti: 9-11.

———. 1982b. Skyes rabs gsol 'debs mu tig dmar po'i phreng ba'i zin thun vaiḍūrya'i mdo 'dzin. In Chokgyur Lingpa 1982a, vol. ti: 61-80.

———. 1982c. Gter chen rnam thar las 'phros pa'i dris lan bkra shis dbyangs snyan bskul ba'i dri bzhon. In Chokgyur Lingpa 1982a, vol. ti: 15-52.

Karma Rinchen Dargye (Kar ma rin chen dar rgyas). 1983. *Gu ru'i thugs dam zab pa skor bdun las mngon spyod drag po'i las kyi zab pa yang gsang thugs kyi phur gcig gi spyi don rnam bsad rig 'dzin rtsal chan rnam gñis kyi zal lun zab don ban mdzod.* Gangtok, Sikkim, Sherab Gyaltsen Lama.

Khakyab Dorje (Mkha' khyab rdo rje). 1981a. *Rgyal dbang mkha' kyab rdo rje'i bka' 'bum.* Paro: Lama Ngodrup.

———. 1981b. Pha rgol 'jom pa'i gtam rdo rje'i me char ma rungs klad 'gems yang dag snang ba'i dga' ston ces bya ba bi ha ra ti sma. In Mkha' kyab rdo rje 1981a, vol. na: 323-409.

Könchog Gyurme (Dkon mchog 'gyur med). 1982. Gter chen mchog gyur bde chen gling pa'i rnam thar bkra shis dbyangs kyi yan lag gsal byed. In Chokgyur Lingpa 1982a, vol. 38: 1-629.

Kunzang Palden (Kun bzang dpal ldan). Undated. *Gangs ri'i khrod kyi smra ba'i seng ge gcig pu 'jam mgon mi pham rgya mtsho'i rnam thar snying po bsdus pa dang gsung rab kyi dkar chag snga 'gyur bstan pa'i mdzod rgyan.* Kathmandu: Shechen Monastery.

Longchenpa Drime Özer (Klong chen pa 'dri med 'od zer). 1992a. Mkha 'gro yang thig. In *Snying thig ya bzhi*, vol. 3-4. Berkeley: Yeshe De Project.

———. 1992b. Gter 'byung Rin po che'i Lo rgyus. In Longchenpa 1992a, vol. 3 (lo rgyus): 1-135.

———. 1992c. Them byang rin chen ljon shing. In Longchenpa 1992a, vol. 3 (them byang): 1-17.

———. 1992d. Tshig don rin po che'i bang mdzod. In Longchenpa 1992a, vol. 3 (tshig don): 588-633.

———. 1992e. Zab don rgya mtsho'i sprin. In Longchenpa 1992a, vol. 3 (zab don) pp. 1-683.

———. Undated. *Chos 'byung rin po che'i gter mdzod bstan pa gsal bar byed pa'i nyi 'od.* No publishing details available. Another version is published by Dodrup Sangyey Lama, Gangtok, 1976.

Mipham Gyatso (Mi pham rgya mtsho). 1984. Gter ston brtag ba chu dwangs nor bu. In *Gangs ri'i khrod kyi smra ba'i seng ge tham cad mkhyen gzigs ma ha' pan di ta Mi pham 'jam dbyangs rnam rgyal rgya mtsho'i bka' 'bum spar gsar*, vol. 14: 475-487. Paro, Bhutan: Lama Ngodrup and Sherab Drimey.

Nyangral Nyima Özer (Nyang ral nyi ma 'od zer). 1976. Slob dpon padma 'byung gnas kyi skyes rab chos 'byung nor bu'i phreng ba zhes bya ba rnam thar zangs gling ma. In Jamgön Kongtrul 1976a, vol. 1: 1-204.

———. 1988. *Nyang ral chos 'byung chos 'byung me tog snying po sbrang rtsi'i bcud*. Lhasa: Bod ljongs mi dmangs dpe skrun khang.

Pawo Tsugla Trengwa (Dpa' bo gtsug lag 'phreng ba). 1986. *Chos 'byung mkhas pa'i dga ston*. Beijing: mi rigs dpe skrun khang.

Pema Yeshe (Pema Yeshe). 1982a. Gter chen mchog gyur gling pa'i thun mong phyi yi rnam thar bkra shis skye ba lnga pa'i dbyangs snyan. In Chokgyur Lingpa 1982a, vol. ti: 81-153.

———. 1982b. Rje gter chen bla ma dbus phebs skor gyi lam yig mdor bsdus bkra shis dpyid kyi rgyal mo'i dbyangs snyan. In Chokgyur Lingpa 1982a, vol. ti: 155-184.

Ratna Lingpa Rinchen Pal Zangpo (Ratna gling pa rin chen dpal bzang po). 1972. *Chos 'byung bstan pa'i sgron me rtsod zlog seng ge'i nga ro*. Palampur, H. P.: Sungrab Nyamso Gyunphel Parkhang.

———. 1977. Gter 'byung chen mo gsal ba'i sgron me. In *Chos rgyal Ratna gling pa'i gter chos*, vol. kha: 1-251. Darjeeling: Taklung Tsetrul Pema Wangyal.

Sok Dokpa Lodrö Gyaltsen (Sog zlog pa blo gros rgyal mtshan). 1998. *Gsang snags snga 'gyur la bod du rtsod pa snga phyir byung ba rnams kyi lan du brjod pa nges pa don gyi 'brug sgra bzhugs*. Beijing: mi rigs dpe skrun khang.

Tsawa Bhande Karma Rinchen Namgyal (Tsha ba bhan dhe karma rin chen rnam rgyal). 1982. Yang gsang thugs kyi phur gcig gi lha khrid gsal bar bkod pa rig pa 'dzin pa'i shal lung. In Chokgyur Lingpa 1982a, vol. tsha: 187-232.

———. 1984. *Dpal gsang ba snying po'i rgyud kyi mchan 'grel nor bu'i sgron me*. Paro, Bhutan: Lama Ngodrup and Sherab Drime.

Tsele Natsog Rangdrol (Rtse le sna tshogs rang grol). 1979. Slob dpon rin po che padma'i rnam thar chen mo las brtsams te dri ba'i lan nges don gsal byed. In *The Complete Works of Rtse le rgod tshang pa padma legs grub*, vol. ga: 397-491. Gangtok: Mgon po tshe brtan.

Unknown. 1982. Gter chen mchog gyur gling pa yi zab bdun gter mdzod bzhes pa'i tshul lo rgyus ngo mtshar lnga ldan. In Chokgyur Lingpa 1982a, vol. na: 341-362.

Urgyen Lingpa (U rgyan gling pa). 1996. *Padma bka' thang*. Beijing: mi rigs dpe skrun khang.

Non-Tibetan Sources:

Aris, Michael. 1989. *Hidden Treasures and Secret Lives: a Study of Pemalingpa* (1450-1521) *and the Sixth Dalai Lama* (1683-1706). London: Kegan Paul International.

Barron, Richard, transl. 2003. *The Autobiography of Jamgön Kongtrul: a Gem of Many Colors*. Ithaca: Snow Lion Publications.

Bischoff, F.A., and Charles Hartman. 1971. "Padmasambhava's Invention of the Phurbu: Ms. Pelliot Tibétain 44." *Etudes tibétaines* 1971: 11-17.

Blondeau, A. M. 1980. "Analysis of the Biographies of Padmasambhava According to Tibetan Tradition: Classification of Sources." *Tibetan Studies in Honour of Hugh Richardson: Proceedings of the International Seminar on Tibetan Studies.* Ed. Michael Aris & A. S. Suu Kyi. Warminster, England: Aris & Phillips Ltd.: 45-52.

———. 1988. "La controverse soulevée par l'inclusion de rituels bon po dans le Rin-chen gter-mdzod. Note préliminaire." *Tibetan Studies. Proceedings of the 4th Seminar of the International Association for Tibetan Studies, Schloss Hohenkammer, Munich,* 1985, J. L. Panglung, ed. München: Kommission für Zentralasiatische Studien, Bayerische Akademie der Wissenschaften: 59-76.

Boord, Martin J. 1993. *The Cult of the Deity Vajrakīla.* Tring, U.K.: The Institute of Buddhist Studies.

———. 2002. *A Bolt of Lightning From the Blue: The vast commentary on Vajrakīla that clearly defines the essential points.* Berlin: edition khordong.

Boord, Martin J., and Losang Norbu Tsonawa, transl. 1996. *Overview of Buddhist Tantra: General Presentation of the Classes of Tantra, Captivating the Minds of the Fortunate Ones.* Delhi: Library of Tibetan Works and Archives.

Broido, M.M. 1988. "Killing, Lying, Stealing and Adultery: A Problem of Interpretation in the Tantras." In *Buddhist Hermeneutics,* ed. Donald Lopez, Honolulu: University of Hawaii Press: 71-118.

Buswell, Robert E., ed. 1990. *Chinese Buddhist Apocrypha.* Honolulu: University of Hawaii Press.

Cabezón, José, and Roger Jackson, eds.1996. *Tibetan Literature: Studies in Genre.* Ithaca: Snow Lion Publications.

Chokgyur Lingpa. 1990a. *Trinley Nyingpo, the Essence of Activity: A Guru Rinpoche Sadhana.* Hong Kong: Rangjung Yeshe Publications.

———. 1990b. *The Concise Manual for Daily Practice According to Lamey Thukdrub Barchey Kunsel, the Guru's Heart Practice, Dispeller of All Obstacles: A Terma Treasure.* Hong Kong: Rangjung Yeshe Publications.

———. 1990c. *The Practice of the Single Form of Vajra Kumara According to the Teaching of Sangtik Nyingpo: A Dharma Treasure.* Hong Kong: Rangjung Yeshe Publications.

Chokling Rinpoche. 2001. *Lotus Ocean: Seeds of the Sublime Dharma.* Kuala Lumpur: Ka-Nying Ling Dharma Society.

Cüppers, Christoph, and Per K. Sørensen. 1998. *Collection of Tibetan Proverbs and Sayings: Gems of Tibetan Wisdom and Wit.* Stuttgart : Franz Steiner Verlag.

Dagyab, Loden Sherap. 1995. *Buddhist Symbols in Tibetan Culture: An Investigation of the Nine Best-known Groups of Symbols.* Boston: Wisdom Publications.

Dargyay, Eva M. 1979. *The Rise of Esoteric Buddhism in Tibet.* Delhi: Motilal Banarsidass.

———. 1981. "A gTer-ston Belonging to the dGe-lugs-pa School." *Tibet Journal* 6 (1): 24-30.

Das, Sarat Chandra. 1970. *A Tibetan-English Dictionary*. Delhi: Motilal Banarsidass.

Davidson, Ronald. 1990. "An Introduction to the Standards of Scriptural Authenticity in Indian Buddhism." In Buswell 1990: 291-325.

——— and Steven Goodman, eds. 1992. *Tibetan Buddhism: Reason and Revelation*. Albany: SUNY Press.

———. 2002a. "Gsar ma Apochypha: The Creation of Orthodoxy, Gray Texts, and the New Revelation." In Eimer 2002: 203-224.

———. 2002b. *Indian Esoteric Buddhism: A Social History of the Tantric Movement*. New York: Columbia University Press.

de Jong, J.W. 1984. "A New History of Tantric Literature in India." *Acta Indologica* 6: 91-113.

Doctor, Andreas. 2002. "Catalogue of the New Treasures of Mchog gyur gling pa." Tibetan and Himalayan Digital Library, University of Virginia (Website: http://iris.lib.virginia.edu/tibet/index.html).

———. 2003. "The Tibetan Treasure Literature: A Study of the Revelations of the Visionary Master Mchog gyur bde chen gling pa (1829 – 1870)." Ph.D. diss., University of Calgary.

Dorje, Gyurme, and Matthew Kapstein. 1991. *The Nyingma School of Tibetan Buddhism: Its Fundamentals and History*. Vol. II. Boston: Wisdom Publications.

Douglas, Kenneth, and Gwendolyn Bays. 1978. *The Life and Liberation of Padmasambhava*. 2 vols. Emeryville: Dharma Publications.

Dowman, Keith. 1973. *The Legend of the Great Stupa*. Berkeley: Dharma Publishing.

———. 1998. *The Divine Madman: The Sublime Life and Songs of Drukpa Kunley*. Middletown: The Dawn Horse Press.

Dudjom Rinpoche. 1991. *The Nyingma School of Tibetan Buddhism: Its Fundamentals and History*. Vol. I. Boston: Wisdom Publications.

Eastman, Kenneth W. 1983. "Mahāyoga Texts at Tun-huang." *Bulletin of Institute of Buddhist Cultural Studies*, Ryukoku University 22: 42-60.

Eimer, Helmut, and David Germano, eds. 2002. *The Many Canons of Tibetan Buddhism: Proceedings of the Ninth Seminar of the IATS*, 2000. Leiden: Brill.

Germano, David. 1998. "Re-membering the Dismembered Body of Tibet: Contemporary Tibetan Visionary Movements in the People's Republic of China." In Goldstein 1998: 53-94.

———. 2002. "The Seven Descents and the Early History of Rnying ma Transmissions." In Eimer 2002: 225-264.

Goldstein, Melvin C., and Matthew Kapstein, eds. 1998. *Buddhism in Contemporary Tibet: Religious Revival and Cultural Identity.* Berkeley: University of California Press.

Goodman, Steven D. 1983. "The 'Klong-Chen Snying-Thig': An Eighteenth Century Tibetan Revelation." Ph.D. diss., University of Saskatchewan.

———. 1992. "Rig-dzin Jigs-med gling-pa and the Klong-Chen sNying-Thig." In Davidson 1992: 133-147.

Gray, David Barton. 2001. "On Supreme Bliss: A Study of the History and Interpretation of the 'Cakrasamvara Tantra'." Ph.D. diss., Columbia University.

Griffiths, Paul J. 1989. "Buddhist Hybrid English: Some Notes on Philology and Hermeneutics for Buddhologists." *Journal of the International Association of Buddhist Studies* 12 (1): 17-32.

Guenther, Herbert V. 1984. *Matrix of Mystery: Scientific and Humanistic Aspects of rDzogs-chen Thought.* Boulder: Shambhala.

———. 1987a. *The Creative Vision: The Symbolic Recreation of the World According to the Tibetan Buddhist Tradition of Tantric Visualization Otherwise Known as the Developing Phase.* Novato: Lotsawa.

———. 1987b. "Buddhism in Tibet." *The Encyclopedia of Religion*, vol. 2, ed. Mircea Eliade. New York: Macmillan Publishing Company.

Gyatrul Rinpoche. 1992. *The Secret Oral Teachings on Generating the Deity.* Taipei: SMC Publishing Inc.

Gyatso, Janet. 1981. "The Literary Traditions of Thang-stong rGyal-po: A Study Of Visionary Buddhism In Tibet." Ph.D. diss., University of California at Berkeley.

———. 1986. "Signs, Memory and History: A Tantric Buddhist Theory of Scriptural Transmission." *Journal of the International Association of Buddhist Studies* 9 (2): 7-35.

———. 1992. "Genre, Authorship and Transmission in Visionary Buddhism: The Literary Traditions of Thang-stong rGyal-po." In Davidson 1992: 96-106.

———. 1993. "The Logic of Legitimation in The Tibetan Treasure Tradition." *History of Religions* 33 (2): 97-134.

———. 1994. "Guru Chos-dbang's gTer 'byung chen mo: an early survey of the treasure tradition and its strategies in discussing Bon treasure." *Occasional Papers - Institute For Comparative Research In Human Culture* 1 (1): 275-287.

———. 1996. "Drawn from the Tibetan Treasury: The gTer ma Literature." In Cabezón 1996: 147-169.

———. 1998. *Apparitions of the Self.* Princeton: Princeton University Press.

———. 1999. "Healing Burns with Fire: The Facilitations of Experience in Tibetan Buddhism." *Journal of the American Academy of Religion* 67 (1): 113-147.

———. N.d. "The Relic Text as Prophecy: The Semantic Drift of Byang-bu and Its Appropriation in the Treasure Tradition." Unpublished paper.

——— and David Germano. 2000. "Longchenpa and the Possession of the Ḍākinī." In White 2000: 239-265.

Hanna, Span. 1994. "Vast as the Sky: The Terma Tradition in Modern Tibet." In Samuel 1994: 1-13.

Harding, Sarah. 2003. *The Life and Revelations of Pema Lingpa*. Ithaca: Snow Lion Publications.

Hartzell, James Francis. 1997. "Tantric Yoga: a Study of the Vedic Precursors, Historical Evolution, Literatures, Cultures, Doctrines, and Practices of the 11th Century Kasmīri, Saivite and Buddhist Unexcelled Tantric Yogas." Ph.D. diss., Columbia University.

Hopkins, Jeffrey. 1977. *Tantra in Tibet: The Great Exposition of Secret Mantra*. London: George Allen & Unwin.

———. 1984. *The Tantric Distiction: An Introduction to Tibetan Buddhism*. London : Wisdom Publications.

Hummel, S. 1952. "Der lamaistische Ritualdolch (phur bu) und die alt-vorderorientalischen Nagelmenschen." *Asiatische Studien* 6: 41-51.

———. 1972. "Vajrakila." *Wiss. Z. Universität Halle* 22.

———. 1974. "Noch einmal Vajrakila." *Wiss. Z. Universität Halle* 23.

———. 1997. "The Lamaist Ritual Dagger (phur bu) and the Old Middle Eastern 'Dirk Figures.'" *Tibet Journal* 22 (4): 23-32.

Huntington, J.C. 1975. *The Phur-ba: Tibetan Ritual Daggers*. Ascona: Artibus Asiae Publishers.

Jackson, Roger. 1985. "Kalachakra in Context." In Sopa 1985: 1-50.

Ju Mipham. 2004. *Speech of Delight: Mipham's Commentary on Śāntarakṣita's Ornament of the Middle Way*. Ithaca: Snow Lion Publications.

Kant, Immanuel. 1960. *Religion Within the Limits of Reason Alone*. New York: Harper Torchbooks.

Kapstein, Matthew. 2000. *The Tibetan Assimilation of Buddhism: Conversion, Contestation, and Memory*. New York: Oxford University Press.

Karmay, Samten G. 1972. *The Treasury of Good Sayings: A Tibetan History of Bon*. London: Oxford University Press.

———. 1975. "A Discussion on the Doctrinal Position of the rDzogs-chen from the 10th to the 13th Centuries." *Journal Asiatique* 263: 147-155.

———. 1988. *The Great Perfection (rDzogs chen): A Philosophical and Meditative Teaching of Tibetan Buddhism*. Leiden: E.J. Brill.

Kawamura, L. S. 1984. "Thus Have I Said – A Preliminary Study of the Tantra." *Tibetan and Buddhist Studies, Commemorating the 200th Anniversary of the Birth of Alexander Csoma de Kőrös*, vol 1: 363-375.

———. 1992. "On 'Jigs-med gling-pa's Dris lan rin po che'i bstan bcos lung gi gter md-zod." *Monograph Series - Naritasan Institute for Buddhist Studies Occasional Papers*, 2: 121-130.

Khenpo Namdrol Rinpoche. 1997. *Vajrakilaya*. London: Dharmakosa.

———. 1999. *The Practice of Vajrakilaya*. Ithaca: Snow Lion Publications.

Khetsun Sangpo Rinbochay. 1982. *Tantric Practice in Nying-ma*. Ithaca: Snow Lion Publications.

Khyentse, Dilgo. 1988. *The Wish-Fulfilling Jewel: The Practice of Guru Yoga According to the Longchen Nyingthig Tradition*. Boston: Shambhala.

Kongtrul, Jamgön. 1996. *Creation and Completion: Essential Points of Tantric Meditation*. Translated by Sarah Harding. Boston: Wisdom Publications.

Kongtrul, Jamgon. 1999. *Light of Wisdom*, vols. 1-2. Kathmandu: Rangjung Yeshe Publications.

Kvaerne, Per. 1983. "The 'Great Perfection' in the Traditions of the Bonpos." In Lai 1983: 367-91.

———. 1987. "Protection Against Natural Dangers: A Translation and Commentary on Tibetan Ritual Texts in The 'Rin Chen Gter Mdzod'." *Bulletin of The School of Oriental and African Studies* 50 (3).

———, ed. 1994. *Tibetan Studies: Proceedings of the 6th International Association of Tibetan Studies Seminar*. 2 vols. Oslo: Insitute for Comparative Research in Human Culture.

Lai, Whalen. 1983. *Early Ch'an in China and Tibet*. Berkeley: Asian Humanities Press.

Lalou, Marcelle. 1953. "Les Textes Bouddhiques au Temps du Roi Khri-sroṇ-lde-bcan." *Journal Asiatique*, 241: 313-52.

Lamotte, Etienne. 1988. *History of Indian Buddhism: From the Origins to the Śaka Era*. Louvain-la-Neuve: Universite Catholique de Louvain.

Lessing, F. D., and A. Wayman. 1968. *Introduction to the Buddhist Tantric Systems*. Repr. Delhi: Motilal Banarsidass, 1983.

Levenson, Claude B., Laziz Hamani.1996. *Symbols of Tibetan Buddhism*. Paris: Editions Assouline.

Linrothe, Robert N. 1999. *Ruthless Compassion : Wrathful Deities in Early Indo-Tibetan Esoteric Buddhist Art*. Boston: Shambhala.

Lopez, Donald S. 1998. *Prisoners of Shangri-la*. Chicago: University of Chicago Press.

Marcotty, Thomas. 1987. *Dagger Blessing: The Tibetan Phurpa Cult – Reflections and Materials*. Delhi: B.R. Publishing Corporation.

Martin, Dan. 1997. *Tibetan Histories: A Bibliography of Tibetan-Language Historical Works.* London: Serindia Publications.

———. 2001. *Unearthing Bon Treasures : Life and Contested Legacy of a Tibetan Scripture Revealer, with a General Bibliography of Bon.* Leiden: Brill.

Mayer, Robert. 1991. "Observations on the Tibetan Phur-ba and the Indian Kīla." *The Buddhist Forum* 2: 163-192.

———. 1996. *A Scripture of the Ancient Tantra Collection: The Phur-pa Bcu-gnyis.* Edinburgh: Kiscadale.

Meredith, G. 1967. "The Phurbu: The Use and Symbolism of the Tibetan Magic Dagger." *History of Religions* 6 (3):236-53.

Mimaki, Katsumi. 1994. "Doxographie tibetaine et classifications indiennes." *Etudes Thematiques. Bouddhisme et cultures locales: Quelques cas de reciproques adaptations.* Paris: École francaise d'Extrême-Orient: 115-136.

Nālandā Translation Committee. 1980. *The Rain of Wisdom.* Boulder: Shambhala.

Nebesky-Wojkowitz, René de. 1956. *Oracles and Demons of Tibet: The Cult and Iconography of the Tibetan Protective Deities.* The Hague: Mouton.

Neumaier, E. K. 1969. "Einige Aspekte der gTer-ma Literatur der rNying-ma-pa Schule." *Zeitschrift der Deutschen Morgenländischen Gesellschaft,* Suppl. 1: 849.

———. 1992. *The Sovereign All-Creating Mind – The Motherly Buddha: A Translation of the Kun byed rgyal po'i mdo.* Albany: SUNY Press.

Newman, John R. 1985. "A Brief History of the Kalachakra." In Sopa 1985: 51-90.

Obermiller, E. 1931-32. *History of Buddhism (Chos-ḥbyung) by Bu-ston.* Heidelberg: Otto Harrassowitz.

Padmasambhava. 1994. *Advice from the Lotus-born.* Hong Kong: Rangjung Yeshe Publications.

Patrul Rinpoche. 1994. *The Words of My Perfect Teacher.* San Francisco: HarperCollins.

Paul, Robert. 1982. *The Tibetan Symbolic World: Psychoanalytic Explorations.* Chicago: University of Chicago Press.

Pemala, Lopon. 1995. *The Treasure Revealer of Bhutan: Pemalingpa, the Terma Tradition and Its Critics.* Kathmandu, Nepal: EMR Pub. House.

Pemba, Lhamo. 1996. *Tibetan Proverbs.* Dharamsala: Library of Tibetan Works and Archives.

Pettit, John. 1999. *Mipham's Beacon of Certainty: Illuminating the View of Dzogchen, the Great Perfection.* Boston: Wisdom Publications.

Prats, R. 1979. "Some Preliminary Considerations Arising from a Biographical Study of the Early gTer-ston." *Tibetan Studies in Honour of Hugh Richardson: Proceedings of the International Seminar on Tibetan Studies.* Ed. Michael Aris & A. S. Suu Kyi. Warminster, England: Aris & Phillips Ltd.: 256-260.

Rangdrol, Tsele Natsok. 1993. *Empowerment and the Path of Liberation.* Hong Kong: Rangjung Yeshe.

Robinson, James Burnell. 1996. "The Lives of Indian Buddhist Saints: Biography, Hagiography and Myth." In Cabezón 1996: 57-69.

Roerich, George. 1953. *The Blue Annals.* 2 vols. Calcutta: Royal Asiatic Society of Bengal.

Sakya Pandita Kunga Gyaltsen. 2002. *A Clear Differentiation of the Three Codes: Essential Distinctions among the Individual Liberation, Great Vehicle, and Tantric Systems.* Transl. Jared Rhoton. Albany: SUNY Press.

Samuel, Geoffrey. 1993. *Civilized Shamans: Buddhism in Tibetan Societies.* Washington, D.C.: Smithsonian Institution.

Samuel, Geoffrey, Hamish Gregor, and Elisabeth Stutchbury, eds. 1994. *Tantra and Popular Religion in Tibet.* Delhi: Aditya Prakashan.

Schmidt, Erik H. 1989. *The Great Gate.* Kathmandu: Rangjung Yeshe Publications.

Schuh, Dieter. 1973a. *Untersuchungen zur Geschichte der Tibetischen Kalenderrechnung.* Wiesbaden: Franz Steiner.

———. 1973b. *Tibetische Handschriften und Blockdrücke,* vol. 5. Wiesbaden: Franz Steiner.

———. 1976. *Tibetische Handschriften und Blockdrücke,* vol. 6. *Gesammelte Werke des kon-sprul Blo-gros mtha'-yas.* Wiesbaden: Franz Steiner.

Schwieger, Peter. 1990. *Tibetische Handschriften und Blockdrücke,* vol. 10. *Die mTshur-pu-Ausgabe der Sammlung Rin-chen gter-mdzod chen-mo, Bände 1 bis 14.* Wiesbaden: Franz Steiner.

Singh, N. 1989. "The Collective Varjakilaya Retreat (Phur Drub)." *Tibet Journal* 14 (2): 49-55.

Smith, E. Gene. 2001. *Among Tibetan Texts: History and Literature of the Himalayan Plateau.* Boston: Wisdom Publications.

Smith, Wilfred Cantwell. 1993. *What is Scripture? : A Comparative Approach.* Minneapolis: Fortress Press.

Snellgrove, David. 1959. *The Hevajra Tantra : A Critical Study.* London: Oxford University Press.

———. 1987. *Indo-Tibetan Buddhism: Indian Buddhists and Their Tibetan Successors.* 2 vols. Boston: Shambhala.

Snellgrove, David, and Hugh Richardson. 1968. *A Cultural History of Tibet.* Rev. ed. Boston: Shambhala, 1986.

Sopa, Geshe Lhundrup, Roger Jackson, and John Newman. 1985. *The Wheel of Time: The Kalachakra in Context.* Ithaca: Snow Lion Publications.

Sparham, Gareth, and Khamtul Rinpoche. 1994. *Dzog Chen Meditation.* Delhi: Sri Satguru Publications.

Thondup, Tulku. 1986. *Hidden Teachings of Tibet: An Explanation of the Terma Tradition of the Nyingma School of Buddhism*. London: Wisdom Publications.

———. 1989. *Buddha Mind: An Anthology of Longchen Rabjam's Writings on Dzogpa Chenpo*. Ithaca: Snow Lion Publications.

———. 1990. "The Terma Tradition of the Nyingmapa School." *Tibet Journal* 15 (4): 149-158.

———. 1996. *Masters of Meditation and Miracles: The Longchen Nyingthig Lineage of Tibetan Buddhism*. Boston: Shambhala.

Tillemans, Tom. 1995. "Remarks on Philology." *Journal of the International Association of Buddhist Studies* 18 (2): 269-278.

Tobgyal, Urgyen. 1988. *The Life and Teachings of Chokgyur Lingpa*. Kathmandu: Rangjung Yeshe Publications.

Tsogyal, Yeshe. 1999. *The Lotus-Born: The Life Story of Padmasambhava*. Boston: Shambhala.

Tsuda, Shinichi. 1965. "Classification of Tantras in dPal brtsegs's lTa ba'i rim pa bshad pa and Its Problems." *Journal of Indian and Buddhist Studies* 13 (1): 42-47.

Tucci, Giuseppe. 1980. *The Religions of Tibet*. Trans. Geoffrey Samuel. Repr. Berkeley: University of California Press, 1988.

Urgyen, Tulku. 1995. *Trinley Nyingpo Commentary '95*. Kathmandu: Rangjung Yeshe Publications.

———. 2000. *The Lineage of Chokling Tersar*. Kathmandu: Rangjung Yeshe Publications.

———. 2005. *Blazing Splendor: The Memoirs of Tulku Urgyen Rinpoche*. Kathmandu: Rangjung Yeshe Publications.

van Schaik, Sam. 2004. *Approaching the Great Perfection: Simultaneous and Gradual Methods of Dzogchen Practice in the Longchen Nyingtig*. Boston: Wisdom Publications.

Vostrikov, A. I. 1970. *Tibetan Historical Literature*. Soviet Indology Series no. 4. Calcutta: R. K. Maitra.

Waddell, L. Austine. 1972. *Tibetan Buddhism*. New York: Dover Publications.

Wangdu, Pasang, and Hildegard Diemberger. 2000. *dBa' bzhed: The Royal Narrative Concerning the Bringing of the Buddha's Doctrine to Tibet*. Wien: Verlag der Österreichischen Akademie der Wissenschaften.

Wayman, Alex. 1977. *Yoga of the Guhyasamājatantra: The Arcane Lore of Forty Verses*. Delhi: Motilal Banarsidass.

———. 1981. "Notes on the Phur-bu." *Journal of the Tibet Society*, 1: 79-85.

———. 1995. *The Buddhist Tantras : Light on Indo-Tibetan Esotericism*. London: Kegan Paul International.

White, David Gordon, ed. 2000. *Tantra in Practice*. Princeton : Princeton University Press.

Williams, Paul. 2001. *Mahāyāna Buddhism: The Doctrinal Foundations*. London: Routledge.

Wylie, Turrell. 1959. "A Standard System of Tibetan Transcription." *Harvard Journal of Asiatic Studies* 22: 261-267.

Zangpo, Ngawang. 1994. *Jamgön Kongtrul's Retreat Manual*. Ithaca: Snow Lion Publications.

———. 2001. *Sacred Ground: Jamgön Kongtrul on "Pilgrimage and Sacred Geography."* Ithaca: Snow Lion Publications.

Index

A

B

C

H

I

J

Q

R

S

T

U